Questioning History

16 Essential Questions That Will Deepen Your Understanding of the Past

Joe Regenbogen
Mosaic Academy, Parkway School District, St. Louis, MO

Vernon Series in Education

Copyright © 2016 Vernon Press, an imprint of Vernon Art and Science Inc, on behalf of the author.

All rights reserved. No part of this publication may be reproduced, stored in a retrieval system, or transmitted in any form or by any means, electronic, mechanical, photocopying, recording, or otherwise, without the prior permission of Vernon Art and Science Inc.

www.vernonpress.com

In the Americas:

Vernon Press
1000 N West Street,
Suite 1200, Wilmington,
Delaware 19801
United States

In the rest of the world

Vernon Press
C/Sancti Espiritu 17,
Malaga, 29006
Spain

Vernon Series in Education

Library of Congress Control Number: 2016941799

ISBN: 978-1-62273-118-3

Product and company names mentioned in this work are the trademarks of their respective owners. While every care has been taken in preparing this work, neither the author nor Vernon Art and Science Inc. may be held responsible for any loss or damage caused or alleged to be caused directly or indirectly by the information contained in it.

To Dana, my truest companion…

Preface

This book represents the culmination of a 37-year teaching career. I have been a high school history teacher since 1979, beginning in an inner-city school in New Orleans, Louisiana, followed by 30 years in the Parkway School District located in the western suburbs of St. Louis, Missouri. This experience, combined with an ample amount of reading, research and reflection, has led me to the belief that the true nature of history requires a style of teaching different from that of any other subject.

In simple terms, history is defined as *"the study of past events, particularly in human affairs."* However, history is anything but simple. Rather than consisting of a litany of events from long ago, it is more about our interpretation of the past as seen through a lens focused by modern-day values. In other words, perception may count for more than reality. It has taken the better part of my life to come to this realization. If history is constantly being rewritten according to an evolving set of standards that distinguishes a new generation of historians, then why even bother including it in the school curriculum?

The answer lies in its inherent power to teach critical thinking. Properly taught, history is a bottomless well from which to draw all of the water that our intellect will require in order to become better-educated citizens. An effective democracy requires not just an informed populace but individuals who can objectively analyze issues and think on their own two feet. What better way to prepare future citizens than by presenting them with a series of broad questions, taken from the past but with relevance to the future? If each question came with a certain amount of background information, it might then serve as a diving platform by which to leap into the intellectual process of becoming an effective citizen in a democratic society.

So, why read this book? First, for any adult who learned and then quickly forgot their textbook history, this book might serve as a means to develop a deeper understanding of the past and how it relates to the present. It will connect the dots and provide much fodder for meaningful reflection. Second, for anyone in the teaching profession, or at least considering such a worthy career choice, it might steer you in a more fruitful direction. I was lucky enough to have a mentor do this for me many years ago, so I am hoping this book might help me to pay it forward, at least a little bit. Finally, this book is intended to generate fervent discussion - heated, zealous, passionate discussion. The greatest learning experiences do not originate from passively listening to lectures, they only come from authentic engagement. Is there anything more memorable or meaningful than participating in a provocative discussion? I feel eternally grateful to two professors, one in philosophy and the other in education that bestowed this experience upon me in my formative years. It is my deepest hope that this book will be the kindling to ignite those same kinds of conversations amongst students and adults.

At the very least, I know this book will help me be a better teacher. I am not fully retired yet, and that day may never happen. Meanwhile, I am already using this book to stir up spirited discussions in my classroom. Seventh and eighth graders have been so engaged they barely notice I am still in the room and they take their conversations with them after the ringing of the bell. Teaching has never been so much fun.

Joe Regenbogen
January 2016

Table of Contents

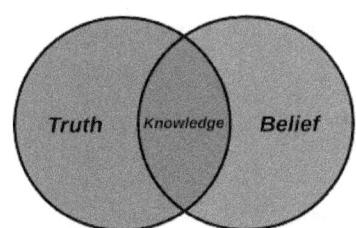

Courtesy of Dando Dangerslice (PD-user)
https://commons.wikimedia.org/wiki/File:Belief_Venn_diagram.svg

Chapter 1 Introduction   1
What are history's essential questions?

Chapter 2 An existential seesaw   13
What is the ideal balance between faith and reason?

Chapter 3 Piety and the past   27
What has been the impact of religion on history?

Chapter 4 History's moral calculus   41
How should civilizations be morally evaluated?

Chapter 5 Stereotypes: The good, the bad and the ugly   57
Why do people ascribe defining characteristics to certain nationalities?

Chapter 6 The best way to slice the pie   75
What is the fairest way for a society to share its wealth?

Chapter 7 A balancing act   99
How much power should be given to the people?

Chapter 8 Sharing the sandbox   115
What is the best way for nations to carry on foreign policy?

Chapter 9 This land is mine   133
How should control of land best be determined?

Chapter 10 I pledge allegiance   153
How should nationalism be assessed in history?

Chapter 11 Let the ruling classes tremble   171
When, if ever, is a rebellion justified?

Chapter 12 War, what is it good for?   189
When, if ever, should a nation go to war?

Chapter 13 Taking off the gloves   211
What limits, if any, should be followed in times of war?

Chapter 14 The flow of humanity   233
What is the best way to control human migration?

Chapter 15 All men are created equal   251
What is the best way to achieve equality?

Chapter 16 In the eye of the beholder   275
What is the best way to evaluate artistic expression?

Chapter 17 The struggle for power   295
Why are there competitive factions in a democratic society?

Chapter 18 Epilogue 323
What is the best way to use essential questions?

Acknowledgements 329

Index 331

Chapter 1
Introduction

Carol Highsmith Collection, Library of Congress, Prints and Photographs Division
LC-DIG-highsm-08336

What are history's essential questions?

The place is Ocala located in central Florida and the date is Sunday, July 12, 2015. Thousands of people are attending a rally in support of flying the Confederate battle flag. Police estimated that 2,000 vehicles, most of them motorcycles and trucks adorned with the Civil War-era flag, took part in the gathering. The event was being held to back a decision by Marion County to return the Confederate battle flag to a display outside of its government complex. This in turn, was a response to the decision made just days before by the South Carolina state government to remove the Confederate battle flag from that state's capitol grounds. This decision had been prompted by the deadly shooting that had occurred just a couple of weeks before at the historic Emanuel African Methodist Episcopal Church in Charleston, South Carolina when 21 year old Dylann Roof killed nine African Americans in a racially motivated shooting spree.

This chain of events brought to the surface an issue that has been imbedded in American history for the last 150 years: what was the real cause of the Civil War? The Lost Cause myth, which had flourished from the days of Reconstruction up until recent times, held that the South had seceded over the issue of states rights and had fought valiantly for the same kind of freedom that had been sought by George Washington, John Adams and Thomas Jefferson in 1776. This view, which was reinforced in films like *The Birth of a Nation* and *Gone With the Wind*, had dominated people's thinking for close to a century, and was part of the decision to fly the Confederate stars and bars on the grounds of the South Carolina state capitol. After all, if states rights and patriotism were the real motives behind the Civil War, it became easier for the South to take pride in its Confederate heritage.

The same debate has recently surfaced in my hometown of St. Louis over whether to keep the Confederate Memorial located in Forest Park. The inscription on the back, written by Robert Catlett Cave reads:

> *To the Memory of the Soldiers and Sailors of the Southern Confederacy who fought to uphold the right declared by the pen of Jefferson and achieved by the sword of Washington. With sublime self sacrifice they battled to preserve the independence of the states which was won from Great Britain, and to perpetuate the constitutional government which was established by the fathers.*
>
> *Actuated by the purest patriotism they performed deeds of prowess such as thrilled the heart of mankind with admiration. Full in the front of war they stood and displayed a courage so superb that they gave a new and brighter luster to the annals of valor. History contains no chronicle more illustrious than the story of their achievements; and although worn out by ceaseless conflict and overwhelmed by numbers, they were finally forced to yield, their glory, on brightest pages penned by poets and by sages shall go sounding down the ages.*

Nowhere on the monument is the word slavery. That is the main reason why the Lost Cause Myth is a myth. By not acknowledging slavery as the primary cause of the Civil War, this vitally important chapter in our nation's history is significantly distorted. The North may have first gone to war to *"preserve the Union,"* and many Southerners may have spent the next 150 years trying to convince themselves the conflict was over states' rights. However, the consensus of most historians today is that slavery was the primary reason why the Civil War was fought. This is clearly seen in the document issued to justify Mississippi's secession from the Union entitled, *A Declaration of the Immediate Causes which Induce and Justify the Secession of the State of Mississippi from the Federal Union*. In describing the *"prominent reasons that have induced our course,"* the document goes on to say that *"our position is thoroughly identified with the institution of **slavery** – the greatest material interest in the world. Its labor supplies the product that constitutes by far the largest and most important portions of commerce of the earth. These products are peculiar to the climate verging on tropical regions, and by an imperious law of nature, none but the black race can bear exposure to the tropical sun."*

The slavery position won the day when South Carolina Governor Nikki Haley signed the legislation to remove the Confederate battle flag from the capitol grounds. It is a shame it took a deadly shooting to revive this debate, although many would say the end result brought us closer to the truth about this important issue from our past. Meanwhile, counter demonstrations continue to take place in Ocala, Florida and the debate goes on.

Just five years earlier, Governor Jan Brewer of Arizona signed House Bill 2281 into law. This legislation targeted public school districts' ethnic studies programs. Arizona School Superintendent Tom Horne, a primary supporter of the bill, claimed the law was necessary because Tucson, Arizona's Mexican American, African American and Native American courses teach students that they are oppressed, encourage resentment toward white people, and promote *"ethnic chauvinism"* and *"ethnic solidarity"* instead of treating people as individuals. Of course, Arizona belonged to Mexico until the mid 1800s when it was taken away as a result of a war, and many of its citizens today are the descendants of the Mexicans that once populated the area. The prejudice directed toward Mexican Americans and other minorities in Arizona has played a significant role in Arizona's history. Should this all be part of the history curriculum in Arizona? Determining what belongs in the secondary history program of any public school classroom is directly connected to determining the truth about the past. The politicians of Arizona and other states may love to argue about what should or should not be taught in the classroom, but part of the problem lies in the ambiguities of history as an academic subject. Whether we acknowledge them or not, history is littered with these types of contentious issues. It is what makes history such a fascinating subject to learn. It also quite possibly makes history the hardest academic discipline to teach.

Why? First, most other subjects are built around a set of indisputable facts. Science teachers love to conduct experiments so that students will learn the value of the scientific method, and there is no denying that this process of developing and testing a hypothesis has value. But much of their curriculum is also built around facts that originated from the scientific method. In other words, the facts taught in chemistry or physics originated from experiments conducted to prove a particular hypothesis. If there is any question about the results, other scientists can replicate the same experiment; and if the same results occur again, the hypothesis is transformed into a scientific fact. The historian, on the other hand, cannot venture back into the past to conduct an experiment. Knowledge about the past can come only from the close examination of the primary source record, and this is often incomplete. In fact, if something important happened in the past, and there are no primary sources available to confirm that it actually occurred, it is not even part of the history curriculum.

The second problem with teaching history is that different historians who look at the same primary sources frequently reach different conclusions. If one historian happened to campaign in 2008 for Mitt Romney while another was an avid supporter of Barak Obama, these two historians living at the same time and in the same city may very well come to significantly different conclusions regarding the truth about the past. On a larger scale, entire societies that possess a different set of values may reach different conclusions from examining the same exact evidence. Imagine how many different ways the Second World War is taught depending on whether the history class is located in Italy, Germany, Japan, Great Britain, Russia or the United States.

To teach this point to my students, I do a quick lesson that begins by dividing the class into two parts. Each is told that a man named Franklin Roosevelt served longer than any other president; this is a historical fact. I then raise the question, was FDR a good president? One half of the class is given a copy of *A People's History of the United States* by Howard Zinn and told to look for information that will help answer this question. The other half is given the same task, but they have to examine a copy of *A Patriot's History of the United States* by Larry Schweikart and Michael Patrick Allen. After given enough time to formulate a good response supported by excerpts from their respective books, the students' discussion continues. As might be expected, the two halves of the class provide very different answers to the question about how good a president was FDR. A little further digging will show that the two books used in this exercise were written with a substantial amount of political bias. In fact, Howard Zinn was considered such a liberal that Governor Mitch Daniels of Indiana, a conservative Republican, once tried to keep Zinn's work out of the hands of K-12 students throughout the state. On the flip side, Schweikart and Allen fall far on the politically right side of the liberal-conservative spectrum. So what's the truth about FDR and the role he played in America's past? Widely respected historians wrote both of the books used in this exercise and both are available in virtually any bookstore in the nation. If nothing else, this activity demonstrates how relative the truth must be in a history class.

A third reason why history is such a challenging subject to teach involves the traditional history textbook. When asked, millions of adults today who say they hated history in school because it was *"so boring"* will frequently point their fingers of blame at the textbook. Not only are the books long, heavy and dull, they also tend to teach about the past as though the information was set in stone. As a result, students who study the past as a set of irrelevant time lines and facts transmitted in these textbooks miss out on the best part of history as an academic discipline. Instead of learning that history is really a dynamic examination and debate over different perspectives and interpretations, they are force-fed a dreary litany of facts.

It is for this reason that I have turned to James Loewen's 1995 treatise, *Lies My Teacher Told Me: Everything Your American History Textbook Got Wrong*. For many years now, this book has been assigned as summer reading to my honors and AP classes. Unlike the traditional and massive textbooks, Loewen does not focus on a chronological core set of facts. Instead, he takes the curriculum taught in these books and explains how much of it has evolved into America's own mythology. Loewen's book does a thorough job of dispelling the myths built around Columbus, the first Thanksgiving and the role in history played by Native Americans. However, there are three other provocative examples that my students are particularly encouraged to note.

The first was John Brown, the radical abolitionist. What I find most intriguing is how the historical view of Brown has varied so much since the Civil War. Those with southern sympathies not only viewed John Brown as a villain who encouraged others to murder people in cold blood, but also saw him as completely insane. However, according to Loewen, more recent accounts of John Brown have suggested that the man with an almost biblical appearance knew exactly what he was doing. There is no denying that John Brown's men killed five proslavery inhabitants at Potawatomie Creek in Kansas or that he attempted to start a violent insurrection at Harpers Ferry, Virginia. If his motives were purely aimed at eliminating the evils of slavery, do these actions make him insane? Perhaps there is a more important question that should be addressed; perhaps what should be analyzed in the teaching of John Brown is the question of when do the ends justify the means?

The second example is the truth about Helen Keller. Anyone who has seen *The Miracle Worker*, the story of how Annie Sullivan displayed incredible fortitude in her quest to break through and reach Helen Keller, knows that both of the main characters are most deserving of our utmost respect. After all, Helen Keller had lost all ability to see and hear, and was completely and hopelessly trapped inside her body. Along came Sullivan and in the film's final scene (spoiler alert), when Helen finally realizes the letters W-A-T-E-R Annie is spelling into her hand represent the fluid being pumped out of the well, many in the audience have been reduced to tears. Clearly, we should all see Sullivan and Keller as representing the kinds of heroes we want our children to emulate, right? Not so quick, according to James Loewen. In *Lies My Teacher Told Me*, we learn that as an adult, Helen Keller not only grew up to become a brilliant writer, but was also a radical socialist who sang the praises of the Russian Revolution. Whether this fact is good or bad is open to debate, but the point is that it hardly fits the image that most people, particularly those who have seen *The Miracle Worker*, hold of Helen Keller. People are never as simple as they are portrayed in the movies or as they are taught in our history books.

Introduction

Helen Keller and Anne Sullivan
Courtesy of the Library of Congress, Prints and Photographs Division
LC-USZ62-78983

The final example from *Lies My Teacher Told Me* involved the man who had been my favorite president growing up: Woodrow Wilson. Wilson's idealism expressed in his Progressive reforms, his Fourteen Points and especially his dream of creating the League of Nations, reflected the same positive outlook I held, or least wanted to hold: through the pursuit of dreams, the world could be made a better place. When I first saw Wilson's grave in the National Cathedral in Washington, D.C., it was almost a religious experience. Nevertheless, like many other mythological narratives that he dispelled in *Lies My Teacher Told Me*, James Loewen burst my bubble when he discussed Wilson's extreme racism. The same president who had created the Federal Reserve System to regulate the nation's banks also used his executive powers to racially segregate the federal government. The same president who pushed to protect American consumers by creating the Federal Trade Commission also stood in the way of providing women the right to vote. Furthermore, the same man who wanted the United States to enter World War One in order "*to make the world safe for democracy*" also ordered American military forces to invade Mexico and to take over Haiti. Once again, the same questions about truth can be raised, and once again, maybe it would be best to focus on a larger question. In this case, maybe the complexities of history should be explored by focusing on the question of what standards should be used to best evaluate political leadership.

President Wilson and his wife
Courtesy of the Library of Congress, Prints and Photographs Division
LC-USZ62-101446

With all of these considerations in mind, what is the most effective way to teach history? After doing the best I could to teach history year in and year out for over three decades, I have finally come to realize that maybe the problem lies in our focus. Yes, to better understand history, people need to become at least somewhat familiar with the chronological events that led us to the present. And yes, when properly taught, people can learn just as much from the compelling historical stories that reflect the human condition as they can from the classics taught in any literature class. But since so many of these facts in history are open to debate, maybe the focus needs to be on the questions, not the answers.

Years ago, like many secondary teachers, I became familiar with the concept of essential questions. The lexicon of educational jargon is so filled with useless vocabulary that comes from the latest passing fad that it might be easy to dismiss this as another one of those expressions. However, the term *"essential question"* seems to have stood up to the test of time; and on a personal level, essential questions have become an integral part of my teaching. If essential questions could lead my students to develop a deeper understanding of the past, could they do the same for everyone else?

So what is an essential question? According to Grant Wiggins, a respected expert in the area of educational reform, in his book, *Understanding By Design*, a question is essential when it:

1. Generates meaningful inquiry into the big ideas and the core curriculum.
2. Causes deep thought, engaged discussion, ongoing inquiry, and new understanding as well as generating more questions.
3. Requires students to improve their decision-making skills by carefully considering the alternatives, weighing the evidence and supporting their idea.
4. Provokes a constant reexamination of traditionally accepted ideas, beliefs and values.
5. Ignites meaningful links between prior learning and current experiences.
6. Encourages the transfer of ideas to new situations and subjects.

In order to apply essential questions to the social studies classroom, I would add the following three standards:

1. Incorporate important historical themes and concepts. Since a focus on broad themes and concepts by itself will deepen the understanding of history, it only makes sense to connect them with essential questions.
2. Not have *"right"* or *"wrong"* answers. As established earlier, the subject of history is dynamic and subject to changing perspectives. The deeper understanding is best reached through the process of inquiry and debate, so a question with a specific correct answer will be of little use.
3. Be timeless. This means the question must be applicable to a variety of times and places. In this way, the question will link different periods of history. By using specific facts from various times to develop an answer to an essential question, the broad idea contained within the question will take priority over the minute trivia that typically dominates the history curriculum of most classrooms.

If these standards are used to develop an essential question that can be plugged into a unit on the Civil War, the best question might be *"when, if ever, should a nation go to war?"* As seen in the discussion of this essential question in chapter 12, the first step in fomenting an answer is to explore the real reason(s) why the Civil War was fought. For over 150 years, those with a predisposition to be more sympathetic to the former Confederacy have argued the war was more about liberty and states rights. Understanding that the purpose of history is to pursue and find the truth about the past, other historians have recently argued that slavery was at the heart of why the Civil War was fought. Like any endeavor, it is impossible to make good decisions without access to the truth. Properly taught, students can be educated to find this truth in their history classes and to then use the information to answer essential questions. The need to find accurate information in order to answer essential questions can provide a new and more meaningful purpose to the primary and secondary sources typically used in a history class. By examining the issue of slavery and its expansion, as well as other factors such as states rights and preserving the union, students can decide if the deaths of over 600,000 Americans in the Civil War were justified. This in turn can be used to help them answer the essential question regarding other wars that have yet to occur. In the near future, it might also help them to better determine who is most deserving from the past to be honored and even what flags should be flown over our state capitol buildings.

In addition, essential questions can be a powerful tool in the classroom. Most history teachers have probably asked their students about the reasons why the United States has engaged in wars from the American Revolution through the recent actions in Iraq and Afghanistan. However, in all likelihood, these conversations have focused on the particular war being studied and there was probably little effort to link the discussion to the present or the future. On the other hand, a Socratic seminar lesson focused on the question, "*when, if ever, should a nation go to war*", enables students to transfer their response from one situation to another. In addition, there is no limit to the time frame for curriculum built around essential questions. An inquiry approach to teaching and learning can use essential questions as the foundation for multi-week units or even the entire course. Over the years, I have used essential questions as the focus of many classroom activities, including structured debates, mock trials, mock Supreme Court hearings, simulations, field experiences and a host of other activities designed to engage students in higher level thinking.

What follows in this book are chapters built around 16 essential questions that have served me well over my 37-year teaching career. They have played a vital role in my curriculum and will serve you well in your efforts to teach or learn history. The questions are linked to particular historical themes or concepts and are then analyzed in great detail by using specific facts from different time periods to support various answers to the question. By the end, the effort to examine the questions and to formulate answers will lead the reader to a deeper understanding of history.

Suggested Reading:

"A Declaration of the Immediate Causes which Induce and Justify the Secession of the State of Mississippi from the Federal Union." *The Avalon Project.* Accessed March 31, 2016. http://www.avalon.law.yale.edu/19th_century/csa_missec.asp.

Gallagher, Gary W., and Alan T. Nolan, editors. *The Myth of the Lost Cause.* Indiana: Indiana University Press, 2010.

Loewen, James W. *Lies My Teacher Told Me: Everything Your American History. Textbook Got Wrong.* New York: Simon and Schuster, 1995.

Schweikart, Larry and Michael Patrick Allen. *A Patriot's History of the United States: From Columbus's Great Discovery to America's Age of Entitlement.* New York: Sentinel, 2004.

Wiggins, Grant J. and Jay McTighe. *Understanding by Design.* Virginia: Association for Supervision and Curriculum Development, 2005.

Zinn, Howard. *A People's History of the United States.* New York: Harper Collins. Publishers, 1980.

Chapter 2
An existential seesaw

John T. Scopes
Courtesy of https://www.flickr.com/photos/smithsonian/2898289055

What is the ideal balance between faith and reason?

The place is Dayton, Tennessee and the year is 1925. A trial is about to begin that many have called the *"Trial of the Century."* A little known biology teacher named John Scopes is about to be brought to justice for violating a recently enacted state law forbidding the teaching of the scientific theory of evolution. Most of the nation is captivated by this legal clash, partially because it pits two well-known personalities against each other; the oft-times presidential candidate William Jennings Bryan, assisting the prosecution, versus Clarence Darrow, the legal titan sent down to Tennessee by the newly formed American Civil Liberties Union. Millions of Americans are listening to the trial on their recently acquired radios complements of WGN operating out of Chicago.

When Darrow attempted to bring in expert witnesses to scientifically prove the theory of evolution, his effort was thwarted by defense objections over their relevance to a trial that was only supposed to focus on whether Scopes had broken the law. The turning point of the entire trial then occurred when Darrow was granted permission to question his opponent, Bryan, who was considered to be an expert on biblical creation. Most observers believed that Darrow destroyed his opponent and left him in a deep state of humiliation. Technically, the trial ended with a legal victory for the prosecution and Scopes was given a fine of one hundred dollars (which was later overturned on appeal). However, in the eyes of much of the world that had been following the trial, the prosecution's case had been thoroughly discredited and the real victor was modern science.

In 1925, roughly half the U.S. population still lived on farms or in small towns while the other half had moved to the nation's growing cities. A dichotomy that had been building since America's earliest days detonated in the mid nineteen twenties like an erupting volcano. While there were plenty of exceptions, the rural areas still represented the religious fundamentalism whose roots ran all of the way back to the establishment of Boston by the Puritans in 1631. Meanwhile, cities like New York, Philadelphia, Chicago and St. Louis had become epicenters of growing modernism that was characterized by the intellectual principles of reason and science that dated back to the Enlightenment of the 18th century. These significant differences in how Americans viewed their existence had been lurking beneath the surface for over 200 years, but the intellectual explosion that occurred in Dayton in 1925 is still seething today in the minds of millions of Americans.

Meanwhile, the evolution versus biblical creation debate has continued right up to the present. According to the Gallup's Values and Beliefs survey conducted in 2014, more than 4 in 10 Americans continue to believe that God created humans in their present form 10,000 years ago. The percentage of the U.S. population choosing the creationist perspective as the closest to their own view has fluctuated in a narrow range between 40% and 47% since the survey's inception in 1982. As recently as 2008, the Louisiana Legislature passed the Louisiana Science Education Act, a controversial decree signed into law by Governor Bobby Jindal. This piece of legislation allowed public school teachers to use supplemental materials in the science classroom that are critical of established science on such topics as the theory of evolution. While proponents of the law state that it is meant to promote critical thinking and improve education, scientific societies collectively representing millions of scientists have opposed the law. The controversy over the origins of human life has continued right up to the present and beneath the surface lurks the deeper clash in fundamental values between faith and reason.

Why has the issue over human origins continued to be so contentious? Like most essential questions, this one has a right answer in the minds of each and every individual, but there is nothing that resembles consensus in the collective minds of the American public. When the subject has been raised in my classes each year, most students first appear to be perplexed. It is obvious that except for a few parents or ministers, no one has ever asked them this question before, and clearly, it has never been raised for discussion in any of their public school classrooms. A few have chosen to dismiss the question by saying it has no real bearing on their present or future lives. However, most students have acknowledged that how they choose to answer the question over humanity's origins will significantly reflect how they view most of the other issues life has in store for them. There is an enormous difference between tracing our roots to Australopithecus versus Adam and Eve, and how one chooses between the two speaks volumes about how he or she would approach other fundamental questions such as the belief in a supreme creator or what happens when one dies.

Regardless of how we began, humans have been attempting to answer those other two questions from the very start. The first issue was not so much over the existence of God, but whether God should be referred to in the singular. Prior to the birth of modern science, there were simply too many questions that could only be answered by giving credit to a deity or a set of deities. Why does the sun rise and set every day? How do you explain the movement of the constellations at night? How do men and women create newborn life? Questions that are easily answered today in a middle school science class could not be answered three thousand years ago except through faith in the ideas provided by an organized religion. Galileo and Newton would change everything, but they did not come along until the 16th and 17th centuries.

For many, the question of an afterlife might be even more fundamental than the existence of God. What happens when we die? Has there ever been a more universally asked question? It has always been the great unknown. Many who are not so certain envy those with complete faith in the existence of heaven or some other kind of eternity after death. Deep inside, just about every person who has walked on this planet has been tormented by this question. Even if one has faith in the answer, there have remained other questions over the requirements necessary to achieve lasting immortality. Is there a connection between the moral acts in this world and the payoff in the next? Can salvation be achieved through individual acts or is the intercession of other people part of the equation? And of course, there has always been the question of what the afterlife will be like. Throughout history, different cultures and societies have wrestled with these questions, and the dichotomy between faith and reason has always provided a foundation for the ongoing discussion.

History is filled with efforts to address these questions. The official state religions in Egypt, Mesopotamia and China involved multiple gods, an accepted set of creation myths, and elaborate beliefs about the afterlife. Although their ideas may not have been codified in writing, the same can be said about the cultures that existed thousands of years ago in North America, South America, Africa and Australia. This pattern was substantially altered about five thousand years ago with the rise of the Hebrews along the eastern shores of the Mediterranean. Most people today are familiar with names like Abraham, Noah and Moses as well as the stories about how the one true God provided them with commandments that should guide their lives. From Judaism, the faith of the Hebrews evolved into two other major monotheistic religions: Christianity and Islam. All three religions preach the existence of one true God, the belief that God was the creator of the universe and the conviction God provided the laws that will lead to eternal life after death. The number of adherents today is hardly even; there are over two billion Christians, one and half billion Muslims and fewer than 15 millions Jews; but the similarities between the world's three monotheistic religions far outnumber their differences. In fact, when one studies the number of times that wars have been fought between these three faiths, it is hard to remember how much they share in common.

A similar review of Hinduism, Buddhism and other eastern religions would reveal that these organized faiths also provide answers to the universal questions about human origins, the role of God(s) and the existence of an afterlife. What needs to be remembered, however, is that these answers are believed largely through faith. Is there any hard evidence to support the existence of God or to resolve the monotheistic – polytheistic issue? What about the existence of heaven or hell? It mostly comes down to faith. What about Abraham, an individual whom more than three billion people – almost half of humanity – venerate as the father, patriarch and spiritual ancestor of their faiths? According to Israel Finkelstein, a biblical archeologist at Tel Aviv University, evidence of Abraham's existence is largely beyond recovery. The need for proof might seem to be an insurmountable burden, but that does not mean there can be no room for reason.

Take Thomas Aquinas for example. The great Catholic thinker, philosopher and theologian from the 13th Century, summarized his cosmological argument in the *Summa Theologia*. In this masterpiece, Aquinas wrote of five ways to prove that God exists. In the first, he argues that there are things in the world in motion (changing) and that whatever is in motion must have been put in motion by another thing in motion. Aquinas holds that, "*whatever is in motion must be put in motion by another*," and that, "*this cannot go on to infinity, because then there would be no first mover.*" Hence, Thomas Aquinas argued that in order to eliminate the infinite chain of motions, there must be a first mover and a source of all motion: God. This was written almost 800 years ago.

Saint Thomas Aquinas
Courtesy of Library of Congress
Prints and Photographs Division

A similar line of thinking emerged during the Enlightenment that dominated England, France and the United States in the 18th century. Thinkers like John Locke, Voltaire and Rousseau encouraged the idea that everything should be viewed through the eyes of reason. While most of their ideas related to science, politics and government, their thoughts also applied to religion. Some, like Voltaire, scorned organized religion as a divisive force that had been the source of many of the planet's wars. However, others applied reason to develop the idea that there had to be a supreme intelligence to explain the origins of the universe as well as the life we see all around us. In *Natural Theology*, published in 1802, William Paley argued that just as it took intelligence to create a watch, the same manifestation of design exists in the works of nature. From this notion that God was a great *"watchmaker"* came the principles of Deism, which manifest themselves today in the Unitarian Church. These ideas had a profound impact on the thinking of some of America's most important founding fathers, including Benjamin Franklin and Thomas Jefferson; and they have been passed down to the scientists of today. It should be noted that as recently as 2009, the Pew Research Center revealed that 51 percent of the members of the American Association for the Advancement of Science expressed faith in a higher power. It should also be pointed out, however, that this is significantly lower than the 95 percent of the American public that professed a faith in God.

The notion that reason could be used to prove the existence of an afterlife has also appeared in recent times. One of the most appealing can be found in *The Grapes of Wrath*, the Nobel Prize winning book by John Steinbeck that for years was required reading in my American History classes. While the plot focuses mostly on the travails of the Joad family as they made their way to California in order to survive the Great Depression, it is easy to overlook one of the main characters: Jim Casey. My students are frequently surprised to learn that Casey's initials are not just a coincidence. After giving up on the hypocrisies that dominated his life as a minister preaching the dogma of organized religion, Casey went on a pilgrimage, and by the end, uncovered the belief that all souls are just a small portion of a larger soul. What then, happens when we die? Using Casey as his mouthpiece, Steinbeck suggests that our soul returns to the one big soul that is a part of everyone. Through discussion, many of the students are usually fascinated by this idea.

On the flip side, the rise of modern science over the last few centuries has contributed to the growth of secular humanism and in its extreme form, atheism. Copernicus, Galileo, Newton, even Christopher Columbus, all contributed to the idea that the use of scientific experimentation, logical observation and the use of reason could potentially answer questions that in the past were only resolved through faith. The apex of this growing movement towards secular humanism was probably reached in the late nineteenth century when Karl Marx published *The Communist Manifesto*. While most people recognize Marx as the father of modern communism, it is also important to remember that Marx was an atheist. When he called religion "*the opiate of the people*," he was arguing that those with wealth and power had used organized religion as a tool for centuries to control the masses. This idea usually emerges in my classes after students have read *Animal Farm* by George Orwell. In this well-known dystopian novel, Moses the Raven spreads the gospel of Sugarcandy Mountain, the place where animals go after they die. Similarly, according to Marx, if the Church told the poor serfs during the Dark Ages that a violent rebellion against the wealthy lord of the manor was a sin and that it would prevent salvation and entry into heaven, the lords were much more likely to retain their wealth and power. Therefore, it is no surprise that when 20th century communism made its way into the world in the form of the Russian, Chinese and Cuban Revolutions, organized religion all but disappeared in those nations. Another name for communism is *"scientific socialism"*, and this was clearly modern science and reason carried to its greatest extreme.

One final way to respond to the question of finding the ideal balance between faith and reason is to use the metaphor of the pendulum. This is the notion that ideas in the past have swung from one extreme to another depending on the time period, just like the swinging of a pendulum within a clock. Take the United States for example. Massachusetts was settled by Separatists; Pilgrims and Puritans who not only came to America in search of religious freedom but also wanted to create what John Winthrop called "*the city upon the hill*" to serve as a beacon for the faithful. The same could be said for the Quakers in Pennsylvania and the Roman Catholics in Maryland. On the other hand, many settlers came to colonies like Virginia in search of gold, land and economic opportunity. From the start, the pendulum was set to swing back and forth between the focus on this world and the next. In the 1730s and 1740s, recognizing that the younger generations in places like Massachusetts were being drawn away from the faith of their fathers and toward greater material comforts, the First Great Awakening was launched. The fiery sermons of men like Jonathan Edwards and George Whitefield, delivered without microphones to audiences of up to 20,000 and designed to return the flock to their faith, represented a time when the pendulum had swung far towards religion. On the other hand, the Enlightenment in the later 1700s, characterized by Ben Franklin's ideas about electricity, and the logic imbedded in Thomas Paine's *Common Sense*, showed the movement of the pendulum in the opposite direction. The early 1800s saw the pendulum swing back again towards faith with the rise of a Second Great Awakening, the start of a new home-bred religion named Mormonism, and new reform movements like Abolitionism. The pendulum has predictably swung more toward reason during times of scientific advances and new inventions, particularly with the rise and spread of the Industrial Revolution. However, during other decades like the 1920s and the 1980s, the growth of religious fundamentalism has brought the pendulum back again.

Looking at the bigger picture, one can see movement by this same pendulum in World History. Obviously, it was stuck on the faith side of the spectrum in ancient times, since religious faith played such a key role in the construction of pyramids in Egypt as well as the Yucatan Peninsula. Furthermore, faith was behind the religious leaders in the governments of Mesopotamia and China and in the writing of the commandments found in Hammurabi's Code as well as the Hebrew Torah. The pendulum then took a significant swing to the other side of the spectrum with the rise of the Greeks. Almost every accomplishment by the Greeks was guided by the use of reason: the political thinking that led to the creation of democracy, the philosophy of Socrates, Plato and Aristotle, the geometric theorems of Euclid, the medicine practiced by Hippocrates, the plays by Aristophanes and Sophocles, and even the history written by Herodotus and Thucydides. The Greeks clearly had their fair share of gods and mythology, but religious faith never played the role in daily life like it did in other ancient societies. Take for example, the philosophy of Epicurus. The adjective, epicurean, is usually associated with hedonistic pleasure. The reality, however, is that this later Greek philosopher simply urged his adherents to live a full life since there was nothing waiting for them in the form of an afterlife – "*death does not concern us, because as long as we exist, death is not here. And when it does come, we no longer exist.*" When the Greeks successfully defended themselves from the invasions by the Persians, whose giant empire represented the greatest traditions and faiths of the East, their victories at places like Marathon and Salamis might be seen as the first time that reason emerged triumphant. The Western world would never be the same. One hundred and fifty years later, when the conquests of Alexander the Great spread Greek culture as far as India, the forces of reason had undoubtedly emerged as a counterweight to balance those of religious faith.

The pendulum remained on the reason side of the continuum for almost another thousand years in the form of the Roman Republic and the Roman Empire. After all, Rome built its civilization on a classical foundation that had first been laid by the Greeks. One glaring exception was the rise of Christianity during the early days of the Roman Empire. Edward Gibbon, in his classic 1776 opus, *The History of the Decline and Fall of the Roman Empire*, went so far as to blame Christianity for Rome's tumble, largely because of its emphasis on pacifism and its belief that a better life existed after death. According to Gibbon, both created an indifference to the mounting challenge of guarding the security of the Roman Empire.

Edward Gibbon
Courtesy of https://www.flickr.com/photos/britishlibrary/11239410994

There is no denying that the fall of Rome in the fifth century ushered in a period of roughly one thousand years where the pendulum was safely back on the faith side of the spectrum. For the most part, the middle ages in Western Europe were a time of ignorance, illiteracy and superstition. There was little in the way of stable governments, education or science, and many of the advances made by the Greeks and Romans were lost or forgotten. The two most dominant institutions during the middle ages were Feudalism, which met certain economic needs, and the Christian Church, which dominated life outside of the economic arena. If the classical civilization of the Greeks and Romans was a time of reason, the Middle Ages were dominated by faith.

In the 16th century, Europe finally crawled out of the period known as the Dark Ages. While it is true that the roots of the Renaissance period that followed can be traced back to Italian writers and artists, this was not a movement that had a clear start. In fact, most people who lived through the Renaissance never understood what it was they were living through. The changes were gradual and uneven. However, with the invention of the printing press and the accompanying rise in literacy, the shifting focus on living in this world rather than focusing so much on life after death, and the rise of modern science despite the resistance of the Church, the Renaissance once again pushed the pendulum away from faith and back towards reason.

"Pendulum" Timeline

	Faith	**Reason**
Before 500 BCE	Egypt, Mesopotamia, Hebrews, China	
500 BCE – 500 CE		Greece and Rome
500 – 1400	Middle Ages	
1400 – 1600		The Renaissance
1600-1750	Pilgrims, Puritans The First Great Awakening	
1750-1800		The Enlightenment
1800-1850	The Second Great Awakening	
1850-Present		The Industrial Revolution, Evolution, Modern Science

Because of the importance of addressing this query regarding faith versus reason in the attainment of a true, liberal arts education, I always began my world history curriculum with an inquiry unit focused on the question regarding the origins of human life. Asking students to take a position on the Evolution versus Creationism issue seemed like a good starting point for any world history class. In addition to finding credible sources to support their thesis, the students were also given a chance to view a debate similar to the one that took place in Dayton, Tennessee more than ninety years earlier. On the Evolution side of this debate, was the chair of the school science department. A religious scholar, however, did not represent the other side. Instead, Dr. David Menton, an anatomist from the Washington University School of Medicine came in to use *"reason and evidence"* in his arguments against Evolution. After all, the debate was taking place inside the confines of a modern public high school where there are now limits imposed by the First Amendment on the teaching of religious faith. The speaker's most persuasive argument centered on the extreme improbability that the human body could ever randomly evolve without some kind of intelligent blue print. When Dr. Menton was asked by the students to explain the source of human origins, he stated that the answer could only be found in religious faith. By the end of the unit, students turned in their papers and participated in their own Socratic seminar. The end result was that most of them engaged in a fiery dialogue they would always remember. In addition, the split between Evolution and Biblical Creation in most classes was relatively even.

As previously stated, the search for the ideal balance between faith and reason is an essential question and by definition, has no correct answer that will garner support from most people. However, it is a vitally critical question that people throughout history have struggled to answer. It has led to wars, it has led to revolutions and it has brought about major social upheavals. A careful examination of this question will enhance an individual's education and possibly provide some insight about one's true self. In addition, it is a good start to achieving a deeper understanding of history.

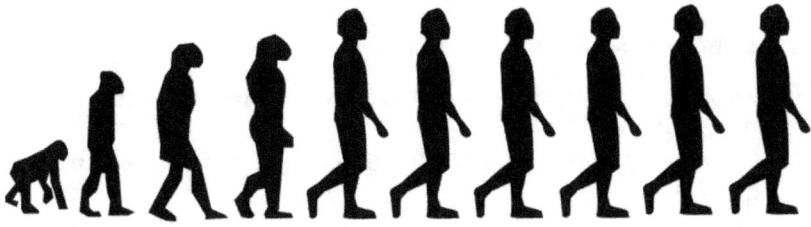

Courtesy of Pixabay CC0

Suggested Reading:

Aquinas, Saint Thomas. *Aquinas's Shorter Summa: Saint Thomas's Own Concise Version of His Summa Theologica.* Bedford: Sophia Institute Press, 2001.

Asher, Neil, and Israel Finkelstein. *The Bible Unearthed: Archaeology's New Vision of Ancient Israel and the Origin of Its Sacred Texts.* New York: Touchstone, 2002.

Bremer, Francis J. *John Winthrop: America's Forgotten Founding Father.* New York: Oxford University Press, 2003.

Emerson, Ralph Waldo. *The Essential Writings of Ralph Waldo Emerson*, Edited by Brooks Atkinson. New York: Classic Books International, 2010.

Epicurus. *The Essential Epicurus.* Amherst: Prometheus Books, 1993.

Gibbon, Edward. *The Decline and Fall of the Roman Empire*, Edited by Hans-Friedrich Mueller. New York: Modern Library, 2003.

Larson, Edward L. *Summer for the Gods: The Scopes Trial and America's Continuing Debate Over Science and Religion.* New York: Basic Books, 1997.

Marx, Karl. *The Portable Karl Marx.* Translated by Eugene Kamenka. New York: Penguin Books, 1983.

Masci, David. "Religion and Science in the United States." *Pew Forum.* November 5, 2009. http://www.pewforum.org/2009/11/05/an-overview-of-religion-and-science-in-the-united-states.

Menton, David. "Evolutionism-Is There Such a Word?" *Answers in Genesis.* November 19, 2013. http://www.answersingenesis.org/theory-of-evolution/evolutionism-is-there-such-a-word/.

Newport, Frank. "In U.S. 42% Believe Creationist View of Human Origins." *Gallup Poll.* June 2, 2014. http://www.gallup.com/poll/170822/believe-creationistview-human-origins.aspx.

Paine, Thomas. *Collected Writings: Common Sense/The Crisis/Rights of Man/The Age of Reason*, Edited by Eric Foner. New York: Classic House Books, 2009.

Paley, William. *Natural Theology*, Edited by Matthew D. Eddy and David Knight. New York: Oxford University Press, 2008.

Chapter 3
Piety and the past

Loaves and fishes mosaic in the Church of the Multiplication
Courtesy of James Every
https://www.flickr.com/photos/seetheholyland/4207408738 (CC BY-SA 2.0)

What has been the impact of religion on history?

The place is the Church of the Multiplication of the Loaves and Fish on the shore of the Sea of Galilee in northern Israel and the year is 2015. More than 5000 people visit the church daily because the modern building sits on the remains of a Fifth Century Byzantine Church that marks the traditional spot of Jesus' miracle of the loaves and fish. It is one of the most popular stops for Christian pilgrims visiting the Holy Land. In the middle of one night in late June, a fire ripped through the church, destroying the roof and causing extensive damage to the inside and outside of the building in what authorities believed was an attack by Jewish extremists. A passage from a Jewish prayer, calling for the elimination of idol worship was scrawled in red spray paint on a wall outside of the church.

The story of the church fire was buried deep within most American newspapers the following day. Compared to other major historical events like the Holocaust or the attacks that took place on September 11th, 2001, the church fire in this remote corner of Israel pales by comparison. However, this deliberate act of arson once again brings to the surface the idea that people will go to great extremes in the name of religion. In fact, from the start of humanity, religion ranks as one of the most powerful forces shaping the course of history.

Religion has existed from the beginning. Early humans who lived in small clans and survived by hunting and gathering worshipped a multitude of gods and followed a collective set of religious traditions. Because of the enormous diversity that has always existed in religions around the world, it is difficult to even provide a definition of the term. We all know a religion when we see it: the large places of worship, the symbols consisting of crosses and stars and the well-established, sometimes bureaucratic organizations. But trying to clarify the difference between an organized faith and a religious cult can be problematic. On a personal level, attempting to answer the question about the impact of religion on human history in a public school history class has also been a challenge. Because of the Establishment Clause of the First Amendment, teachers can and should teach about religion as a force in history, but they must be careful not to cross the line that would violate the barrier between church and state. In addition, many of my students, possibly because they have learned about the separation of church and state at an early age, have subtly displayed some discomfort in discussing a topic that many perceive to be personal in nature.

Therefore, as might be expected, religion has generally been introduced into my history classes in a cautious and conciliatory manner. We usually start by stating the obvious; that religion has always been a powerful force in history. For a definition, students usually agree that religion has been a timeless search to find meaning in the universe and those different cultures in the past have turned to religion to answer the unanswerable. The next step has always been to establish that our study of world religions, particularly the "big five" (Judaism, Christianity, Islam, Hinduism and Buddhism), will take place through a field trip to different religious sites so that comparisons can be made. On a typical trip, my classes have started by visiting a Jewish synagogue, then moved on to a Catholic monastery, then an Islamic mosque and finally we end up at a Hindu Temple. The religious sites we have visited vary a little from year to year, but regardless of where the school busses have taken us, the students have always been guided by the same set of essential questions. What do the faiths believe is the true nature of god or gods? How do the religions explain the creation of the universe and the start of the first humans? What does each religious faith have to say about the afterlife? What does one have to do in order to insure the best situation after death comes? Finally, what is the purpose of life; and related to this question, what is expected of the religion's adherents in terms of moral obligations? These questions are briefly explained before the day of the field trip. Students are told they should respectfully raise the questions on the day of the trip and should take careful notes on how each religion answers them. They also understand that the answers they receive will vary widely from one religious site to another.

As might be expected, the trip has always proven to be a mind-blowing experience for most of the students. Many have only started to wrestle with their own answers to these essential questions. When they hear how much the organized religious faiths differ on how to define the true nature of god, to explain the emergence of the first humans or what happens after we die, they are left more confused than ever. I usually respond by saying, "*welcome to a deeper understanding of religion.*" Once again, they are reminded that one major reason why religions first appeared was to provide answers to the unanswerable. The biggest surprise for most is the realization that established religions can differ so much in their answers. The other revelation that usually follows is the conclusion that some of the greatest differences exist within the same religion.

Take Judaism for example. Orthodox Jews rigorously follow 613 commandments, not just the better-known ten; separate women from men in their religious services and leave little room for how they interpret the Torah. On the other hand, Reform Jews have no trouble accepting the tenets of Evolution, are frequently guided by women rabbis and are much more open to a wider reading of the Bible. Many students observe that the differences between a Reform Jew and an Orthodox Jew may be greater than those between a Reform Jew and an Episcopalian Christian. Before the field trip experience and the follow-up discussions, most students would probably lay out the names of the world's major religions on some kind of visual continuum. Afterwards, they quickly realize that the real religious spectrum should probably place *"liberal"* or *"reformed"* at one end and terms like *"fundamentalist"* or *"orthodox"* at the other. As more discussion takes place, students usually gain even greater insight into the amazingly wide gulf that separates most of the world's religions today. If there is so much disagreement in the present, a time when science has been able to at least partially answer some of the unanswerable questions, how much disagreement has there been in the past?

For the most part, religion has been a divisive force in world history. While this has frequently led to wars, persecution and oppression, it also must be acknowledged that religion has played a positive role in shaping the world's diverse cultures and moral codes. Before reviewing examples of both the positive and the negative, one other dilemma needs to be addressed: can religious truth be both universal and relative? The answer to this question is relevant in any analysis of the impact of religion on history.

The question of universal standards versus relativity transcends the subject of religion and will receive greater attention in the next chapter. For now, the question simply poses a dilemma that has confronted just about every organized faith in history. The original Jews believed that there was only one god, which meant that all other gods being worshipped by all other civilizations were false gods. Christians saw Jesus Christ as the lord and savior of all who have faith, and other deities were never intended to share this status. The same can be said for the Islamic view of Allah. The Hindu and Buddhist ideas regarding reincarnation do not only apply to Hindus or Buddhists. In every case, the doctrine of each religion was intended to apply to all humans and should therefore be considered universal.

Yet in modern times, with the advent of religious freedom, at least in western cultures, it has become increasingly common for individuals to see religious ideas in relativistic terms. How many times does a Christian, with good intentions, say to his/her Jewish friend, *"We believe in Jesus Christ as our lord and savior, but we respect your right not to hold this belief"*? In our democratic society, different religions can hold conflicting beliefs and yet one set of ideas should not be considered more correct than another. This has spawned increased toleration and peace, but at some level, defies common sense. This development, along with the increased ability of modern science and reason to answer questions that formerly were the domain of religious faith, has reduced the impact of religion in today's world. In fact, in a Harris Poll taken in 2013, the percentage of people proclaiming absolute certainty that there is a God dropped to 54 percent from 66 percent in a span of just ten years. This can all be traced back to the Enlightenment of the 18th Century and to the ensuing freedom of religion contained within the First Amendment of the U.S. Constitution.

The founding of the earliest American colonies contained the seeds for the rise of religious freedom. The Pilgrims that settled Plymouth and the Puritans that established Boston came to the New World seeking the right to worship God in their own way. Once established as the Massachusetts Bay Colony, however, that did not mean they wanted to necessarily grant that same freedom to others. Therefore, as early as 1636, Roger Williams, Anne Hutchinson and other religious dissenters left Massachusetts to settle the colony of Rhode Island. It soon became a place of religious freedom and as a result, Jews and other denominations seeking an escape from religious persecution soon arrived. Congregation Jeshuat Israel was established in Newport, Rhode Island around 1658 and soon morphed into Touro Synagogue; the oldest surviving Jewish Synagogue building in North America.

Colonial American History still suffered for many years from the tension that resulted from the universal truth versus religious relativity issue. Yet while Quakers led by William Penn settled the colony named after their founder, they too granted religious freedom. Some colonies proved to be more tolerant than others, but the seeds for religious freedom had been sown. Thomas Jefferson, like many of our founding fathers, had come under the influence of the Enlightenment, and strongly believed that religion was a personal choice that should be free from government interference. Therefore, in 1779, he introduced the Bill for Establishing Religious Freedom in Virginia. Ten years later, as a compromise to win over support for the ratification of the Constitution, James Madison would propose the Bill of Rights, which included the principles of religious freedom in its very first amendment.

Touro Synagogue in Newport, Rhode Island
Courtesy of the Library of Congress, Prints and Photographs Division
HABS RI, 3-NEWP, 29—1

Most Americans know that freedom of religion is one of the key rights expressed in the First Amendment, but not everyone is familiar with the issue that has emerged from its two separate clauses. The First Amendment, which is basically just one, long, run-on sentence, begins with *"Congress shall make no law respecting the establishment of religion, or prohibiting the free exercise thereof..."* The first part of this statement, known as the Establishment Clause, creates a wall of separation between church and state, and is the reason why there have been numerous Supreme Court cases that have prohibited prayer in public schools or the posting of the Ten Commandments in public courthouses. The next part, the Free Exercise Clause, is what grants each of us the right to worship any god or gods we might choose. Could these two clauses from the First Amendment ever clash with each other? Yes, and this has led to some interesting hair-splitting by the Supreme Court.

Over the past several decades, the Supreme Court has wrestled with some tough issues involving the subject of religion. Can a community that is predominantly Christian be allowed to exercise their freedom by erecting Christmas symbols in their town square? The answer has been yes if the symbol is largely secular, such as a Christmas tree; but no to something as religious as a nativity scene. What if a football team representing a public high school wants to prepare for the big game by reciting a prayer? Technically, the answer is no, but this sort of thing goes on all over the nation on Friday nights. How about references to God on our money or in the Pledge of Allegiance? Is it okay for Congress or even the Supreme Court to start off their sessions by mentioning the Almighty? In the economic arena, should religious institutions receive breaks in property taxes, even if a church or a synagogue is located on some of the most expensive real estate in town? The answer to all of these questions has been a resounding yes; the Supreme Court has allowed all this. We live in a nation that has always been dominated by a Protestant majority, and from the very beginning, religion has played a large role in American history. However, what is truly amazing is that despite the enormous influence of religion in American society in the form of mega churches, televangelism and the rise of the Moral Majority in politics, the First Amendment has created a balance that has led to unprecedented religious harmony and toleration. Most people would assume that Israel, with 6.1 million Jews, would be the nation with the biggest Jewish population, and because of a recent rise in fertility, this has become true. With 5.7 million Jews, the United States runs a close second. France comes in a distant third with only 475,000. Why are there so many Jews in the United States? A quick glance at the First Amendment is good starting point to answer that question.

Even if one agrees that the rise of religious freedom combined with the growing influence of modern science has reduced the impact of religion on the modern world, there is no denying that it has played an enormous role throughout world history. So much of that impact has been deadly and destructive that at one point, Voltaire, the great philosophical thinker in France during the 18th Century Enlightenment, called Christianity "*the most ridiculous, the most absurd and bloody religion that has ever infected the world.*" He based this notion on the large number of people who had died as a result of religious wars fought between different denominations that each felt had cornered the truth about such topics as the true nature of God or how one should achieve salvation. While this is clearly a controversial point, there is no denying the numbers. In the Crusades that occurred when Christian armies from Western Europe traveled to the Middle East to try to recapture *"the Holy Land"* from the Muslims in the 12th and 13th Centuries, it is estimated that between one and three million people lost their lives. In the late 16th Century, when Catholics fought against Protestants for control of France, estimates of the number killed range between two and four million. A short time later, when the Thirty Years War consumed most of Western Europe from 1618 to 1648, the number of dead is estimated to have run between three million and 11 million. While political issues also complicated this war, the start of the Protestant Reformation a century earlier is what began the chain reaction of events that pitted Catholics against Protestants. The numbers killed in religious conflicts is by no means limited to the distant past. Up to a quarter of a million people died in Lebanon's civil war that involved Shiite Muslims, Sunni Muslims and Christians between 1975 and 1990. In the Second Sudanese War, which again concerned Christians and Muslims in a bloody conflict that ran between 1983 and 2005, there were between one to two million casualties. As previously stated, religion has been a divisive force in history, and its greatest negative impact has manifested itself in a long series of religious wars.

Voltaire
Courtesy of the Library of Congress
Prints and Photographs Division LC-USZ62-72043

These conflicts have not been limited to Europe or to the West. The subcontinent of Asia is a giant graveyard for people who have died in religious conflict. After the dissolution of the British Raj in 1947, a decision was made to create two new sovereign nations: India for the Hindus and Pakistan for the Muslims. The subsequent partition of India displaced up to 12.5 million people, with estimates of loss of life varying from several hundred thousand to a million. What makes this situation even scarier, however, is the fact that the conflict between Hindu India and Muslim Pakistan continues up to the present, and that both nations possess nuclear weapons. My students are generally shocked when they learn that the religious cold war in the Asian subcontinent has lasted longer than the one they are more familiar with between the United States and the Soviet Union.

In addition to wars and conflicts, religion has been a combustible fuel that has ignited may acts of intolerance and persecution throughout history. The legacy of anti-Semitism dates back thousands of years and has appeared in a variety of forms. Jews were expelled from England in 1290, faced torture and expulsion from Spain in the Inquisition that began in the late 15th Century and were systematically exterminated in the Holocaust during the Second World War. At different times and in different places, almost every faith has been guilty of persecuting another faith. The situation has not improved much in modern times. In Nigeria, for example, the numbers are shocking. According to the U.S. Commission on International Religious Freedom, 12,000 people have been killed in a cycle of violence between Christians and Muslims stretching back more than a decade. Egypt imprisons members of the Baha'i faith and members of minority Muslim sects; additionally, some are also fired from their jobs, kicked out of universities and barred from having bank accounts, driver's licenses, even birth certificates. In Myanmar, the government attempted to control Buddhist institutions through coercive means, including the intimidation, torture and murder of monks. After monks played an active role in the protest movements against military dictatorships in 2007, the state cracked down on Buddhist monks and monasteries. A thorough review of the examples of religious persecution from both the past and the present would more than fill the pages of this book, but the point should be clear.

While it is tempting to tout the progress made as a result of the increased tolerance in recent times, religion still imposes major restrictions on individual freedom throughout the world. While officially abolished, the caste system in India that resulted from the long-standing traditions of Hinduism still lead to daily examples of prejudice directed at the untouchable castes. Women accused of adultery can still be stoned to death in many Islamic societies. Orthodox Jewish women living in arranged marriages wishing to receive a divorce or *"get"* cannot receive one unless their husbands agree. Furthermore, for the over one billion Roman Catholics around the world, there is not a single woman priest. All of these examples (and many others) are shrouded in controversy, but there is no denying that at their core, there is an organized religious faith imposing restrictions on someone's individual freedom.

It would be a serious error, however, to discuss only the negative impact that organized religion has had on the course of world history. Although it is almost impossible to prove this point with any quantifiable evidence, religion has clearly had a significant impact on the moral structure of every society, past and present. Requirements posed by the gods in any ancient, polytheistic culture, from the Egyptians and Mesopotamians to the Greeks and Romans, have shaped the way people treated each other. The same can be said for Hinduism, Buddhism and Taoism in the East as well as for tribal cultures in Africa, the Western Hemisphere and Oceania. Confucius heavily focused on the li, the principle of maintaining proper relationships and rituals that will enhance the life of the individual, the family and the state. The Buddha taught that the only way to break free from the endless cycle of reincarnation was to take steps to end the human suffering that is found all around us. It would be difficult to find any religious faith that did not have something to say on the subject of moral values.

The rise of Judaism followed by the evolution of Christianity and Islam as related monotheistic faiths placed an even sharper focus on morality. The narrative of the ancient Hebrews is clouded by a lack of reliable historical evidence, and as a result, stories from the Old Testament are not usually included in history textbooks. Were there really an Adam and Eve? An Abraham? Noah? Moses? Great debates have been held over these questions, but while there may never be reliable historical proof that Moses received the Ten Commandments from God on Mount Sinai, there is no denying that Jewish people ever since have maintained they were chosen to receive the Ten Commandments. From these commandments came an emphasis on moral behavior that was unprecedented.

As the Hebrews found themselves repeatedly subjugated by the Babylonians, the Greeks and finally the Romans, they managed to survive by clinging to the moral values found in their Torah; but they also remained small in population and on the fringe of most ancient societies. Their moral values had little appeal to the vast majority of people who were not Jewish. The addition of new moral ideas introduced by Jesus of Nazareth, who was considered a Hebrew up until the day he died on a Roman cross, completely changed everything. Thanks to the efforts of disciples like Paul, the teachings of Jesus, especially those that emphasized brotherhood, love and a more peaceful universe, had much broader appeal and slowly spread throughout the Roman Empire. Even with the fall of Rome in the late 5th century and the rise of the Middle Ages in western Europe, Christianity continued to spread and flourish. So did Judaic-Christian morality.

Finally, by the early 7th century, Muhammad introduced the third major monotheistic faith to the world: Islam. Once again, a new set of moral values was built on a foundation of Jewish and Christian ethics, and once again, the moral precepts were codified in a religious book; in this case, the Koran. Over three billion people today, Jews, Christians and Muslims; practically half of the planet's population, live by the morality found in the Torah, the New Testament of the Bible and the Koran. Legal systems around the world that spell out laws dealing with murder, theft, lying, adultery, family commitments and a host of other legal obligations can all be traced to these religious roots. It is impossible to say, but how much worse would the world be today if the major religions had not prescribed their moral values to the millions of their adherents?

In fact, most organized religions go further than simply setting requirements to guide humans in how to get along. Most, if not all, have expectations regarding charity, giving alms and doing missionary work. Granted, some of their motivation may stem from the desire to spread their particular faith, but the end result is that religion has motivated millions of people to try to make the world a better place. For example, Jews have always been guided by the principle of tzedakah, the act of giving aid, assistance and money to the poor and needy and to other worthy causes. This was to be done not because it would lead to any kind of reward, but because it is simply the right thing to do. To emphasize this point, ideally, tzedakah should be done anonymously. For thousands of years, Christians have been expected to tithe, to give a tenth part of one's salary to the causes supported by the Church; and Christian missionaries have built and established schools, hospitals and homeless shelters around the world. In fact, at the core of Christianity is this principle from Luke, that *"when you give a feast, invite the poor, the crippled, the lame, the blind."* And within Islam, giving alms to the poor is one of the Five Pillars, the basic expectations that Allah maintains for every devout Muslim. Buddhists do not directly focus on maintaining soup kitchens or providing clothes for the poor, but they do make a concerted effort to work with the root problems of greed, anger and mental confusion. They maintain the belief that if everyone did this, there would be a lot more generosity, kindness and wisdom in the world; and the hungry would be fed and the homeless housed. Once again, just about every organized religion puts forth the effort to make the world a better place.

Finally, anyone who has travelled even a short distance from home can see ample evidence of the cultural contributions that have been made by the world's religious faiths. Visit the Hagia Sophia in Istanbul, St. Peter's

Basilica in the Vatican, or the Pagoda of Kofuku-ji, which is the Buddhist temple in Nara, Japan, and you can see just three of the thousands of examples of religious architecture around the world. Some of the planet's most beautiful examples of structural design were built as a tribute to people's religious passion and faith. Read Greek or Roman mythology, or better yet, take a look at the Hindu Bhagavad-Gita to see examples of religiously inspired literature. The same can be said for art, music, dance and most other forms of creative expression. If nothing else, just listen to Christian gospel music or enjoy the carols that accompany the Christmas season to witness how religion has enriched American culture.

No matter where one falls on a spectrum of religious faith, there is no getting away from religion. According to the *Washington Times*, 84% of the world's population still has faith, and this number was undoubtedly higher in the past. Religion definitely played a role in the burning of the Church of the Multiplication of the Loaves and Fish. It has also exerted a profound if not indirect influence over the atrocities committed by ISIS, the harsh dictates of the Taliban in Afghanistan and the destruction of Buddhist temples by the Chinese government in Tibet. There is no denying the destructive and divisive force that religion has played and continues to play throughout the planet.

However, while the world's major religions tend to divide people from each other, the same can be said for politics, economics and geography. While this divisiveness has led to wars and persecution, it has also enriched our lives with diversity and cultural expression. As might be expected, the vast majority of the students in my classes have professed some sort of religious faith, and most have said that by definition, faith encapsulates beliefs and ideas that are held without evidence. If you need proof to back up a belief in God or the existence of an afterlife, then this knowledge is the result of reason; it does not come through faith. Throughout the ages, the vast majority of people have always possessed some form of religious faith, and despite all the advances in science, there is no reason to believe this is about to change. The need for religious faith is a universal characteristic of being human, and for the better as well as the worse, this fact has had an indescribable impact on the course of history.

Prevailing World Religions Map, 2007

Courtesy of LilTeK21, (CC BY-SA 3.0)
https://commons.wikimedia.org/wiki/File:Prevailing_world_religions_map.png

Suggested Reading:

Harper, Jennifer. "84 Percent of the World Population Has Faith; a Third Are Christian." *Washington Times*. December 23, 2012. http://www.washingtontimes.com/blog/Watercooler/2012/dec/23/84-percent-world-population-has-faith-third-are-ch/.

Liben, Paul. "United States Commission on International Religious Freedom 2013 Annual Report ." *United States Commission on International Religious Freedom.* April 2013. http://www.uscirf.gov/sites/default/files/resources/2013 USCIRF Annual Report(2).pdf.

Missal, Larry Shannon. "American's Belief in God, Miracles and Heaven Declines." *The Harris Poll.* December 16, 2013. http://www.theharrispoll.com/health-and-life/Americans_Belief_in_God_Miracles_and_Heaven_Decline.html.

Smith, Huston. *The World's Religions.* New York: Harper Collins, 1991.

Voltaire, Francois-Marie. *The Portable Voltaire,* Edited by Ben Ray Redman. New York: Penguin Books, 1977.

Chapter 4
History's moral calculus

A campaign against female genital mutilation – a road sign
near Kapchorwa, Uganda
Courtesy of Amnon Shavit(CC BY-SA 3.0)
https://commons.wikimedia.org/wiki/File:Campaign_road_sign_against_female_genital_mutilation_%28cropped%29_2.jpg

How should civilizations be morally evaluated?

The place is the Newark International Airport and the year is 1996. A 17-year-old girl named Fauziya Kassindja has just arrived seeking asylum. She has fled her native country of Togo, a small West African nation, to escape what people call excision. Excision is a permanently disfiguring procedure that is sometimes called female circumcision although it has little resemblance to the Jewish ritual. In the West, it is more commonly referred to as genital mutilation. According to the World Health Organization, the practice is widespread in 26 African nations, and two million girls each year are excised. In some cases, excision is part of an elaborate tribal ritual, performed in small traditional villages; and some girls look forward to it because it signals their acceptance into the adult world. In other instances, the practice is carried out in cities on young women who desperately resist.

Fauziya Kassindja was the youngest of five daughters in a devoutly Muslim family. Her father, who owned a successful trucking business, was opposed to excision, and he was able to defy the tradition because of his wealth. His first four daughters were married without being mutilated. But when Fauziya was 16, he suddenly died. Fauziya then came under the authority of her grandfather, who arranged a marriage for her and prepared to have her excised. Fauziya was terrified, and her mother and older sister helped her to escape.

In America, Fauziya was held for two years while authorities decided what to do with her. She was finally granted asylum, but not before she became the center of a controversy over how to regard the cultural practices of other peoples. A series of articles in the *New York Times* encouraged the idea that excision is a barbaric practice that should be condemned. This might be called the universal moral standards position because it is based on the thinking that there is a set of universal moral standards by which ALL civilizations should be guided and judged. Other observers were reluctant to be so judgmental – live and let live, they said; after all, our practices probably seem just as strange to other cultures. They insist that there is no cultural-neutral moral standard to which we may appeal. Let's call this the cultural relativism position. While this controversy made headlines just about 20 years ago, the deeper issue it represents has existed throughout history.

Relativity is a broader subject that has roots in modern physics. The saying that everything is relative is frequently applied to commonplace subjects like speed, height, and even intelligence. When someone says they can run fast, we all know that while they may win many footraces, they could not begin to compete with a car or an airplane. When parents brag about the intelligence of their child, this usually means they make good grades in school, but compared to Albert Einstein, they may not be so smart. It is all relative. I'm frequently the tallest person in the room at certain family gatherings, but at five foot, nine, I never considered a career in the NBA.

Carried over to the subject of history, the subject of relativity becomes relevant anytime a civilization, past or present, is morally evaluated by a different civilization. When teaching about Marco Polo's arrival in the court of the Kublai Khan, Columbus' first contact with the indigenous people of North America or 19th Century Imperialism, comparisons between two or more different cultures become inevitable. Many teachers might choose to avoid the issue, but that approach will not satisfy the curious students who wonder why Columbus felt justified in enslaving the people he called Indians. A better approach might be to address the questions head on. Through migration patterns, wars, conquests and trade, civilizations have been encountering each other for thousands of years. Therefore, an examination of the cultural relativity versus universal standards question can only yield a deeper understanding of the subject.

Cultural relativists regard universal standards as little more than the arbitrary dictates of the more powerful nations of the world, engaging in some form of colonization by imposing their values on less powerful nations. From this perspective, there is little reason to argue that international norms or universal standards should supersede a state's history, religion or culture. What is the basis for this position? First, cultural relativists are understandably nervous about interfering in the social customs of other peoples. Europeans and their cultural descendents in America have a shabby history of destroying native cultures in the name of Christianity and Enlightenment, not to mention self-interest. Second, the relativists feel, rightly enough, that we should be tolerant of other cultures. Tolerance is seen as a virtue; a tolerant person is willing to live in peaceful cooperation with those who see things differently. The result will be a more peaceful world. Finally, the cultural relativists are reluctant to judge a practice like excision because they know that there are practices within our own culture that would be scorned by other civilizations. They are aware that American culture has been accused of being violent, self-indulgent and overly materialistic, and they are familiar with the phrase about those who live in glass houses.

James Rachels, an American philosopher who specialized in ethics, pointed out that cultural relativists have advanced several distinct claims. First, different societies have different moral codes and the moral code of one society has no special status; it is merely one among many. According to Rachels, there is no universal truth in ethics, no moral truths that holds for all people at all times. This means there is no objective standard that can be used to judge one society's code as better than another's. It is mere arrogance for us to try to judge the conduct of other peoples. We should adopt an attitude of tolerance towards the practices of other cultures.

Even if one tends to reject this line of thinking, there are still two lessons that can be learned from cultural relativity. First, relativists remind us about the danger of assuming that all of our preferences are based on an absolute rational standard. They are not. Many of our practices are merely peculiar to our society, and it is easy to lose sight of this fact. There are many matters we tend to think of in terms of objective right and wrong that are really nothing more than social conventions. Should women cover their breasts? A publicly exposed breast may be scandalous in our society, whereas in other cultures, it is unremarkable. Objectively speaking, it is neither right nor wrong.

The second lesson has to do with keeping an open mind. In the course of growing up, we have all acquired some strong feelings. When applied to countries, according to Herodotus, the Greek *"father of history"*, any individual, when given the opportunity of choosing from amongst all the nations of the world the set of beliefs which he thought best, would inevitably, after careful consideration of their relative merits, choose that of his own country. Everyone without exception believes his own native customs, and the religion he was brought up in, to be the best. Realizing this can result in avoiding arrogance and having more open minds. We may then be more open to discovering the truth, whatever that might be.

Portrait statue of Herodotus along the balustrade
Courtesy of the Library of Congress, Prints and Photographs Division
Lc-DIG-highsm-02110

In order to jump into the opposing position of universal moral standards, let's examine the Inuit Eskimos. The customs of the Inuit up until the early 1900's were very different from our own. The men often had more than one wife, and they would share their wives with guests, lending them for the night as a sign of hospitality. Moreover, within a community, a dominant male might demand and get regular sexual access to other men's wives. The women, however, were free to break these arrangements simply by leaving their husbands and taking up with new partners. Overall, the Eskimo practice was a capricious scheme that had little resemblance to what we call marriage.

However, it was not only their marriage and sexual practices that were different. The Eskimos also seemed to have less regard for human life. Infanticide, for example, was common. Knud Rasmussen, one of the most famous early explorers, reported that he met one woman who had borne 20 children but had killed ten of them at birth. Female babies, he found, were especially liable to be destroyed, and this was permitted simply at the parents' discretion, with no social stigma. Older people, when they became too feeble to contribute to the family, were also left out in the snow to die. So there seemed to be, in this society, remarkably little respect for life.

At first glance, the advocates for the universal moral standards would seem to have a field day with this example. How could the cultural relativists possibly defend wife sharing, infanticide and leaving senior citizens out to die in the snow? However, a closer examination by anthropologists would suggest an even more universal standard: survival. Killing babies is not even the first option considered. Adoption is common and childless couples are especially happy to take a more fertile couple's *"surplus."* Killing is only the last resort. However, the Eskimos live in a very harsh environment, and when resources become scarce, infants and seniors may have to make the ultimate sacrifice. The Eskimos' values are not all that different from our own. However, life forces choices upon them we do not have to make. Survival is a universal standard and combined with others, like honesty and the avoidance of unnecessary killing, we do have a set of universal values by which to morally evaluate all civilizations.

The obvious question that can be raised with the advocates of the universal moral standards position is what are the universal moral standards? According to Dr. Kent M. Keith, an American writer and leader in higher education, there is a universal moral code consisting of a list of fundamental moral principles that can be found throughout the world. Created by

Keith in 2003 while writing a book on morality and ethics, the code incorporates basic, universal ideas about how we should live and how we should treat each other. The code is divided into two complementary sets of statements. The first set consists of negative statements about not doing harm: do not lie, steal, cheat, commit incest, murder and so on. The second is to do good: be generous, be faithful to your family and friends, be kind to strangers, respect all life, etc. This simple set of principles reflects the culmination today of thousands of years of codified moral rules dating back to the Ten Commandments and the teachings of Confucius.

In addition, the proponents of universal moral standards maintain that there are certain human rights that have been guaranteed by international treaties and conventions. The United Nations Charter identifies one of the organization's primary objectives as *"promoting and encouraging respect for human rights and for fundamental freedoms for all without distinction as to race, sex, language or religion."* Under the aegis of the United Nations, numerous human rights declarations, treaties and conventions have been drafted. One of the most fundamental declarations adopted by the U.N. General Assembly is the Universal Declaration of Human Rights. It sets forth the basic rights and freedoms that the international community committed itself to respecting and protecting. The declaration's preamble states that it is to serve *"as a common standard of achievement for all peoples and all nations."* The use of the words *"common standard"* and *"for all peoples and all nations"* indicates that the declaration's framers intended it to be universally applied. The Universal Declaration has been followed by a number of treaties that elaborate on its basic rights and freedoms. These treaties protect civil, political, economic, social and cultural rights. They prohibit governments from interfering with freedom of thought, conscience and religion or from engaging in actions such as torture or genocide. The treaties also prevent racial and gender discrimination. The fact that nations did not have these standards to enforce prior to World War Two meant that no one intervened in a timely manner or at all as the Nazis repressed, persecuted and then exterminated millions of people. This serves as evidence to the world community of its tragic failure to develop and enforce a set of universal moral standards.

Finally, those in favor of a universal standards approach not only question the sanctity of culture, but also disagree with the view that international human rights standards are little more than arbitrary legal pronouncements by those with power or wealth to control those lacking power or wealth. The standards that came into existence after the Second World

War were not legislated by a few powerful nations. To the contrary, representatives from many diverse nations drafted them. These drafters agreed that state sovereignty or unique cultural traditions could never justify certain practices, such as genocide or torture.

When applied to an examination of history, the case for cultural relativity first began to build in the days of the ancient Greeks. Once again, it was Herodotus who originally raised the subject in his *History* by noting that Darius, the king of ancient Persia, was intrigued by the variety of cultures he encountered in his travels. He had found, for example, that the Callatians, a tribe of Indians, customarily ate the bodies of their dead fathers. The Greeks, or course, did not do that; the Greeks practiced cremation and regarded the funeral pyre as the natural and fitting way to dispose of the dead. Darius thought that a sophisticated understanding of the world must include an appreciation of such differences between cultures. Therefore, he invited in representatives from the Callatians and representatives from the Greeks and told each group about the funerary practices of the other group. As might be expected, each group was disgusted by what they heard.

The story of the ancient nations-Darius the Great
Courtesy of https://www.flickr.com/photos/internetarchive-bookimages/14582629340

This story recounted by Herodotus illustrates the recurring issue of cultural relativism throughout history. Different cultures have always had different moral codes. What has been thought right within one group may be utterly abhorrent to the members of another group, and vice versa. Should we eat the bodies of the dead or burn them? If you were a Greek, one answer would seem obviously correct; but if you were a Callatian, the opposite would seem equally certain. And what about today? Most people in our Western Culture would probably side with the Greeks. However, to the Callatians, eating the flesh of the dead could be understood as a sign of respect. It could be taken as a symbolic act that says we wish this person's spirit to dwell within us. To the Callatians, burying the dead could be seen as an act of rejection, and burning the corpse as positively scornful.

The story of Darius shows us that there were cultural relativists thousands of years ago. However, back then, just as today, the majority of people believed their own cultural norms were superior and were the ones to be followed; and unfortunately, this played out time and time again throughout history. The Greeks clearly viewed their culture as more advanced and saw victories in battles like Marathon and Salamis against the Persians as the salvation of their Western values in the face of the *"barbarism"* that threatened from the East. They then proceeded to build colonies throughout the Mediterranean world to better spread their civilization. The later conquests of Alexander the Great put the Greeks into the offensive and helped to spread their *"advanced"* Hellenic civilization as far as Egypt and India. This resulted in the Hellenistic Era, which was characterized by the spreading influence of Greek values, ideas and cultural achievements. A couple of centuries later, the Romans built an enormous empire on the cultural foundation first established by the Greeks. While the Romans lasted as long as they did partially because of the tolerance they displayed toward the cultures they had conquered, make no mistake, there is a reason why we say, *"all roads lead to Rome."* The common practice of enslaving large numbers of subjugated people also supports the idea that the Romans displayed a high level of cultural arrogance.

Cultural ethnocentrism also existed in the Far East. There are numerous times when the Japanese and the Chinese waged wars against each other, at least partially because each saw the other as culturally inferior. Unlike the West, this sometimes led to deliberate acts of isolation rather than empire building. The Great Wall was built primarily to keep out the *"barbaric hordes"*, and under the shoguns, Japan expelled all foreigners. In fact, Japan did not open itself up to the world they had scorned for so many centuries until American warships forced the issue in the mid 19th Century. Even

History's moral calculus

then, although foreigners from the West were imported to help the Japanese modernize their economy, technology and military, the Japanese still viewed their culture as superior to that of all of their Asian neighbors. This fact goes a long way towards explaining the military aggression Japan took in the 1930s that finally culminated in the attack on Pearl Harbor and America's entry into World War Two.

The fall of the Roman Empire in the western half of Europe led to a thousand years of cultural decline commonly known as the Middle Ages. When the Renaissance of the 15th Century pushed the Europeans into a stronger position, newly created nations like Portugal, Spain, France and England wasted no time in exploring the New World *("discovered"* by Columbus), and they soon were making efforts to export their Christian religion and their *"superior"* way of life to most of North, Central and South America. This, in turn, later led to the subjugation by Europeans of Australia, most of Africa and much of the Asian subcontinent; and in the case of the Africans, the rise of a horrific slave trade to better meet the labor needs in their new western colonies.

To better understand these developments, I have my students conduct a nighttime mock trial at the end of every school year where the defendant is Hernando Cortez, and the charges are crimes against humanity because of the manner in which this Spanish conquistador subjugated the Aztecs. The jury is composed of their parents. The students understand in advance that the central issue of this case involves the moral assessment of two different cultures. Each side prepares an opening statement, calls to the stand and questions three witnesses, cross-examines the other side's witnesses and sums up their case in closing statements.

Reception of Hernando Cortez by the Emperor Montezuma
Courtesy of the Library of Congress, Prints and Photographs Division
LC-USZC4-741

The prosecution tries to prove that Cortez and the Spaniards viewed the Aztecs as barbaric heathens who would not only benefit under the influence of the Catholic Church and the political control of the Spanish king, but would also provide gold and silver to enrich Cortez and his imperial highness in Madrid. The defense usually counters by focusing on the point that Cortez brought an end to the Aztec practice of sacrificing between 20,000 and 250,000 people per year (estimates vary widely). In some cases, young women had their hearts cut out of their chests and the Aztec priests would then bite into the hearts while they were still beating. Surely, the indigenous people of Mexico would be better off living in the colony of New Spain than under this brutal Aztec control. The prosecution counters this point by bringing up the fact that Spain had already launched its Inquisition, characterized by the heavy use of torture and the burning at the stake of thousands of *"infidels."* Did the alleged cultural superiority of the Spanish justify the conquests by Cortez? By the end of the trial, the parents on the jury are forced to deliberate by applying the essential question about cultural relativity to a relevant historical example. More often than not, the trial usually ends with a hung jury.

Cultural condescension has also played a significant role throughout American History. This has been seen in the rise of modern racism created to justify the African slave trade and in the series of land grabs, broken treaties and wars that forced the indigenous people off their land. In fact, my U.S. History classes have also ended their school year with a mock trial that also focuses on the same essential question. In this case, the defendant is President Andrew Jackson and the charge revolves around his determination to pass and enforce the Indian Removal Act of 1830. In particular, the Cherokee, who had adopted many American cultural practices such as Christianity and formal education, resisted the efforts to force them beyond the Mississippi River not on the battlefields, but in the courts. Under chief justice John Marshall, the Supreme Court sided with the Cherokee; however, President Jackson refused to abide by that decision and instead, decided to force the Cherokee to move. The Prosecution usually maintains that Jackson's attitude toward Native Americans was paternalistic and patronizing, and later resulted in the lost lives of hundreds of the Cherokee along the infamous Trail of Tears. The defense once again usually counters with the argument that the Cherokee would be better off living in what is now Oklahoma rather than continuing to resist the intrusion of white settlers who were hungry for their land.

By the end of the 19th Century, the American government did not know what to do about the *"Indian Question."* The policy in the past had been to force the different tribes onto reservations consisting of land that was essentially unwanted by most white settlers. However, by the late 1800s, this policy fell out of favor. The Dawes Act of 1887 carved up reservations into individual plots of land and encouraged Native Americans to take up farming as a way of life. In addition, with the encouragement of groups like the Friends of the Indian, native children were encouraged to attend boarding schools in the East like the one located in Carlisle, Pennsylvania. The pendulum had now swung from one extreme to another. Rather than attempting to isolate the native cultures that were seen as inferior, the plan was to force them to assimilate into the great American melting pot. At Carlisle, young boys had their hair cut, were forced to attend church and had their mouths washed out with lye soap if they were caught speaking their tribal language. Lurking beneath the surface of these events was the deeply held attitude that white civilization was superior to that of the indigenous tribes.

Overseas, during this same time period, cultural arrogance can best be seen in the rise of modern imperialism. Between 1880 and 1914, the entire African continent, except for Ethiopia and Liberia, was carved into colonies by European nations in the name of what the English writer, Rudyard Kipling, called "*The White Man's Burden.*" India became the crown jewel of a British empire upon which "*the sun never set.*" The French controlled Laos, Cambodia, and Vietnam. The Dutch *"owned"* Indonesia, and after a brief conflict between the United States and Spain in 1898, the Philippines became American.

Modern imperialism emerged for several reasons, including the rise of modern nationalism and the economic need to provide industry with cheap natural resources and emerging markets. India had ten times the population of Great Britain, its *"mother country"*, so this provided a huge market for British textile products that were being manufactured from Indian cotton. However, the desire to impose cultural standards that were perceived as superior was a big motive behind British imperialism. This same rationale infected American thinking in the late 19th Century and it was clearly seen in the debate over what to do with the Philippines after it had been liberated from Spain. Some famous Americans such as William Jennings Bryan and Mark Twain took a position against colonialism in places like the Philippines, but the imperialists, led by Theodore Roosevelt, won the day. In the end, it took two years and up to 200,000 Philippine casualties before the United States had firm control over its first Asian colony, but America had become an imperial power and was now in a position to export its *"advanced Christian civilization."*

The mid 20th Century has witnessed a different variation of cultural arrogance by the United States in the guise of the Cold War. In its efforts to contain the spread of Soviet communism between the end of World War Two and the fall of the Berlin Wall in 1989, the United States interfered in the affairs of nations around the globe. This sometimes took the obvious form of military interventions in places like Korea, Vietnam and Cuba. Some actions were more covert, such as the overthrow of world leaders in places as far flung as Chile, Iran and Cambodia. Even American actions that were purely altruistic on the surface contained the seeds of cultural arrogance. The Marshall Plan of the late 1940s simply involved American dollars to help rebuild European nations from the ashes of the Second World War. However, it must also be acknowledged that another goal of the money was to inoculate these nations from the *"evils"* of communism. When President Kennedy called for a new generation to go forth via the Peace Corps to work in developing nations, the underlying goal was to spread knowledge and civilization to the unenlightened corners of the world. In both cases, there is no denying that there were good intentions, but these actions were based on the belief that America's democratic way of life was superior. In these locales, U.S. military and economic might was used to spread American values and to win the hearts and minds of the local populace. The results may have been mixed, but the effort alone contributed to the rise of *the "ugly American"* image that the U.S. has earned around much of the world.

Over the past 25 years, the adversary has changed, but not the arrogance. Communism may have been vanquished, but it has only been replaced by the *"evils"* of modern terrorism. Ever since the attacks on September 11, 2001, the United States has sent military forces to Afghanistan and Iraq. More important, covert activities have taken place in many other countries, particularly in the Middle East. Accounts about taking out bad guys with missiles launched by unmanned drones in nations like Yemen and Pakistan have become so common they are no longer front-page news stories. While there is no question that America has a legitimate right to protect itself on U.S. soil, taking the war into other nations carries with it the perception of American cultural arrogance.

The same can be said about the distribution of military bases around the world. According to a September 2015 article in *The Nation* by David Vine, there are now around 800 US bases in foreign countries. There are still 174 base sites in Germany, 113 in Japan and 83 in South Korea according to the Pentagon. Hundreds more are scattered in around 80 nations; including Aruba, Australia, Bahrain, Bulgaria, Colombia, Kenya and Qatar. It should be noted that there are no freestanding bases staffed by foreign nations located in the United States. While few Americans realize it, the United States has more bases in foreign lands than any other people, nation or empire in history. Americans may take pride in this fact, and most certainly feel a greater sense of security. However, how does the 95 per cent of the world's population not living in the United States view this fact?

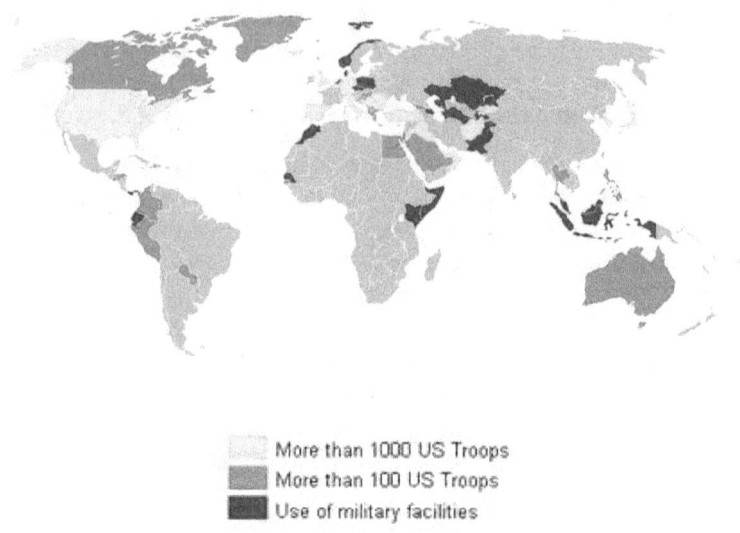

U.S. Military Bases In the World, 2007
Courtesy of Tree Sign (PD-user)
https://commons.wikimedia.org/wiki/File:US_military_bases_in_the_world_2007.PNG

While those who support the principle of universal cultural standards might have a difficult time defending the application of this position throughout much of our history, this does not diminish their position in the modern world. Twelve million people died in Nazi concentration camps and the majority of the sixty million people who died in World War Two were innocent civilians. Roughly one and a half million Cambodians died in the killing fields of that nation in the mid 1970s and the Hutu majority in Rwanda butchered over half a million Tutsis during the mid 1990s. Mass murder, torture and human rights violations are still commonplace in many parts of the world, and those who believe in fixed moral standards feel like these developments cannot be ignored in the name of respecting cultural variation. Women and other minority groups are still commonly subjected to major violations of their human rights. Wars, beheadings, torture and acts of genocide still appear on a regular basis on the nightly news. Furthermore, as previously stated, the nations of the world have signed treaties, created global organizations and a World Court, and have passed international legislation designed to establish and maintain universal standards around the planet. Despite the long record of cultural arrogance throughout history, one hundred per cent adherence to the tenets of cultural relativity could lead to a repeat of the Holocaust, and in a world of nuclear weapons, this could prove to be cataclysmic.

Of all the questions discussed in this book, this may be one of the toughest. It is almost impossible to dogmatically support only the position of cultural relativity or that of universal cultural standards. To achieve a sense of closure at the end of a class that takes up the discussion of this essential question, I usually present the students with a one to ten spectrum to indicate where they fall on the *"moral evaluation of civilizations"* continuum. Even then, many students admit to being confused and conflicted over this issue.

When first told about Fauziya and her dilemma, the majority of students surprising take the culturally relativist position and argue that while excision may seem abhorrent to most Americans, we are not in a position to tell other cultures how to behave. However, after some intense discussion and some reflective thinking, many students change their minds. The end result is a fairly even split. While a class may be divided over such practices as female excision, most students come to appreciate the importance of the broader essential question. They see the important role the question has played in both the past and the present, and most come to appreciate that a deeper level of understanding of the cultural relativity essential question may lead to fewer global conflicts and more respect for the widespread diversity that engulfs our planet.

Suggested Reading:

Briant, Pierre. *Darius in the Shadow of Alexander.* Translated by Jane Marie Todd. Cambridge: President and Fellows of Harvard College, 2015.

Casas, Bartolome de Las. *A Short Account of the Destruction of the Indies.* Translated by Nigel Griffin. London: Penguin Books, 1992.

Dugger, Celia W. "A Refugee's Body Is Intact But Her Family Is Torn." *New York Times.* September 11, 1996. http://www.nytimes.com/1996/09/11/nyregion/a-refugee-s-body-is-intact-but-her-family-is-torn.html?pagewanted=all.

"Female Genital Mutilation." *World Health Organization.* February 2016. http://www.who.int/mediacentre/factsheets/fs241/en/.

Herodotus. *The Histories,* Edited by John M. Marincola. London: Penguin Books, 2003.

Inskeep, John. *Jacksonland: President Andrew Jackson, Cherokee Chief John Ross, and a Great American Land Grab.* New York: Penguin Press, 2015.

Keith, Kent M. "The Universal Moral Code." 2003. http://www.universalmoralcode.com.

Levy, Buddy. *Conquistador: Hernan Cortes, King Montezuma, and the Last Stand of the Aztecs.* New York: Bantam Books, 2009.

Rachels, James and Stuart Rachels. *The Elements of Moral Philosophy.* New York: McGraw Hill Education, 2014.

"The Universal Declaration of Human Rights." *United Nations Organization.* December 10, 1948. http://www.un.org/en/universal-declaration-human-rights/.

Vine, David. "The United States Probably Has More Foreign Military Bases Than Any Other People, Nation or Empire in History." *The Nation.* September 14, 2015. http://www.the nation.com/article/the-united-states-probably-has-more-foreign-military-bases-than-any-other-people-nation-or-empire-in-history/.

Chapter 5

Stereotypes: The good, the bad and the ugly

Draft riot in New York City, 1863
Courtesy of the Library of Congress
Prints and Photographs Division LC-USZ62-47037

Why do people ascribe defining characteristics to certain nationalities?

The place is New York City and the date is July 13, 1863. Thousands of white, working-class men, primarily ethnic Irish, are taking to the streets to riot. Over the next three days, they burned down buildings and attacked blacks wherever they could find them. Known at the time as Draft Week, this outbreak of violence was the culmination of working-class discontent with the new laws passed by Congress that year to draft men to fight in the ongoing

American Civil War. In particular, what stirred up the most resentment was the allowance made for the wealthy that permitted them to pay a $300 commutation fee (equivalent to $5,766 today) to hire a substitute and therefore avoid the draft. The riots remain the largest civil and racial insurrection in American history, aside from the Civil War itself. Ironically, they occurred in the middle of the Civil War, just days after the battle of Gettysburg: the bloodiest battle in U.S. history.

Initially intended to express anger at the draft, the protests turned into a violent race uprising when white rioters turned their anger on free blacks, which they perceived as the cause of the war. The riots became so deadly and destructive that President Lincoln was forced to divert several regiments of militia and volunteer troops from the Gettysburg battlefield to control the city. At one point, conditions were such that Major General John E. Wool, commander of the Department of the East, said on July 16 *"Martial law ought to be proclaimed, but I have not a sufficient force to enforce it."* The military did not reach the city until after the first day of rioting, when mobs had already ransacked or destroyed numerous public buildings, two Protestant churches, the homes of various abolitionists or sympathizers, many black homes and the Colored Orphan Asylum; which was burned to the ground. In the end, the official death toll was listed at 119.

How does one explain this outbreak of violence in the midst of the most violent conflagration in American history? The more immediate answers include the perceived ambiguity at the time over the reasons for fighting the war and the class conflict that was fueled by the recent arrival of millions of Irish immigrants. After all, most had come to escape death by starvation back in Ireland due to a potato blight that had infected the one crop by which so many Irish peasants had come to depend. They had come to America looking for economic opportunity, not to fight in a bloody civil war that aimed to free up to four million slaves, thereby creating more job competition and lower wages. Today, most Americans are either unfamiliar with the New York City draft riots, or only know about them because they have seen the 2002 Martin Scorsese film, *Gangs of New York*. Even the movie is so loaded with violence that it is inadvisable to show to most high school students.

In order to achieve an understanding of this time period, any attempt to explain the draft riots might require a deeper examination of the essential question regarding the defining characteristics of a certain nationality; in this case, the American people. Granted, civil wars have existed all over the planet, both past and present. However, the American Civil War took the lives of over two percent of the entire population, one out of every fifty people. Amongst the population of young males, the percentage was considerably higher. When asked, most of my students have a difficult time imagining what this would mean to them in today's world. In July of 1863, just after a battle with roughly 50,000 casualties, our largest city witnessed three days of arson, lynching and mayhem. Could violence of this nature occur in any nation, or is there something about the American people that gives them a propensity to use carnage in order to resolve their conflicts? If there are defining characteristics that might help explain events like the New York draft riots in U.S. history, could similar explanations be uncovered to help elucidate on other events that have taken place around the globe?

Before going any further, a particular word must be defined and examined. That word is **stereotype**. By definition, a stereotype is a widely held but fixed and oversimplified image or idea of a particular type of person or thing. Within this definition, the word *"oversimplified"* is the main reason why so many people avoid any discussion of stereotypes. Even if there might be a grain of truth attached to a particular stereotype, the fact that this truth is also considered to be an oversimplification means that there will be many exceptions. Therefore, why use stereotypes at all? They will just stir up angry debate at best and contain the potential to generate ugly prejudice at the worst. Any sentence that begins with *"Most_____* (fill in with the name of a minority group or a particular nationality) *tend to be _____* (fill in with any particular adjective)" is bound to shake up a hornet's nest.

While any discussion focused on stereotypes is like tiptoeing through a minefield that does not mean they should be completely ignored. After all, they are prevalent in the minds of most people, and that certainly includes the students in all of our classes. If stereotypes are ignored in class discussions, they will still germinate conversations amongst teenagers, and without the presence of a teacher to facilitate, there is no telling where these discussions might lead. Therefore, I have always been of the belief that stereotypes should be openly acknowledged, but with some ground rules. First, students must fully understand the definition of a stereotype and that some may be completely false. Second, even if there is a degree of truth to a stereotype, students must know that the truth is still a broad generalization and that there will be plenty of exceptions. Finally, and most important, students must recognize that every stereotype has a historical explanation by which to explain the existence of the stereotype.

Searching for the original reason behind a stereotype will generally require the deeper understanding of history that is the basis for this book. That said, let's tiptoe a little further into the minefield for a minute and throw out one other explanation behind stereotypes, one that typically conjures up accusations of prejudice or even racism: genetics. Most people usually turn to genetics in order to explain physical features such as eye color, height or maybe athletic skills. But can genetics also be used to explain human behavior? Any dog breeder will say that a dog's disposition is at least partially the result of its genetic breeding. Could the same be said for humans? The best way to answer this question is to take a brief look at something called eugenics.

Eugenics refers to a set of beliefs and practices that aims at improving the genetic quality of the human population. It is a social philosophy advocating the improvement of human genetic traits through the promotion of higher rates of sexual reproduction for people with desired traits, or reduced rates of sexual reproduction and sterilization of people with less-desired or undesired traits; or both. While eugenic principles have been practiced as far back in world history as Ancient Greece, the modern history of eugenics began in the early 20th century when a popular eugenics movement emerged in Britain and spread to many countries, including the United States and most European nations. In this period, eugenic ideas were espoused across the political spectrum. Consequently, many countries adopted eugenic policies meant to improve the genetic stock of their people. Such programs often included both positive measures, such as encouraging individuals deemed particularly *"fit"* to reproduce, and negative measures such as marriage prohibitions and forced sterilization of people deemed unfit for reproduction. People deemed unfit to reproduce often included those with mental or physical disabilities, people who scored in the low ranges of different IQ tests, criminals and deviants, and members of disfavored minority groups.

As might be anticipated, the eugenics movement became negatively associated with Nazi Germany and the Holocaust: the murder by the German state of approximately 12 million people. After all, the *"scientific"* basis behind most of Hitler's social policies was the belief that he could take the German *"master race"* and genetically abolish all impurities. Many of the defendants at the Nuremberg trials at the end of World War Two attempted to justify their human rights abuses by claiming there was little difference between the Nazi eugenics programs and the American eugenics programs. In light of this perceived hypocrisy and with the increased emphasis placed on human rights after the war, many countries gradually abandoned eugenics policies; although some Western nations, among them Sweden and the United States, continued to carry out forced sterilizations for several decades.

Eugenics Protest circa 1971
Courtesy of Southern Studies Institute(CC BY 3.0)
http://www.southernstudies.org/2011/06/institute-index-justice-for-the-souths-forced-sterilization-victims.html

There is absolutely no question that following a eugenics policy in order to improve human behavior traits will place major restrictions on individual freedom and will lead to dangerous consequences. That said, as an explanation for the existence of a particular stereotype, genetics might still have some merit. For example, when examining why a certain population came to inhabit a particular region like a desert or a tropical rain forest, a genetic predisposition that might enable the people to better survive in that region would be part of the explanation. Africans who were genetically more resistant to malaria possessed a trait that would help to shield them, at least for a while, from the intrusion of Europeans who did not possess this genetic safeguard.

Beyond genetics, the more common explanation for the existence of a particular stereotype involves history. One example might be one that is blatantly anti-Semitic: the perception that Jewish people have a talent when it comes to handling money. Growing up as a Jew in the American suburbs, this was the one I frequently heard. Like most, I assumed there was absolutely no basis to this stereotype. However, I was eventually forced to acknowledge that Jews were disproportionately represented in certain professions such as law, medicine and yes, finance. This cannot be the result of random chance. How is this best explained?

There is a reasonable answer to this question that dates back to medieval times, but the problem with the explanation is that no matter how it is framed, it still lies on the brink of speculation. There are indisputable facts, but when put together, the explanation may be perceived as a broad generalization open to interpretation or even debate. However, as previously stated, this is often the nature of history. Unlike math or science, not every question about the past has a definitive answer. That does not mean, however, that the question should be ignored.

In this particular case, it is a fact that during the Middle Ages, Jews throughout much of Europe were forbidden to own land or to engage in any form of agriculture. It is also a fact that the Church discouraged Christians, who comprised most of the population, from going into money lending or any business enterprise that earned a profit at the expense of their neighbors. Growing food or engaging in a craft was doing God's work; loaning money and charging interest was seen as a sin. Therefore, for generations, Jews became the moneylenders; which at the time, was seen as a pejorative term. Over time, Jewish moneylenders evolved into modern bankers. One in particular, a Jew in Frankfort by the name of Mayer Amschel Rothschild, came up with the brilliant idea of sending his five sons out to different countries, thereby creating what is today referred to as international banking. Because of the trust between brothers, the Rothschilds created an international banking system, and within a century, they were among the wealthiest families in the world. They would remain so until the Nazis confiscated everything in the 1930s.

Mayer Amschel Rothschild
Courtesy of Project Gutenberg
http://www.gutenberg.org/files/
23595/23595-h/23595-h.htm

Within the enclosed European Jewish community, the value placed on banking and other business enterprises was passed down from one generation to the next. Many Jews went into money lending 700 years ago because they had few other choices, but the success earned in this field has survived up to the present. To many gentiles, this helped to create the stereotype that Jews were good with money, that they liked money, that they could even be tight with money. These simple historical facts combined with the anti-Semitism that has existed for the last 2000 years helped to create an ugly stereotype.

That said, many of the students in my class are well aware of the fact that while Jews make up only 2.2 percent of the American population, they play a disproportionate role in banking and finance; including the hedge fund industry, the private equity industry and even the Federal Reserve System. In fact, several Jews have served as chairmen of the Fed; including Ben Bernanke, Alan Greenspan, and the current chairwoman, Janet Yellen. Should this fact be ignored in the classroom, or is it better to directly confront the inevitable development of stereotypes in their formative stage and use historical explanations as a way to destroy the myths and explain the reality?

Here is another common stereotype built around a kernel of truth and explained by a simple historical generalization. The stereotype is that Asian Americans as a whole tend to be smart and do quite well in school. Over my 37 years as a high school teacher, there does seem to be a degree of truth to this stereotype. The data also supports this truth. Asian Americans have the highest educational attainment of any racial group in the country; 49.8% have at least a bachelor's degree (nation-wide, the percentage is about 30%). Since the 1990s, Asian American students often have the highest math averages on standardized tests such as the SAT and the GRE. While their verbal scores generally lag, their combined scores are usually higher than those of white Americans. The proportion of Asian Americans at many selective educational institutions far exceeds the national population rate. Asians constitute around 10 to 20 percent of those attending Ivy League colleges and other elite universities. These are facts that are difficult to conceal from most high school students. Is there something from the past that might help us better understand these facts?

For thousands of years, a large percentage of the Chinese people managed to scrape by as peasants growing rice on a few acres of land. Even if a child was precocious, there was not much hope for a better life. Then, beginning over 2000 years ago with the Han dynasty, a system of civil service exams was instituted to select office holders for the imperial government. This system, perfected in the mid-Tang dynasty, became the major path to office, and remained so until its abolition in 1905. Since China has always had an enormous population, the state bureaucracy required to provide for the needs of hundreds of millions of people also grew in size. If the parents of a bright child wanted him to have a brighter future than working as a rice farmer, they would do everything in their power to encourage literacy in a written language based on a complex alphabet and an education focused on Confucian teachings that were the basis of the exams. This unique set of circumstances helped to nurture the growth of a cultural value placed on learning and education that has survived to the present. The Asian American education stereotype might also be explained by other theories, but this one should certainly be considered. Once again, this can only happen if the stereotype is directly confronted with information taken from the past.

Stereotypes obviously hang over the heads of most of the minority students currently sitting in classrooms across the United States. Three in particular: Native Americans, Hispanics and African Americans, are all forced to wrestle with stereotypes rooted in the prejudice and discrimination of their past. In teaching units on the Civil Rights Movement over the years, I have always included a Socratic seminar focused on this essential question so that these stereotypes can be systematically examined in a controlled environment. Before going any further, it would be helpful to briefly explain the nature of Socratic seminars and the role they can play in the classroom.

Elfie Israel wrote about Socratic seminars in *Inquiry and the Literary Text: Constructing Definitions in the English Classroom* (2002). According to her, a Socratic seminar is a more formal discussion based on a text and focused on open-ended queries. Within the discussion, students should listen carefully, think critically and ask thoughtful questions. In addition to the facilitation of higher level thinking skills, Socratic seminars should encourage the growth of behavior traits based on cooperation and civility. In a history class, the students are encouraged to apply what they have learned from primary and/or secondary sources to the discussion of a particular essential question. The ground rules for a Socratic seminar can vary from teacher to teacher, and in my case, from one essential question to another. However, at their core, every Socratic seminar should encourage students to keep an open mind, ask questions rather than just spouting opinions and apply a high level of reason to the issues at hand.

With many Socratic seminars, a student usually volunteers to facilitate the discussion and I sit back as a silent observer. Because of the sensitive nature of stereotypes, as well as the racial diversity of most of my classes, I usually play a more enhanced role in this Socratic seminar. After reviewing some basic ground rules, including the need to be respectful as well as honest, the seminar begins by addressing a common stereotype associated with African Americans: the connection between blacks and crime. Students are shown a copy of the chart below:

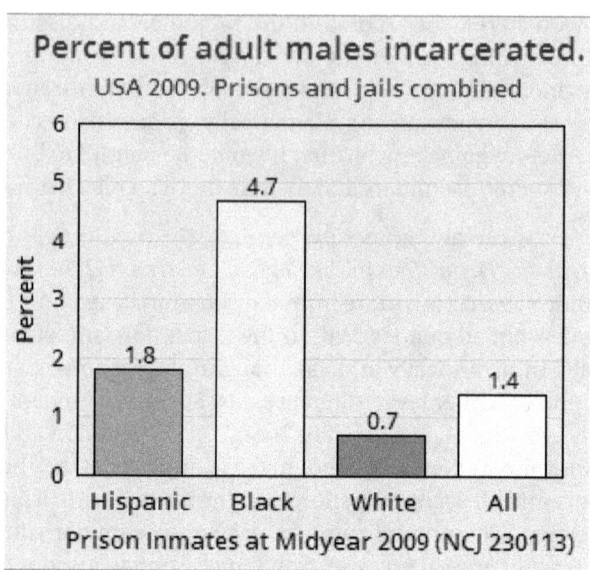

Courtesy of Department of Justice, U.S. Bureau of Justice Statistics
http://www.bjs.gov/index.cfm?ty=pbdetail&iid=2200

After a brief interpretative discussion to be sure students understand how this chart shows the gross overrepresentation of blacks in American prisons, the seminar begins by asking students to suggest reasons behind this phenomenon. Although it is usually not necessary, the genetic explanation is quickly dismissed because the association between race and prison is unique to the United States and only at the present time. Besides, students are quick to recognize that in this context, a genetic theory is unacceptably racist. They are then steered towards history in search of other viable theories.

In the course of most of these seminars, two basic ideas emerge. The first is directed at the historical experience encountered by most African Americans. Students generally agree that 250 years of slavery where education was completely forbidden wiped out much of the culture previously rooted on the African continent. Although the end of the Civil War in 1865 finally abolished slavery, another century of Jim Crow segregation, widespread discriminatory policies, and a dearth of economic opportunity followed. The modern Civil Rights Movement of the 1950s and 1960s effectively ended most segregation policies and removed most barriers to the ballot, but a large percentage of blacks were still left in a state of poverty.

Students recognize that all races commit crime and someone always points out that the 0.7 per cent of white adults in prison is comparable to the total number of blacks. However, since history has deposited the vast majority of white males in a superior position in terms of their options and opportunities, history can be useful in explaining why a few more blacks turn to a life of crime.

The second theory focuses more on the current state of our criminal justice system. According to Andrew Kahn and Chris Kirk in an August 9, 2015 article in *Slate*, when comparing blacks to whites, African Americans are:

1. Three times more likely to have their cars searched by the police.
2. Twice as likely to be arrested for drugs.
3. More likely to be jailed while awaiting trial.
4. More likely to be offered a plea deal that involves prison time.
5. Serving on average 10 per cent longer sentences for the same crime.
6. More likely to have their probation revoked.

Additionally, in most classes, students of color provide ample anecdotes of personal confrontations with the police. Their stories open the eyes of their white classmates to an existence most had never contemplated. It does not take long for classes to reach a consensus that the police, the courts, and the corrections systems still do not treat blacks and whites the same. Combined with the historical explanations, the stereotype linking blacks to crime makes sense to most students by the end of these Socratic seminars. For closure, the historical explanations and the more subtle forms of racism still endemic in our society are applied to other racial stereotypes. These include gaps in education, wealth, and even why African Americans, who make up about 13 per cent of the overall population, constitute 75 percent of the basketball rosters in the NBA. Many teachers shy away from these types of discussions and Socratic seminars out of fear that nerves will be touched and feelings might be hurt. However, most students are aware of the disparities and the stereotypes; and as previously stated, it is preferable to examine these in a classroom setting with a teacher present than to simply let students do so on their own.

There are many stereotypes that exist for many different groups, but to better answer the essential question regarding the characteristics of certain nationalities, it would probably help to look at our own reflection in a mirror and examine what defines an American. Every year in my U.S. History classes, I ask my students this question: "*What makes Americans unique from other nationalities?*" In this lesson, students are asked to brainstorm a list of the positive attributes as well as the negative. What kind of image does the American tourist project when traveling abroad? How much truth is there to the *"ugly American"* image? Narrowing down the list, the three most positive traits recognized by the students are that Americans tend to be more **generous**, more **democratic** and more **individualistic**. On the flip side, the consensus for the three most negative attributes is that Americans tend to be more **materialistic**, more **arrogant** and more **violent**. The students also point out that connected to their willingness to use more violence is the American love affair with guns.

Assuming there is some basis of truth to these perceptions, the next obvious question is why do Americans possess these qualities? On a rare occasion, a student will find a diplomatic way to suggest a genetic cause. To support this contention, one student used the metaphor of a magnet. If iron particles are blended with sand, a powerful magnet will sift the iron from the silicon. The point the student was making is that for over 400 years, America has been this magnet. It has always attracted a certain type of person from the Eastern Hemisphere; one who may have been more ambitious, adventurous, willing to take greater risks. After all, who in their right mind would board tiny ships like the *Susan Constant* making its way to Jamestown in 1607 or the *Mayflower* headed towards Plymouth in 1620? Not only was the journey long and dangerous; survival in the new settlements also involved incredible risk. The student pointed out that it takes a particular type of person to make this journey, and if there is any kind of genetic component underlying certain behavioral traits, then America became the magnet sifting the risk-takers from the more cautious. If those genes were passed down over the next 20 generations, constantly being fertilized by the genes of other risk-taking immigrants, would that not create a unique set of characteristics for what defines an American?

As stated before, suggesting a genetic explanation for any national trait is difficult to prove and potentially dangerous in light of what transpired with the Eugenics Movement over the last century. Nevertheless, the idea is a bit intriguing and cannot be easily dismissed. The student understood that the process of evolution occurs over a much longer period than just 400 years, and he was not suggesting that Americans have *"evolved"* to become gun-toting cowboys. However, if a dog breeder wanted to create a more vicious watchdog, the effort would be made to mate two animals with a greater propensity toward aggression. There may not have been any conscious effort to *"breed"* a more thrill-seeking human, but the risk required to come to America may have served the same purpose.

In the search to find a more historical rationale to explain the unique attributes of the typical American, the next step used in my classes has been to examine the Turner Thesis. In 1893, the American historian Frederick Jackson Turner presented a paper entitled *"The Significance of the Frontier in American History"* to the American Historical Association in Chicago. This paper was largely the result of the U.S. Census of 1890 that officially declared the frontier to be dissolved. According to Turner, this meant the *"frontier"* which had existed from the earliest colonial days no longer existed. He reacted to this development by sounding an alarm, speculating as to what it meant to lose this energy source within U.S. society that had fueled America's innovation and democratic ideals.

Frederick Jackson Turner
Courtesy of The World's Work, 1902 (PD-US)
http://archive.org/stream/worldswork04
gard#page/2318/mode/2up

According to the Turner Thesis, American democracy was formed by the frontier experience. He stressed the process: the ever-moving frontier line and the impact it had on pioneers going through the experience. He also stressed results. Especially that American democracy was the primary result; along with the accompanying egalitarianism, a lack of interest in high culture, and a stress placed on violence. *"American democracy was born of no theorist's dream; it was not carried in the Susan Constant to Virginia, nor in the Mayflower to Plymouth. It came out of the American forest, and it gained new strength each time it touched a new frontier,"* said Turner. In the thesis, the American frontier established liberty by releasing Americans from European mindsets and eroding old, dysfunctional customs. The frontier had no need for standing armies, established churches, aristocrats, or for landed gentry who controlled most of the land and charged heavy rents.

Frontier land was free for the taking and therefore offered limitless opportunities and a new way of life for anyone willing to confront the high level of risk. To mitigate this risk, pioneers formed communities based on mutual support and egalitarian values. Leadership was crucial, but it was exercised in a democratic manner where every adult had a stake and an equal say. In order to secure food and more important, to provide protection from the hostile indigenous tribes that were attempting to protect their land, guns and violence became a part of everyday life. As the frontier line spread from the piedmont lands east of the Appalachians all the way west to the Pacific Ocean, it left in its wake a unique culture and way of life. According to Frederick Jackson Turner, this culture created the American as a unique human being and it has left a permanent imprint.

For over one hundred years, the Turner Thesis has been discussed, debated and criticized. Such is the nature of history. In particular, it has been lambasted for ignoring other factors that have helped to shape U.S. culture, such as America's industrial experience. It has also taken a hit for minimizing the role played in the West by indigenous tribes, Mexican Americans and women. According to Western historian, Patricia Nelson Limerick, Turner was ethnocentric and nationalistic. English-speaking white men were the stars of his story; Indians, Hispanics, French Canadians and Asians were at best supporting actors and at worst, invisible. The same could be said of women of all ethnicities. Overall, like any historical theory, it has been attacked for oversimplifying a complex subject. That said, the Turner Thesis, despite its flaws, is a good starting point in attempting to explain the unique qualities that define American culture. In fact, every year, I assign a position paper for students to write where they must develop their own thesis to explain what makes Americans distinct from other societies. They are told to begin with the Turner Thesis and to then move on from there.

As an application exercise, the knowledge and understanding gained by students from the experience of writing this paper was recently applied to an event taken from the headlines. On May 17, 2015, a shootout erupted at a Twin Peaks restaurant in Waco, Texas. The killing involved members of several motorcycle clubs including the Banditos and the Cossacks who had gathered for a regularly scheduled meeting about political rights for motorcyclists. Waco police, including a SWAT team, had gathered to monitor them from outside, and opened fire on the bikers after the shootout started. Nine bikers were killed and 18 were injured. The conflict allegedly began over a parking spot where *"someone had their foot run over,"* and the fighting escalated from there. Although all of the deaths were due to gunfire, other weapons seized after the conflict included chains, brass knuckles, knives, clubs and batons. The mêlée involved shooting by both gangs as well as the police, and it was difficult afterwards to determine who shot whom.

The discussion in class first revolved around whether an event of this kind could happen in just any nation or were there characteristics of American culture that made it more likely to occur here. A quick glance at the 2015 Global Peace Index provided by the Institute for Economics and Peace ranked the United States 94th out of 162 countries according to its level of violence. (Iceland was ranked first for possessing the least amount of violence.) Except for Russia and a few other nations in Eastern Europe, America is clearly more violent than any other economically developed nation. The discussion then turned to the question of **why** events like the shooting in Waco are much more likely to occur in the United States than in nations like Denmark, Canada, Portugal, Australia or Japan. Anything approximating a consensus usually involves a combination of the genetic magnet principle discussed earlier and the lasting influence of the Turner Thesis. As usual, there is no clear right or wrong answer, but much is gained intellectually through the process of discussing the question.

The reality is that almost every ethnic group, religion and nationality has certain stereotypes for which they are commonly known. Some are relatively harmless: Germans are incredibly efficient, Canadians are exceptionally polite, and Italians make great lovers. Others are obviously racist or disparaging in other ways. In the classroom, most teachers I know purposely go out of their way to avoid any mention of these stereotypes. After all, in the *"politically correct"* universe we inhabit, any comment taken out of context can lead to parental complaints or even worse. Therefore, of all the essential questions discussed in this book, addressing the issue of why people ascribe defining characteristics to certain nationalities contains the greatest risk for generating controversy.

However, while it might be safer or easier to avoid this question altogether, students in our classrooms are still well aware of the stereotypes. If a history class is taught in an open and honest fashion, students are bound to raise sensitive questions. We can either teach our classes like ostriches with our heads buried in the sand, or we can have the courage to help students make sense of the world in which they live. The latter choice may involve some risk; yet, if handled with openness, honesty, and most importantly, discretion and sensitivity, students will benefit not only in terms of their knowledge and understanding, but also their tolerance towards others different from themselves.

Suggested Reading:

Bernstein, Iver. *The New York City Draft Riots: Their Significance for American Society and Politics in the Age of the Civil War.* New York: Oxford University Press, 1990.

Black, Edwin. *War Against the Weak: Eugenics and America's Campaign to Create a Master Race.* Westport: Dialog Press, 2012.

"Global Peace Index 2015." *Institute for Economics and Peace.* 2015. http://Economicsandpeace.org/wp-content/uploads/2015/06/Global-Peace-Index-Report-2015_0.pdf.

Grobman, Gary M. "The Holocaust-A Guide For Teachers: Stereotypes and Prejudices." *Remember.org.* 1990. http://remember.org/guide/history-root-stereotypes.

Holden, James, and John S. Schmit, eds. *Inquiry and the Literary Text: Constructing Discussions in the English Classroom(Classroom Practices in Teaching English).* Urbana: National Council of Teachers, 2002.

Kahn, Andrew, and Chris Kirk. "What It's Like to Be Black in the Criminal Justice System." *Slate.* August 9, 2015. http://www.slate.com/articles/news_and_politics/crime/2015/08/racial_disparities_in_the_criminal_justice_system_eight_charts_illustrating.html.

Le, C.N. "14 Important Statistics About Asian Americans." *Asian Nation.* March 16, 2016. http://www.asian-nation.org/14-statistics.shtml.

Limerick, Patricia Nelson. *The Legacy of Conquest: The Unbroken Past of the American West.* New York: W.W. Norton and Company Ltd., 1987.

McGarty, Craig, and Vincint Y. Yzerbyt. *Stereotypes as Explanations: The Formation of Meaningful Beliefs about Social Groups.* Cambridge: Cambridge University Press, 2002.

Turner, Frederick Jackson. *The Frontier in American History.* New York: Dover Publications, 1996.

Chapter 6
The best way to slice the pie

Bonus Army Camp
Courtesy of the Library of Congress, Prints and Photographs Division LC-H2- B-5267

What is the fairest way for a society to share its wealth?

The place is an open area within sight of our nation's capital building in Washington, D.C. and the date is July 28th, 1932. There are about 2,000 veterans and their family members camped out in a shantytown and President Hoover has decided they should disband. Until recently, the group was much larger, somewhere between 10,000 and 20,000; but after the Senate voted down a bill that would have given each veteran a $500 *"bonus"* for services rendered during the First World War, most of them packed up and returned home. Two thousand remained, however, hoping to meet with the president. After all, like much of the nation, they were out of work, homeless and hungry. The Great Depression had begun with the Stock Market Crash three years earlier, and now the unemployment rate was approaching 24%. This was at a time when there was no food stamps, no Medicaid, no federal government handouts of any kind.

Congress had already approved the bonus for veterans back in 1924, but it was supposed to be paid out in 1945 in the form of cash and a life insurance policy. In light of the growing desperation sweeping the land, Congressman Wright Patman had proposed that the bonus be paid out immediately. Former veterans and their families arrived from all over the nation to support the bill, and despite the fact that President Hoover considered most of them to be *"communists and people with criminal records,"* he supported the marchers' right to peaceful assembly. He even provided food and supplies for their growing shantytown. After the Senate voted down the Patman Bill on June 17th, however, Hoover called on the Bonus Army marchers to leave. Most did, but when the 2,000 refused, Hoover decided to send in the military against the former American soldiers.

Led by General Douglas MacArthur and his aide, Major Dwight D. Eisenhower, a force of 1,000 troops was sent in to drive out the veterans and to destroy their camp. A. Everette McIntyre, a government official watching from a nearby office, recalled what happened next.

> *The 12th Infantry was in full battle dress. Each soldier had a gas mask and his belt was full of tear gas bombs... At orders, they brought their bayonets at thrust and moved in. The bayonets were used to jab people, to make them move. Soon, almost everybody disappeared from view, because tear gas bombs exploded. The entire block was covered by tear gas. Flames were coming up where the soldiers had set fire to the buildings to drive these people out... Through the whole afternoon, they took one camp after another.*

Before it was over, more than 1,000 people were gassed, including an 11-month-old baby, who died; and an 8-year-old boy, who was partially blinded. Two people were shot and many were injured. Most Americans were stunned by the government's treatment of veterans and this event contributed to President Hoover's landslide loss to Franklin Delano Roosevelt in his bid for reelection three months later. At the time, most people were living from one day to the next and were just trying to survive. In retrospect, however, what was lurking beneath the surface was a classic essential question: how should a society fairly distribute its wealth?

To introduce this question to my students every year, I play a dirty little trick that has always proven to be deviously fun. I tell them our current grading system has always irked me as being unfair because some students barely study and still get A's on most everything, while others spend hours and hours studying, and are lucky to pull a C. I then distribute a handout describing a new grading policy that will be fairer and tell them to take it home and discuss it with their parents. The new approach will encourage greater cooperation and sharing amongst students. In every imaginable way, students under this new policy will be encouraged to help each other so that everyone can learn as much as possible. At the end of the marking period, an average for the entire class will be computed, and every student will then receive that grade: the SAME grade. After the apoplectic reaction that I typically get from the A students, particularly in an honors class, I explain that the proposal is just an idea being considered and that it is open to discussion. I also make clear that until a decision is made, I do not want to receive any calls or emails from parents. The plan is simply to chat about the idea.

During the ensuing discussion, students come to realize that grades in a high school class are similar to wealth out in the real world. Good grades will lead to good colleges, which in turn, will lead to good jobs and a higher income. By the end of class, about a third of the students say they would support the plan, about third are opposed and the final third want to think about it some more. At this point, I explain that I am not changing the grading policy and that if I did, I would have plenty of opposition from parents and administrators as well as some of the students. I sometimes have to duck to avoid airborne projectiles, but before students leave, they have begun to see that just like the wealth of society at large, grades given in class are like an apple pie. The question is how should the pie be shared. Should some, who work harder or contribute more or are simply blessed with greater talents than others, receive a bigger piece of the pie, or should everyone get a slice that is the same size?

Every society, past, present and future, has had to wrestle with this question. A cursory glance at American society today shows that the pie is hardly divided in a manner that gives every individual the same size piece.

In fact, the United States has a wider disparity of wealth between rich and poor than any other nation in the developed world. According to the Federal Reserve's Survey of Consumer Finances, an in-depth survey of the assets of some 6,000 American families collected in 2013, the top three percent of the American population controls 54.4 percent of the nation's wealth. The top three percent now holds double the wealth of America's poorest 90 percent of families. In addition, America's richest 10 percent holds 85 percent of the nation's financial assets. The Forbes 400, listing the nation's richest 400 people, shows that the inequality is only getting more unbalanced. In 1982, the year Forbes began annually listing America's richest 400, the United States had only 13 billionaires. To make the list of 400 in 2014, a wealthy American needed a fortune of at least $1.55 billion. When race and ethnic background are taken into account, the disparity is even more pronounced. According to a Pew Research Center analysis, the typical white family held a net worth six times greater than the typical black family at the end of the 20th Century. That gap has now doubled. The wealth chasm between white and Hispanic households has widened as well. Whether talking about real estate, financial assets or income, the pie is not even close to being equally shared. This should not come as much of a surprise to anyone.

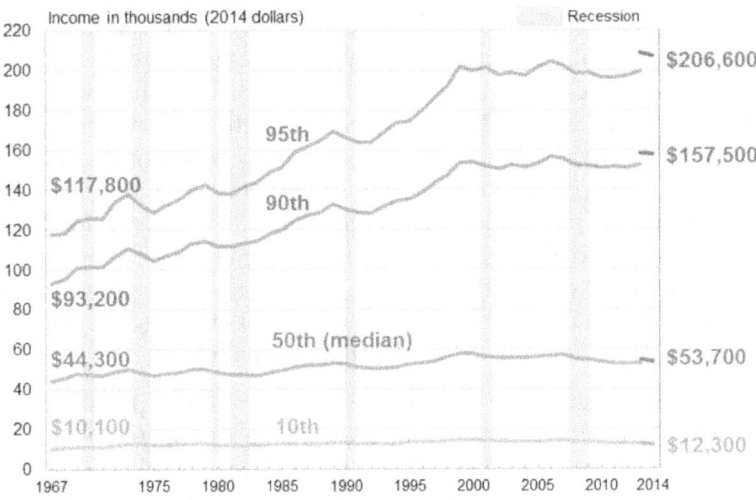

Courtesy of the U.S. Census Bureau
http://www.census.gov/hhes/www/income/inequality/index.html

   Naturally, the question concerning the fairest way to distribute wealth raises a great deal of controversy. Why do some Americans, mostly Republicans, want individuals to keep most of the wealth they earn while others, mostly Democrats, want the government to exercise its powers to reduce the gap between the rich and the poor? The answer is inextricably linked to a debate I first encountered as a freshman in a college philosophy class; the issue of free will versus determinism. Although many of us may never have given this subject much consideration, it lurks beneath the surface of so many other issues. Take the average, everyday criminal for instance. A supporter of free will would say that the criminal was exercising his free will when he chose to commit a crime, and should therefore face a punitive form of retribution from the corrections system so that next time, he will choose to follow the law. In addition, the knowledge of stiff punishments will deter future criminals from making the same bad choice. On the other hand, the determinist would say that the criminal committed his crime because it was determined for him by factors or forces beyond his control. After all, none of us gets to choose our parents or what we genetically inherit from them. We also do not get to choose the environment in which we are raised. A combination of these forces put the criminal on a path that led to his crime, so the solution afterwards is some form of rehabilitation that will determine a more law-abiding path in the future.

The philosophical issue of free will versus determinism was a fun issue to debate in college, but since then, I have come to see this issue everywhere. It is not only a divisive force in the world of criminal corrections. Religious scholars have been debating for centuries whether an individual can choose a path towards salvation or whether an all-powerful deity determined who would achieve salvation long before the individual was born. In the world of psychology, Behaviorists like B.F. Skinner, who argued that external reinforcers or punishments shape human behavior, have disagreed for many years with humanistic psychologists like Abraham Maslow, who believed that the freedom to choose is not only possible but also necessary if we are to become fully functional human beings.

As previously stated, free will versus determinism plays a key role in helping Americans to make the political choice between the Democrats and the GOP. When it comes to the essential question about the distribution of wealth, it should come as no surprise that a proponent of free will typically argues that since we all have the freedom to make choices in a competitive economy, those who exercise hard work, creative thinking or perseverance are entitled to the larger share of the pie they have earned. On the flip side, the determinist will argue that since we are all really the product of the confluence between biology and the environment, we should all have a relatively equal share of a society's wealth. I learned in my first year of college that most people are not absolute determinists or complete supporters of free will; most of us, once we understand the issue, will lean one way or the other.

To give the essential question about wealth distribution an economic framework, it is necessary to briefly review the two basic economic systems that have dominated the world for close to 200 years: capitalism and socialism. Capitalism is the older of the two and some might argue it has recently won the battle with the different forms of socialism around the world. However, like almost everything else, the two systems are not absolutes, and almost every society, past or present, exhibit at least some attributes of both.

The "*father*" of capitalism, also known as free enterprise, was the English economist, Adam Smith. He first wrote about its basic principles in *The Wealth of Nations*, which interestingly enough, was published in 1776. The economic principles he advocated have had a profound influence on the growth of capitalism in the United States. Smith believed that private interests should have a free reign and in order for this to happen, the government should practice a policy of laissez-faire, which means that the government should leave the economy alone. As long as markets were free and competitive, he said, the actions of private individuals, motivated by self-interest, would work together for the greater good of society. Smith did favor some forms of government intervention, mainly to establish the ground rules for free enterprise; but it was his advocacy for laissez-faire that earned him favor in the United States, a nation built on faith in the individual and distrust of government authority.

Adam Smith
Courtesy of the Library of Congress
Prints and Photographs Division LC-USZ62-17407

The principles of capitalism are really quite simple. With only a minimal role for the government, individuals should have maximum freedom to own their own property, run their own businesses and make unlimited profits. The only restrictions they will face come from the unwritten law of supply of demand, which restricts the setting of prices, and the competition that should take place with other businesses. Otherwise, the profit incentive, which is the linchpin of free enterprise, provides ample motivation to invent, to innovate and to outwork the competition. The fact that wealth is NOT evenly distributed is the primary force behind the profit incentive and the fuel that powers the capitalist engine.

When examining the arguments in favor of capitalism, it is worth remembering something I am constantly telling my students, that there are two basic types of arguments: moral and pragmatic. The moral justification for free enterprise is based on the fundamental principle of fairness; an individual should be able to keep what he or she earns. Say a person exercises her free will and chooses to come up with a new product that will improve the standard of living for others. Say this person takes the risk to create and market the new product and works hard make her business a success. Morally speaking, shouldn't she be able to keep all profits earned from her business? In addition, there is a moral argument to be made in defense of the right to own property. John Locke argued that people are entitled to the fruits of their labor. *"When individuals mix their labor with the natural world, they are entitled to the results."* All things being equal, it would certainly seem immoral for someone to seize your crops after you worked all year to grow them.

The pragmatic argument is also quite simple: capitalism works. The profit incentive provides plenty of motivation for individuals to constantly invent new products and bring them to market. Because creativity, innovation and efficiency will all be rewarded by added profits, the free enterprise economic system has been the most productive throughout history. Yes, the downside may be that there will always be an element of society that does not succeed, and as a result, there may always be a percentage of people who live in a state of poverty. But this is more than compensated for by the constantly rising standard of living.

Another pragmatic defense of capitalism comes from Wendy Milling in a March, 2013 op-ed article in *Forbes*. She argues that as long as the government meets it obligation to provide equality under the law, even those born into unfortunate circumstances will have ample opportunities to become successful. She observes that at the present, everyone possesses a reasonable shot at economic achievement. Upward mobility is a reality that is easily observed in the countless rags-to-riches stories that dot the American landscape. People have risen from slums to become wealthy. Fortunes have been made despite all kinds of physical and even mental incapacitation. The only true impairment, according to Milling, is a lack of motivation; and that is not the responsibility of an economic system, or a government, to fix.

While the roots of capitalism go back several centuries, socialism primarily arose in response to the evils of the Industrial Revolution in the 19th Century. Socialism stood capitalism up on its head by reversing just about all of its basic principles. Under socialism, the government controls the economy, the means of production are not privately owned, and most importantly, everyone receives an equal share of the wealth. There are many different ways to establish a socialist economic system, but regardless of the means, the end is a society where individuals contribute what they can to the betterment of everyone else and each person should share equally in the wealth that is generated. In terms of the grading proposal, giving every student the same class average grade is the socialist equivalent.

Courtesy of International Publishing Company Cleveland, Ohio(PD-anon-1923)
https://commons.wikimedia.org/wiki/File:Pyramid_of_Capitalist_System.jpg

By the late 19th Century, industrialization may have been improving the standard of living for millions in the long term, but it was also creating misery for millions in the short. Workers in factories and mines were slaving away for 12 hours a day under deplorable conditions and for low pay. Child labor was common and families were forced to live in crowded slums and tenements. Because of laissez faire government policies, there was no unemployment insurance, senior pension programs, minimum wage requirements, restriction on hours, or protection from dangerous machinery and unhealthy workplaces. Some workers tried to form unions and others sought relief from their government leaders. Many, however, particularly in European nations, turned to socialism.

From the start there was disagreement as to how socialism should best be established. Some recognized that socialism would never be accepted by the majority as an alternative to free enterprise, so they therefore decided to withdraw from the larger world into utopian socialist communities. One of the best-known examples of this approach was the town set up at New Harmony, Indiana. Established by Robert Owen, a Welsh industrialist and social reformer, the intent was to create a utopian society where every person would share in the work and in the wealth generated. While Owen's social experiment was an economic failure just two years after it began, the community made some important contributions to American society. Most utopian communities did not last, but they did provide one alternative to the downside of capitalism.

Other socialists were more patient and willing to work within the established democratic system. They organized political parties, ran candidates for office and supported any legislation designed to improve the lives of the working classes. They were natural supporters of the rise of labor unions and pushed hard to impose progressive taxes on the wealthier classes. While these moderate socialists never came close to establishing control over our national government, they did play a role in enacting reforms on a state or local level. Robert La Follette, the governor and senator from Wisconsin in the early part of the 20th century, successfully advocated a number of socialist policies; and in 1912, Eugene Debs, who had been a candidate for president five times for the Socialist Party of America, earned 6% of the popular vote. The influence of these democratic socialists can best be seen in the expansion of government policies that took place later in the 1900s.

Eugene Debs
Courtesy of the Library of Congress, Prints and Photographs Division
LC-DIG-ggbain-36502

Finally, there was a small but vocal element of socialists who believed that those with wealth and power would never voluntarily give it up without a violent struggle. Their most prominent leader was Karl Marx, who wrote his ideas in pamphlets like *The Communist Manifesto* and who worked to organize the communist political party on an international level. Marx was an economic determinist who argued that the wealthier classes had always found ways to exploit the workers throughout history. He predicted that with the rise of industrialization in the more advanced capitalistic societies, the workers would finally "*throw off their chains*" and use violence to overthrow the established free enterprise order and replace it with a workers' state where everyone would share equally in society's wealth. This extreme form of socialism has been called scientific socialism, but it also goes by a more recognized name: communism.

Socialism in its various forms can also be supported by moral and pragmatic arguments. Morally, a different variation of fairness can be used to defend socialism. In a typical factory, one individual may be the owner who took the risks, built up the organization and made decisions on a daily basis. Another person may have simply worked on the factory floor helping to run the assembly line that manufactures the widgets or whatever the factory produces. Following a deterministic line of thinking, the owner was probably born with genetically innate abilities to run the factory, or was raised in an environment that provided many advantages, or in some cases, simply inherited his position. The factory worker also came from a background not of her own choosing that put her on a path that led to work on the factory floor. If they both put in full day contributing what each is most capable of doing, shouldn't they both earn the same salary? According to the Economic Policy Institute, the CEO-to-Worker compensation ratio in 2013 was 295.9 to 1. A socialist would argue that it is morally unconscionable for the head of a company to make $300 for every dollar earned by one of his workers.

Another moral argument is based on the principle that true wealth is almost always the product of the combined efforts of many people. As Senator Elizabeth Warren of Massachusetts pointed out, there is no one in America who got rich on his or her own. According to Warren, the goods produced in someone's factory were moved to market on roads paid for by the rest of us. The workers in the factory were educated in schools paid for by the rest of us. The factory was kept safe by the police and fire forces financed by the rest of us. Warren feels that the factory owner is entitled to reasonable portion of the profits created, but part of the underlying social contract is that the entrepreneur should pay something forward for the next person who comes along.

On a pragmatic level, a socialist can point out that every member of a socialist society has a respectable standard of living. By sharing equally in society's wealth, each person can earn a decent education all the way up through college, have access to good health care, look up at a roof over his or her head, and enjoy food on the table. In other words, there is no poverty. In addition, there are none of the problems that plague capitalist economies related to the business cycle. With little to no government intervention, the economy under the free enterprise model fluctuates like a flag in the breeze. One year may bring a strong economy with full employment, although this is sometimes accompanied by inflation that will eat away at the standard of living for those on fixed incomes. The next year might bring an economic slowdown in the form of a recession or even a more severe depression. This will mean rising unemployment, business losses and a rise in poverty rates.

Just as the defenders of capitalism love to tout how well free enterprise works on a practical level, comparable arguments have been made in defense of socialism. In 1949, the brilliant physicist, Albert Einstein, wrote that a socialist economy deliberately adjusts production to the needs of the community. He argued that a planned economy distributes the work to be done among all those able to work and guarantees a livelihood to every man, woman and child. The education provided to each individual in a socialist state, in addition to promoting innate abilities, would attempt to develop in him a sense of *"responsibility for his fellow human beings in place of the glorification of power and success in our present society."*

Others have also seen more inherent goodness in socialism than in capitalism. Fidel Castro, the communist revolutionary leader of Cuba, found capitalism to be repugnant. He said that it was *"gross and alienating… because it causes war, hypocrisy and competition."* The greed inherent in capitalism has been blamed for imperialistic expansion, modern slavery and the exploitation of the masses. While capitalists frequently point out the failure of socialism in places like the former Soviet Union and the *"democratic republics"* of Eastern Europe, Castro has asked, *"where is the success of capitalism in Africa, Asia and Latin America?"* The success of both capitalism and socialism is somewhat relative. When compared to the standard of living in capitalist nations like the United States, life in communist China or Cuba may seem less appealing. However, when life in those two communist nations is compared to their situations before the Chinese or Cuban revolutions, it must be conceded that significant progress has been made, particularly in terms of their housing, health care and educational systems.

When applied to history, the essential question of wealth distribution falls largely within the last two hundred years. After all, prior to the start of the Industrial Revolution in England during the latter part of the 18th Century, wealth was primarily based on the ownership of land. While there may have been gross inequalities in this arena between wealthy landowners at one extreme and feudal serfs or peasants at the other, most people accepted this arrangement as the status quo. There were instances where radicals during the French Revolution sought to redistribute land in a manner that resembled an early form of socialism, but otherwise, there were few instances where people collectively tried to alter the way wealth was divided within their respective societies.

As stated earlier, the rise of industrialization changed everything. By the end of the 19th Century, wealth was generated more and more by factories rather than by agriculture, and this accentuated a growing gap between the rich and the poor. As a result, while many workers turned towards the ideas of socialism or even communism in Europe, most American workers either joined labor unions like the Knights of Labor or the American Federation of Labor, or they began to organize politically. By the 1890s, millions of factory workers and farmers had united to join the Populist Movement. For the first time in American history, a significant number of people began to push for a federal government that would do more than just collect tariffs on imports, maintain a relatively small military and deliver the mail.

On the federal, state and local levels, the Populists pushed for more government to restrict hours, abolish child labor and improve working conditions. They were also becoming increasingly concerned about the rise of huge, multi-million dollar corporations led by industrial titans like Andrew Carnegie in steel, John D. Rockefeller in oil, Cornelius Vanderbilt in railroads and J.P. Morgan in just about everything. Populists saw the consolidation of business into massive monopolies and trusts as a development that would lead to less competition and higher prices, thus harming all consumers. The apex of the Populist Movement occurred in the 1896 presidential election that pitted William Jennings Bryan, nominated by the Populist Party, against William McKinley. Bryan's loss may be seen as the beginning of the end for the Populist Movement, but it must be acknowledged that the Populists established a foundation for what was to follow by setting the precedent that the federal government could and should play a larger role in the economy.

Many would attribute the mixed success achieved by the Populists to the fact that farmers and factory workers had limited political clout. When the growing middle class took up the Populist cause at the dawn of the 20th Century, the result was the Progressive Movement that lasted almost 20 years and dramatically increased the government's role in the economy. After reading books and magazine articles written by such muckraking journalists as Upton Sinclair, whose book, *The Jungle*, publicized the horrors that existed in the meatpacking industry, a large number of people with more education, money and political influence began to support a growing role of government at every level. After the horrific fire in 1911 at the Triangle Shirtwaist Factory in New York took the lives of 146 garment workers, important reforms came about on the state level. Under the leadership of Theodore Roosevelt, William Howard Taft and Woodrow Wilson, the federal government also increased its role. This resulted in government regulations on meatpacking plants and most other industries that marketed food and drugs, government lawsuits to break up trusts like Standard Oil, and improved recognition of the rights of labor unions. It also increased protection of the nation's land and natural resources, created the Federal Reserve System to better regulate the nation's banks, and led to an amendment to the Constitution enabling the federal government to finance its increased role through an income tax. The U.S. decision to enter World War One in 1917 may have taken the wind out of the sails for the Progressive Movement, but by then, the government had at least accepted its role as an umpire in the U.S. capitalist system to better insure greater equality of opportunity for all Americans.

As might be expected, developments in Europe were even more extreme. The Communist International had growing influence in many European nations, and this finally exploded into the Russian Revolution of 1917. By the end of this cataclysmic episode, the Czar of Russia and his entire royal family were dead; and Russia was engaged in a bloody civil war that finally succeeded at putting Karl Marx's communist theories into practice. Under the leadership of Vladimir Lenin, Leon Trotsky and eventually, Joseph Stalin, Russia was transformed from a land of a few wealthy nobles and tens of millions of poor peasants into the *"modern"* Soviet Union where everyone was supposed to share equally in the nation's wealth. Many people around the world applauded this development, and one of them was the English writer, George Orwell. Because of his socialist leanings, Orwell was delighted by the early stages of the Russian Revolution. When he saw how Stalin's schizophrenic and brutal leadership undermined the Marxist principles of the revolution, the result was his classic book, *Animal Farm*. I have assigned this book to my students for years, and they always get a kick out of learning that each of the farm animals that overthrew Farmer Jones in this classic parable represent different individuals or groups from the Russian Revolution.

While these events were unfurling in Russia, Europe was rebuilding from the horrors of the First World War and the United States was experiencing massive economic growth during its *"Roaring Twenties."* Every president during the twenties was a pro-business Republican who wanted to pull back on the increased role of government that had been established in the Progressive Era. Once again, the pendulum had swung back from one extreme to another. Then, in October of 1929, everything changed.

The crash of the stock market ushered in the Great Depression, the longest and most severe economic downturn in our nation's history. By the late 1920s, the United States had become the wealthiest and most productive society in history. How could there now be 25% unemployment? Before it was all over, millions of people saw their savings wiped out in bank closures, thousands of businesses went belly up, and there was homelessness, hunger, even starvation in a nation that had known so much plenty. Historians still debate the long term causes of the Great Depression, but there is no getting away from the fact that its impact was severe and global. The one nation that did not really feel its effects was the Soviet Union because as stated before, one advantage of a socialist or communist system is that it immunizes the economy against diseases such as runaway inflation or depressions. In fact, during the Great Depression of the 1930s, 100,000 Americans picked up and moved to the Soviet Union because they thought capitalism was on its deathbed and that communism represented the wave of the future.

To guide the United States through its most stressful economic period in the nation's history and to save its capitalism from complete annihilation, Franklin D. Roosevelt was elected president in November of 1932. He immediately got busy putting millions of the unemployed back to work. In fact, the huge volume of legislation passed just in the first one hundred days of his administration completely transformed the nation forever. Collectively known as the New Deal, Roosevelt created about two dozen new programs designed to stabilize banks, shore up farming, provide senior pensions, regulate the stock market, and most important, create jobs. Despite his efforts, the Depression continued throughout the 1930s and did not end until the start of World War Two finally pulled the United States out of its economic doldrums, and as a result, there were some who criticized Roosevelt for not doing more.

Probably the most famous was the Louisiana governor and senator, Huey P. Long, whose *"Share-the-Wealth Program"* would have limited annual incomes to one million dollars, capped inheritances at 5.1 million and provided every family with a homestead allowance of not less than one-third of the average family wealth of the country. Long was assassinated in 1935, so we will never know how far he might have taken this plan, but his popularity clearly showed how far the nation had come in its thinking about wealth distribution. In the long run, most historians credit FDR's New Deal with enabling the U.S. to survive the Great Depression without experiencing a violent communist revolution or turning to the leadership of a fascist dictator.

Huey P. Long
Courtesy of the Library of Congress, Prints and Photographs Division
LC-H2- B-6816

Combined with the gargantuan growth of federal government necessary for the United States to fight and win the Second World War, America entered the postwar era after 1945 with a gross domestic product greater than the rest of the world combined, a government that played a significantly larger role in the economy and a growing middle class that helped reduced the gap between the rich and the poor. In addition, despite the pessimistic predictions made about the economy returning to a dramatic slowdown when millions of soldiers returned from the war to resume their civilian lives, the pent-up demand for new products like cars, washing machines and televisions after the war led to the longest sustained period of economic growth in the nation's history.

After the Axis powers surrendered in 1945, different forms of democratic socialism spread to Great Britain and other Western European nations as they rebuilt from the ashes of the war. Eastern European nations went even further as Soviet tanks helped to spread and protect new communist regimes in nations like Poland, Hungary, Czechoslovakia and East Germany. As new wealth was being generated in these societies, it was clearly being shared in a more equitable manner. Beginning in 1945, the United States waged a Cold War with the Soviet Union to *"contain"* the spread of communism. However, despite the intense competition in propaganda, the arms race, the space race and many other indirect conflicts designed to win support in the new emerging nations of the world, the pendulum within the United States was gradually swinging towards a more equitable sharing of wealth. The Civil Rights Movement that emerged in the 1950s helped to at least offer the promise of greater economic opportunities for African Americans and other minorities, and when President Johnson decided to *"declare war on poverty"* in the 1960s, the result was a slate of new government programs collectively called the Great Society.

By 1968, the Great Society had created Medicare, Medicaid, Project Head Start, Food Stamps and the Department of Housing and Urban Development. Combined with a number of other programs, liberal Democrats in the 1960s truly believed that a nation with the wealth of the United States could eliminate or dramatically reduce poverty in this nation. Many, to this day, insist that if ten times as much money had not been spent to fight the war in Vietnam as was being spent to wage war against poverty, the Great Society would have been a rousing success. Be that as it may, by 1980, the majority of the American public had grown weary of expanded federal programs that were increasingly funded by rising taxes and were clearly not working. This was made crystal clear in 1980 with the election of President Ronald Reagan.

The Reagan *"Revolution"* represented a significant swing of the pendulum back in the direction of less federal government and more wealth falling into the hands of fewer and fewer people. In his first term, federal income taxes were cut 25%. Government regulations over industries ranging from aviation to banking were appreciably reduced as was spending on most social programs. In fact, the only area where federal spending went up was for the military. Republicans applauded this counter to the direction the nation had been following ever since the start of the New Deal in 1933. At the present, almost any Republican candidate for office wants to be identified with Ronald Reagan, the *"Great Communicator"* and his conservative economic policies. On the other hand, liberal Democrats were livid. They knew that in the years to follow, the income gap between the rich and everyone else would widen. In fact, wages for the average worker declined in the 1980s and the nation's homeownership rate fell as well. During

Reagan's two terms in the White House, which were boon times for the rich, the poverty rate in cities grew.

While President Reagan's supply side economic policies based on lower taxes, increased investment and fewer economic restrictions are still being debated to this day, his military build up and tough stance towards the Soviet Union draws almost universal acclaim. The reason why is because after the appointment of Mikhail Gorbachev as the leader of the U.S.S.R. in 1985, free elections were allowed and the communists were voted out of power. This set off a chain reaction of events: the break up of the Soviet Union into 15 separate states, the end of communist rule in the nations of Eastern Europe, significant reductions in the stockpiles of thousands of nuclear weapons and the rise of a free market economy in place of what had been 70 years of communism. Historians are still trying to come to grips with who deserves the most credit for ending the Cold War and for bringing down its most despised symbol, the Berlin Wall. Was its Reagan's tough policies, Gorbachev's openness to reform, or some sort of combination?

While it is easy to see these events as *"proof"* of capitalism's superiority to socialism, the reality is not so simple. In theory, the tenets of socialism still have broad appeal around the world, and roughly 20 per cent of the planet's population still lives under some form of socialism or communism. Therefore, the explanation for the fall of communism in the Soviet Union and in the nations of Eastern Europe has more to do with their unique circumstances than to Mikhail Gorbachev simply caving in to President Reagan's pressure from the West. In his 2009 book, *The Rise and Fall of Communism*, Oxford historian Archie Brown, stated that nationalism contributed greatly to the collapse of communism in Eastern Europe. In addition, he claims the combination of new political ideas and political choices led to the demise of the Soviet Union. Others point out that the 70 years of communist rule in the U.S.S.R. never included much time for communism to prosper. Ronald Suny, the editor of a recent volume on 20th Century Russian history, suggests that the total number of lives destroyed by the Stalinist regime in the 1930s is between 10 and 11 million. In the following decade, the Nazi invasion of the Soviet Union took another 22 million Russian lives, almost 10 per cent of the total population. Under these extreme conditions, how well would any economic system prosper?

History is never simple. Examining the past to find examples of the success or failure of either the capitalist or socialist economic models can prove to be an exasperating experience. In theory, there are positive and negative points that can be made about both systems, but when applied to particular cultures, political systems or historical circumstances, it becomes much harder to carry on a simple debate. Nevertheless, it is incumbent on every history teacher to bring up this essential question regarding the best way for a society to distribute its wealth in order for students to grow into effective citizens in a democratic society.

Few Americans today remember or even know about the fate of the Bonus Army in 1932. While many might be shocked to learn that American troops physically attacked American veterans and their families, it is not difficult to understand the broader issue lurking beneath the violent clash. After all, even though we are not currently suffering through a nightmarish economic calamity comparable to the Great Depression, in many respects not much has changed. Only a small fraction of Americans control a huge percentage of our nation's wealth. While a much larger percentage of the public accepts this situation possibly under the guise that they too may one day acquire greater wealth, a significant percentage of the population is becoming increasingly frustrated. Just look at the Occupy Wall Street demonstrations, the recent rise of the Black Lives Matter Movement or even the large crowds attending speeches by the Democrat/Socialist candidate for president, Bernie Sanders. Capitalism may seem to rule for the present, but socialism has not disappeared, and all it will take is another major economic downturn to bring it back to the surface.

As can be seen above, the issue of how much a role the government should play in our nation's economy and the related essential question over how our nation should best divide its wealth are probably the single biggest wedges separating Democrats from Republicans today. Debates are constantly taking place between the two political parties over income taxes, business regulations, social programs like social security or Medicaid, and even the minimum wage. Lurking beneath the surface of all of these issues is the essential question over the fairest way for our society to share its wealth. A deeper understanding of this essential question will go a long way towards helping people figure out the basic differences between modern-day Democrats and modern-day Republicans. This in turn, will help people to be better citizens in our democratic society.

Suggested Reading:

Brown, Archie. *The Rise and Fall of Communism.* New York: Harper Collins, 2009.

"Changes in U.S. Family Finances from 2010-2013: Evidence Survey of Consumer Finances." *Federal Reserve.* September, 2014.
http://www.federalreserve.gov/pubs/bulletin/2014/pdf/scf14.pdf.

Collins, Chuck, and Josh Hoxie. "Billionaire Bonanza: The Forbes 400 and the Rest of Us." *Institute For Policy Studies.* December 1, 2015. https://www.ips-dc.org/billionaire-bonanza/.

Dickson, Paul, and Thomas B. Allen. *The Bonus Army: An American Epic.* New York: Walker and Company, 2004.

"Einstein's Defense of Socialism." *The Luxemburgist.* September 5, 2010.
http://www.luxemburgist.wordpress.com/2010/09/05/einsteins-defense-of-socialism.

Kane, Robert. *A Contemporary Introduction to Free Will.* New York: Oxford University Press, 2005.

Kochhar, Rakesh, and Richard Fry. "Wealth Inequality Has Widened Along Racial, Ethnic Lines Since End of Great Recession." *Pew Research Center.* December 12, 2014.
http://www.pewresearch.org/fact-tank/2014/12/12/racial-wealth-gaps-great-recession/.

Marx, Karl, and Friederich Engels. *The Communist Manifesto.* Southkingstown: Millennium Publications, 2015.

McElvaine, Robert S. *The Great Depression: America 1929-1941.* New York: Three Rivers Press, 1984.

McGerr, Michael. *A Fierce Discontent: The Rise and Fall of the Progressive Movement in America, 1870-1920.* New York: Oxford University Press, 2005.

Milling, Wendy. "Without Question, Capitalism Is Supremely Moral." *Forbes.* March 21, 2013.
http://www.forbes.com/sites/realspin/2013/03/21/without-question-capitalism-is-supremely-moral/#2ee2bcfe5dc7.

Mishel, Lawrence, and Alyssa Davis. "Top CEO's Make 300 Times More than Typical Workers." *Economic Policy Institute.* June 21, 2015.

http://www.epi.org/publication/top-ceos-make-300-times-more-than-workers-pay-growth-surpasses-market-gains-and-the-rest-of-the-0-1-percent/.

Orwell, George. *Animal Farm.* Orlando: Harcourt Brace and Company, 1945.

Smith, Adam. *The Wealth of Nations.* Introduction by Alan B. Krueger. New York: Oxford University Press, 2008.

Suny, Ronald Grigor, ed. *The Cambridge History of Russia Volume 3: The Twentieth Century.* Cambridge: Cambridge University Press, 2006.

Terkel, Studs. *Hard Times: An Oral History of the Great Depression.* New York: The New Press, 1970.

Williams, T. Harry. *Huey Long.* New York: Alfred A. Knopf, 1969.

Chapter 7
A balancing act

Socrates Holding Cup of Hemlock
Courtesy of Library of Congress, Prints and Photographs Division LC-USZ61-1503

How much power should be given to the people?

The place is Athens, Greece and the date is 399 BCE. Socrates, the famous (or infamous) educator and philosopher best known for the precept that "*the unexamined life is not worth living*," has just been convicted on two charges: corrupting the youth and impiety. More specifically, Socrates' accusers cited two impious acts: "*failing to acknowledge the gods that the city acknowledges*" and "*introducing new deities.*" In reality, the conviction is the result of the philosophical questions Socrates had been raising with his pupils and his encouragement that they should question everything and think for themselves. A majority of the dikasts voted to convict Socrates, and consistent with practice, the dikasts voted that his punishment should be death by drinking a hemlock-based liquid.

While these events took place more than 2400 years ago, the information regarding the trial comes by way of two of Socrates' students, Plato and Xenophon. The trial and the resulting execution stand out as one of the most famous injustices in the history of the world, and many lessons have since been drawn from these proceedings. The lesson, here, however, involves the dikasts. To this day, Athens remains one of the best examples of pure democracy that history has ever provided. All big decisions were the result of a vote taken by the Athenian Assembly, and every citizen of this Greek city-state was a member. Granted, women, slaves and the foreign-born were excluded from citizenship, so the Assembly did not represent a majority of the population. However, with between 6,000 and 43,000 members (estimates vary widely), there is probably no better historical example of a society that entrusted its populace with so much power. In addition, in order to minimize the accumulation of too much political power in the hands of a small number of career politicians, the individuals charged with executing and interpreting the laws were periodically chosen by lot. That included the dikasts, the jurors who voted to convict Socrates.

In retrospect, the decision to try, convict and execute a philosopher for raising questions that challenged the status quo might be seen as a momentous error in judgment and a terrible injustice. But should a decision of this magnitude have been left up to ordinary people? By definition, a democracy entrusts all or most of its political power to the people, but are the masses up to the challenge? This question has been debated for many centuries, and it has been thoroughly vetted in all of my history classes. The initial reaction by my students may be a bit surprising – they tend to fear the masses. Over the years, they have been quick to point out numerous examples of where the people "*blew it*" in a particular election. After all, it was the American people (through the electoral college) that voted to send James Buchanan, Warren G. Harding and Richard Nixon to the White House. (U.S. News has listed these three among the ten worst presidents in history.) In my early days of teaching in New Orleans, students were too quick to remember the "*democratic*" mobs that participated in violent lynching's; and in 1989, the people of Louisiana elected David Duke, a well-known Ku Klux Klan leader, to the state House of Representatives. In the world history classes, the more knowledgeable students usually point out that Adolph Hitler was appointed as the German chancellor only after his Nazi Party led all other political parties by receiving over 37% of the votes.

It is usually at this point that I remind them of Winston Churchill's famous quote that *"it has been said that democracy is the worst form of Government except for all those other forms that have been tried from time to time."* Before going any further, we then agree to identify and define those other forms of government. We start by agreeing that in a democracy, the people govern, but we also distinguish between those rare examples of pure democracy like Ancient Athens and the more common representative democracies also known as republics. After all, most democracies are much too large to fit all of the citizens into one assembly, so while the final say may rest with the people, representatives are elected by the citizens to make and carry out the laws. In the United States, only 535 representatives are elected to Congress to make the laws for over 300,000,000 people.

When asked to identify the form of government that sits on the opposite end of the spectrum from democracy, the answer is a monarchy or a dictatorship. Here, the power resides with just one person, and the only difference between a monarchy and a dictatorship is over how that one person comes to power: monarchs inherit their position while a dictator is either chosen or simply uses force to take the power. In between are forms of government like aristocracies, where once again, the power is usually inherited; and oligarchies, which can be simply defined as governments where the power sits with only a minority of the population. There are obviously other specific forms of government – theocracies, meritocracies, etc., but the point to the use of this linear spectrum approach is to keep the focus on how many people have a share in a society's political power:

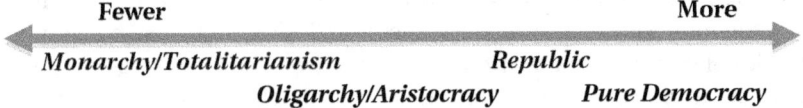

Fewer		**More**
Monarchy/Totalitarianism	*Republic*	
	Oligarchy/Aristocracy	*Pure Democracy*

Usually at this point I introduce a hypothetical situation to my students. Since we now live in the age of computers and the Internet, the question is raised as to whether we really need Congress. After all, 435 U.S. Representatives and 100 Senators are only .00000178% of the U.S. population, and in a *Rasmussen Reports* survey taken in February, 2016, only 11% of the U.S. population believed Congress was doing a good or excellent job, while 60% rated Congress poorly. What if the people instead decided the major issues currently voted on by Congress? Once a week, a major issue could be debated by *"experts"*, or better yet, average people sitting in front of their computer terminals could be randomly picked to offer their opinions for others to consider. In addition, the news media, which already acts as the *"fourth branch of government"*, could provide relevant information and fact-checking services. Commercials and advertisements could be run and a certain amount of time might be allowed for informal discussion to take place across the nation. Then, at an appointed time, people could vote from the comforts of their own living rooms. In this manner, the citizens themselves could decide whether to raise their own taxes, restrict abortions or approve the military budget. Thanks to modern technology, we could transform our nation, with the world's third largest population, into a pure democracy. When a student invariably mentions the cheating that might take place, I remind him that if my son or daughter could take their law school final exams online without cheating, we can certainly create a secure method to conduct the voting. Beside, security is not the issue; the question is whether we should trust the masses with the same power we currently give Congress.

At this point, some of the students usually become intrigued by the idea, and we generally agree that the next step should be to examine the pros and cons of the proposal. Those who lean toward becoming a pure democracy point out that if the people are trusted with the power to directly make the big decisions, they will care more about what is taking place around them and will be less apathetic. Giving people more of a stake in their government is certainly preferable to the less than 37% of the electorate that turned out in the 2014 congressional election, is it not? The next point usually made in defense of greater democracy is the attack that is usually fomented against the other forms of government. When power resides with just one person or is in the hands of a small minority, what will guarantee that the interests of everyone will be considered? History is filled with examples of corruption and/or the abuse of power whenever kings or oligarchies are in charge. As the famous line by Lord Acton says, *"Power tends to corrupt and absolute power corrupts absolutely."* Finally, there are always some students that just have an implicit faith in the people. For whatever reason, they are populists by nature and feel that if given a proper civic education, the people can be trusted to rule. With a little research, they will bring in quotes like the following:

> *"It is an axiom in my mind that our liberty can never be safe but in the hands of the people themselves, and that, too, of the people with a certain degree of instruction."*
>
> Thomas Jefferson

> *"I am a firm believer in the people. If given the truth, they can be depended upon to meet any national crisis."*
> Abraham Lincoln

> *"Democracy is worth dying for, because it's the most deeply honorable form of government ever devised by man."*
> Ronald Reagan

To give this side of the debate a little more support, and also because it is an appealing activity, I usually propose at this point that we engage in a simulation called "*Lost on the Moon.*" In this activity, which is readily available online from Kagan Cooperative Learning, students are told to pretend they are members of a space crew originally scheduled to rendezvous with a mother ship on the lighted surface of the moon. However, due to mechanical problems, their ship was forced to land at a spot 200 miles from the rendezvous point. There are 15 items available to help with the journey to the mother ship, but since taking them all may prove to be problematic, the items should be ranked according to how useful they will be to guarantee survival. The items include a box of matches, five gallons of water, a magnetic compass and two 100-pound tanks of oxygen. The students are then told to rank the items from one to fifteen on their own without any discussion. After this is accomplished, the students are divided into groups of five or six and then given a reasonable amount of time to discuss the situation. Each group is then told to create a collective ranking of the same 15 items. When this is accomplished, the correct NASA ranking of the fifteen items is distributed, and students are told to calculate the error for each item. For example, if they rated the compass a three for being the third most important item, the error would be 11, since NASA actually ranked the compass 14th. (The magnetic field on the moon is not polarized, so it is worthless for navigation.) The error for all 15 items is then totaled for each individual and for each group. Obviously, the lower the total, the better the score for the decisions made. While there are a few individual exceptions, the average score for the groups has generally been better than the average individual scores. What does this mean? The students are usually forced to acknowledge that at least in some situations, a larger number of people will make better decisions through discussion and the sharing of ideas than they will as individuals.

After completing the case for doing away with Congress and becoming a more democratic society, the other side is allowed to develop their arguments. The first point usually made is that democracy tends to be too slow and inefficient to get things done. Both the United States and Germany faced similar economic disasters in 1933 as each nation confronted the worst year of the Great Depression. However, when Adolph Hitler and his Nazi henchmen took over the reigns of power in Germany, money was immediately spent on massive public works projects that put people back to work in armaments plants or constructing the Autobahn. Within months, Germany had effectively clawed its way out of the Great Depression. Meanwhile, President Franklin Roosevelt had to deal with Congress, the Supreme Court, and plenty of critics from all sides. While New Deal legislation did help to mitigate some of the worst symptoms of the Depression, unemployment remained relatively high throughout the remainder of the decade. Unlike Hitler, the fascist dictator, there were limits on the powers of Roosevelt, the elected president.

Franklin Delano Roosevelt
Courtesy of Library of Congress, Prints and Photographs Division
LC-DIG-hec-47384

The great journalist, H.L. Mencken, once said that *"under democracy one party always devotes its chief energies to trying to prove that the other party is unfit to rule - and both commonly succeed, and are right."* Roosevelt, a Democrat, had to tackle the Republicans in his bids to seek reelection in 1936, 1940 and 1944; additionally, he was also facing a growing number of Republicans in Congress after 1936. Furthermore, the Supreme Court had declared some of his New Deal legislation to be unconstitutional. Is it no wonder that the popularity of fascism was on the rise around much of the world at the same time that democracies were struggling to handle the worst economic crisis the modern world had ever known?

The other arguments against giving too much power to the people are usually aimed directly at the people. The masses are generally accused of being too ignorant, too selfish or both. While Winston Churchill has been quoted as saying that democracy may be the best government when one considers the other options, he also said *"the best argument against democracy is a five-minute conversation with the average voter."* And James Bovard once said in *Lost Rights: The Destruction of American Liberty*, that *"democracy must be something more than two wolves and a sheep voting on what to have for dinner."* Ask any member of a school district what often happens when the voters are requested to improve their schools by passing a tax referendum. While there may be a significant number of people who do take their roles as citizens seriously by staying informed about their options, the majority often tends to be apathetic, unaware and self-centered. The result more often than not tends to be bad decision-making and a high tolerance for corruption. This fear of the people abusing their power helps to explain why men like James Madison and Alexander Hamilton worked so hard to place many limits within the Constitution on the powers of the people. As stated in Federalist No. 51, Madison argued, *"If men were angels, no government would be necessary. If angels were to govern men, neither external nor internal controls on government would be necessary. In framing a government which is to be administered by men over men, the great difficulty lies in this: you must first enable the government to control the governed; and in the next place, oblige it to control itself."* He went on to say in Federalist No. 10 that *"Democracies have ever been spectacles of turbulence and contention; have ever been found incompatible with personal security, or the rights of property; and have, in general, been as short in their lives as they have been violent in their deaths."*

Finally, the students themselves generally raise a valid, pragmatic concern: time. In our modern world, filled with all of its complexities, would the average person have the time to work a jam-packed job by day and then come home at night and have additional time to become a legislator? The members of Congress, despite their perceived shortcomings, do not simultaneously pursue other careers that will compete with their time or energy to be full time legislators. When a bill is proposed, they serve on committees, call in experts to testify and have assistants to conduct research. There are many chores to be completed, and as anyone who is familiar with the procedures of Congress knows, the real work gets done in committees. When Congress passed the Affordable Care Act (Obama Care) in 2010, there were over 20,000 pages of details. Most in Congress had not read all of these pages, so how many average voters would be able to do this if Congress were abolished?

The pro-democracy students usually rebut this point by stating that the field of journalism could provide enough experts to sift through the mountains of data before a law is passed. In addition, they say that if given enough civic education, the people can be trusted to vote for the greater good of society and not just to enrich themselves. To this point, their opposition usually mentions the Dictator Game. In this game, the first player, *"the dictator"*, determines how to split an endowment (such as a cash prize) between himself and a second player. The second player, *"the recipient"*, simply receives the remainder of the endowment left by the dictator. The recipient's role is entirely passive, as he has no input into the outcome of the game. Studies show that 40% of the *"dictators"* end up keeping all of the money, and the average amount given to the recipients is only 20%. Can a proper civic education ever hope to root out this high level of greed among the general populace? Only the most eternally optimistic could ever say yes. As much as we may like to tout our democratic system as the greatest the world has ever seen, many Americans, including a majority of my students, get very nervous at the prospect of our system ever becoming a pure democracy.

When reviewing the historical record for insight on how to best answer this essential question, there was very little to go on prior to the year 1215. With the exception of some of the Greek city-states and possibly the Roman Republic before the rise of demagogues like Julius Caesar, power was usually in the hands of a single person. The titles varied: king, queen, emperor, Caesar, Kaiser, Czar, chief; but the reality was that one person possessed most of the power within any given society. Things began to change in England in 1215 when a group of lords managed to force King John to seek and receive their approval before taxes could be raised. The king agreed to these terms by signing the Magna Carta and many have come to see this document as the birth certificate of our modern democracy. Over time, this council of lords evolved to become Parliament, but even four hundred years later, there were still English kings competing with Parliament over who should have the most power.

The issue was finally resolved in 1688 when Parliament decided to peacefully remove James II as the king and replace him with William of Orange, a distant relative that could not even speak English. If Parliament could remove one monarch and replace him with another, the power pendulum had shifted to Parliament, and it has never shifted back. John Locke, the first great thinker and philosopher of the Age of Enlightenment, defended this move by developing his Theory of Natural Rights. According to Locke, all humans are born into a state of nature with three natural rights: life, liberty and property; and that in order to protect these rights, the people should create a government through a social contract. The purpose of government is simply to protect these rights, and if the government abuses this responsibility, the people can then void the contract by overthrowing the government and replacing it with another. This principle, along with others ideas contributed by French philosophers like Voltaire, Montesquieu and Rousseau, formed the foundation for the American and French Revolutions of the late 18th Century. Liberal revolutions in some form or fashion have been spreading around the planet ever since.

John Locke
Courtesy of Library of Congress
Prints and Photographs Division
LC-USZ62-59655

However, it must be noted that by 1800, there was still a long way to go before authority really rested with the people. In Great Britain, power may have shifted from the monarchy to an elected Parliament, but most adults in England still could not vote in Parliamentary elections, and they certainly had no direct say in passing English law. It was not until passage of the Reform Acts of the mid 19th Century that most men in England gained the right to vote, and women's suffrage did not come about until the first half of the 20th century.

Meanwhile, across the pond, England's 13 colonies began to wage a war for independence after the first shots were fired outside of Boston in 1775. While battles waged from New England to South Carolina, the Continental Congress in Philadelphia wrote the Articles of Confederation to create a government for the emerging nation. Mostly out of fear that a powerful federal government could be just as dangerous as the British government that was currently being replaced, the Articles gave very little authority to Congress and instead, left most power with the individual states. Within each state, however, only white, male landowners could vote. Also, with a Congress that could not collect taxes and lacking a president or a Supreme Court to enforce or interpret the law, the new nation was soon faced with the prospect of coming apart. When Daniel Shays led a rebellion of farmers from western Massachusetts in 1786 against the state government in Boston over taxes and other economic issues, the rest of the nation took notice and quickly realized the Articles needed some major reform.

The result was the Constitutional Convention of 1787. This meeting in Philadelphia lasted months and was filled with contentious debates. As might be expected, one of the central issues involved how much power should be given to the people. Should all adults be able to vote? The answer: let's leave it up to the states, and for the immediate future, the vote was only given to white, male landowners. Should these voters be able to vote for the members of Congress? The answer: yes, in the case of the House of Representatives, which was intended to have a closer connection to the people, but no in the case of the Senate. The people could elect their friends and neighbors to the state legislatures (although even here, property requirements meant that legislatures would usually be composed of wealthy, well-educated white men), and the state legislatures would elect the state's two senators. This would not change until 1913 when the 17th Amendment finally provided for the direct election of senators. Should the people be empowered to elect their president? The answer: no. Once again, the state legislature would pick a group of electors (the number would be based on the state's population), and the electors would come together as an Electoral College to pick the president. In an age where there was no radio, television or Internet, and since a large number of people had no access to newspapers or were unable to read them, it is amazing that the members of the Constitutional Convention trusted the people as much as they did. The United States had a long way to go in the dissemination of political power amongst the people.

After 1787, two developments in America helped to move the pendulum a little closer towards greater democracy. One was the addition of a Bill of Rights to the Constitution. Since many Americans threatened to hold up the ratification of the Constitution over the fear that it was creating a government that might easily abuse its new powers, another compromise was proposed that if the Constitution were approved, a set of amendments would soon be added to the Constitution to limit these powers. However, it should be noted these amendments were primarily intended to be limits on the powers of the government. After all, the First Amendment does not begin, *"The people should have freedom of religion."* It states, *"Congress shall make no law respecting the establishment of religion, or prohibiting the free exercise thereof..."* In other words, despite the fact that the Bill of Rights has been interpreted to make us a more democratic society, the reality is that the first 10 amendments were really just intended to check the powers of the government.

The second development occurred with the election of Andrew Jackson as president in 1828. It came about more because of his image as a man of the people rather than through specific actions taken by Jackson. Even his inauguration party, which almost brought down the White House, was seen as ushering in the new *"Age of Jackson"*; a more democratic period in American History. Probably the single most important development during this time was the decision by the states to drop the property requirements to vote. Making the franchise more available to all white men rather than just wealthy white men was a step towards spreading political power out to a larger number of stake-holders. The Age of Jackson laid a foundation for the expansion of the right to vote from the 1830s up to the 1960s.

Andrew Jackson
Courtesy of Library of Congress
Prints and Photographs Division
LC-USZ62-5663

After the Civil War was concluded, Reconstruction ushered in three more amendments to the Constitution, including the 15th Amendment, which gave the right to vote to former slaves. However, this progress was largely dismantled when southern states found major loopholes in the 15th Amendment. These loopholes allowed for the creation of poll taxes, literacy tests and grandfather clauses to keep African Americans out of the voting booth.

During the Progressive Age between 1900 and 1920, two more amendments were added to the Constitution. As previously stated, the 17th gave American voters the power to directly elect their senators. Then, in 1920, as a culmination to the Women's Suffrage Movement that had first begun in Seneca Falls, New York way back in 1848, women were finally granted the right to vote. Forty-four years later, the 24th Amendment abolished poll taxes, and a short time afterwards, the 26th Amendment lowered the voting age from 21 to 18. This development made perfect sense in light of the fact that young men aged 18 to 20 were being sent off to fight, kill and die for their country in Vietnam without the ability to elect the leaders who were sending them off to fight.

This brings us back to the present and to the essential question at hand. How much power should be given to the people? As can be seen, this is purposely not a yes or no question and might best be answered on a spectrum. If the number one represents giving the masses no say at all and the number 10 is the opposite position where we become a pure democracy, most of my students over the years have veered toward the lower numbers. Even though the Digital Revolution has given us new technology that has effectively allowed us to create an assembly with hundreds of millions of members, the majority of my students have opposed this idea. Instead, they prefer we continue the current system of checks and balances as first envisioned by men like John Locke, the Baron Montesquieu, John Adams and James Madison. The fear of entrusting too much power to one person, a small group or everyone, has led to the principle that power should be shared between different branches of government, as well as between different levels of government; and that each should be able to check the abuse of power by the others. After all, it is hard to argue with what appears to be over two centuries of political success.

There is one final consideration. Which political system provides the best government when it comes to effectively meeting the needs of the most people? Citizens in the western democracies would argue that the answer to that question should be a representative democracy. This form of government not only allows each citizen to vote based on individual concerns, but also insures that no one person or group will gather enough power to threaten the existence of the current government. A representative democracy, in which the people elect legislators to vote on their behalf, also offers a more responsive and efficient governing body than a direct democracy. A pure democracy would require cumbersome popular votes to decide every issue and the service of amateurs as opposed to professionals to execute the decisions made.

Further support for representative democracy comes from the World Bank, which ranks nations according to a government effectiveness score, based on how well each government meets the needs of the people. The countries that rank highest on this scale include the United States, the United Kingdom, Germany, Australia and several Scandinavian nations; all maintain some form of bicameral, multi-party, representative government. By contrast, nations that were part of the former Soviet Union such as those located in Sub-Saharan Africa, in addition to nations in Southern Asia, rate poorly. Countries scoring lowest are likely to have a one-party system, a military or a monarchy, or a state of government so disordered it is best described as anarchy.

Based on this thinking, it can be argued we have come a long way since the death of Socrates 2400 years ago. It seems unimaginable that a group of ordinary Americans would force him to drink the hemlock today. On the other hand, it was the elected members of Congress that passed such horrible acts of intolerance as the Indian Removal Act in 1830 and the Chinese Exclusion Act in 1882. It was elected members of Congress during the Red Scare of the early 1950s that jailed Dalton Trumbo for his association with the Communist Party. And for that matter, it was juries composed of ordinary citizens serving a vital role in our democratic society that sent many of the two million people to our nation's jails and prisons. Yes, most of these people are guilty of serious crimes, but according to the Innocence Project, studies indicate that somewhere between 2.3 to 5 per cent of these inmates were wrongly convicted. This means that despite the best of intentions, somewhere between 46,000 to 100,000 people are serving time for crimes they did not commit. With this in mind, one has to wonder what would happen to a modern-day Socrates.

In the final analysis, most students have usually come to the conclusion that as much as they might complain about our current system of government, they would not make any significant changes to our present system. Our current representative democracy might be tweaked in certain ways, like abolishing the Electoral College and replacing it with a national election where all citizens over 18 can directly choose their president. The students fully understand the imperfections of the human race; so after a careful examination of this essential question, they usually come to the conclusion that any form of government will also be imperfect. Otherwise, the question over how much power to give the people is purely academic. In a democratic society like our own, it is guaranteed to lead to heated debate but also a healthy exchange of ideas.

Suggested Reading:

Bovard, James. *Lost Rights: The Destruction of American Liberty.* New York: St. Martin's Press, 1994.

Brands, H.W. *Andrew Jackson: His Life and Times.* New York: First Anchor Books, 2006.

Churchill, Winston. *The Power of Words,* Edited by Martin Gilbert. Boston: Da Capo Press, 2012.

"Congressional Performance." *Rasmussen Reports.* February 22, 2016. http://www.rasmussenreports.com/public_content/politics/top_stories/congressional_performance.

Hamby, Alonzo L. *Man of Destiny: FDR and the Making of the American Century.* New York: Basic Books, 2015.

Hamilton, Alexander, and James Madison. *The Federalist Papers,* Edited by Richard Beeman. New York: Penguin Books, 2012.

"How Many Innocent People Are There In Prison?" *Innocent Project.* Accessed October 12, 2015. http://www.innocenceproject.org/faqs/how-many-innocent-people-are-there-in-prison.

Kagan, Spencer. *Cooperative Learning Resources for Teachers.* Oakland: University of California Press, 1990.

Locke, John. *The Second Treatise of Government and a Letter Concerning Toleration.* New York: Dover Publications, 2002.

Plato. *The Trial of Socrates: Four Dialogues.* Translated by Benjamin Jowett. New York: Classic Books International, 2010.

Chapter 8
Sharing the sandbox

USS Arizona, following Japanese attack on Pearl Harbor
Courtesy of the Library of Congress, Prints and Photographs Division
LC-USZ62-104778

What is the best way for nations to carry on foreign policy?

The place is Pearl Harbor, Hawaii and the date is December 7th, 1941. A calm Sunday morning is suddenly disturbed by the sounds of hundreds of Japanese dive-bombers and torpedo planes screaming out of the sky. Sailors still hung over from partying the night before in downtown Honolulu scramble to climb out of their bunks and man their battle stations. When a

Japanese bomb detonates in the magazine of the battleship, the U.S.S. Arizona, the ensuing explosion immediately sinks the iron-plated behemoth, killing 1,177 officers and crewmen. By the end of the day, the U.S. Pacific fleet based in Hawaii is mostly destroyed and 2,400 Americans are dead. The following day, President Franklin D. Roosevelt calls December 7th, 1941, a *"date that will live in infamy,"* and less than an hour later, Congress obliges the president's request and declares war on Japan. The United States finally joins in the Second World War, a conflict that had begun over two years earlier.

Most people are quite familiar with this story, including my high school students. When asked about the significance of the attack on Pearl Harbor, the standard response is that it either started World War II or it dragged the United States into the conflict. Most people, however, do not see it as a major turning point in American diplomatic history; but considering that one hundred and fifty years of foreign policy tradition came to an abrupt end in a single day, the Japanese attack also played this role.

Ever since President George Washington warned the nation in his 1796 Farewell Address that *"the true policy (of the United States) is to steer clear of permanent alliances with any parts of the foreign world,"* America had been following a foreign policy tradition called isolationism. This policy was based on the assumption that our new nation would best grow and prosper by exploiting its natural geographic advantage of having two major oceans serve as protective barriers from the destructive conflicts that had always dominated the Old World. While there were a number of glaring exceptions, this policy had largely succeeded. Then, in a single day, the Japanese use of new technology, in particular, airplanes launched off the decks of aircraft carriers, clearly demonstrated that the oceans would no longer protect American security interests. Within days after the attack on Pearl Harbor, U.S. control of the Philippines was also challenged, and thousands of Americans from Seattle to San Diego were on the lookout for a Japanese attack anywhere along the West Coast. The United States was no longer safe, and isolationism could no longer be followed as a foreign policy. What would take its place?

Put in a larger context, the real question is how should the United States, or for that matter, any nation, conduct a foreign policy with the other nations of the world? On a planet where there are tens of thousands of nuclear warheads, no question is probably more important, and yet no question gets a duller reaction in my classes. Why does the subject of foreign policy garner such apathy from high school students? The answer is purely anecdotal, but decades of frustrated efforts have shown that high school students in the United States tend to take much for granted. Most live comfortable lives in a large, affluent nation where they feel well protected. Most seem to develop a parochial attitude from the time they are young children, which creates a resistance among many to even study a language beyond their own. And most find foreign policy to be dizzyingly complex.

On the other hand, an examination of the history behind this subject proves that it can be approached on a simple level. In fact, while there were plenty of wars, treaties and conflicts, most nation-states prior to 1789 were largely just concerned with either expansion or survival. History is filled with examples of one kingdom or empire looking to expand at the expense of a neighbor, but as a rule, there was no overarching foreign policy that played a part in world affairs prior to the onset of the French Revolution in 1789. However, when the French beheaded King Louis XVI and his wife, Marie Antoinette in 1793, everything changed.

The guillotining of the French king and queen sent shivers down the spines of other European leaders. The powerfully appealing ideas of liberalism and nationalism were also perceived as a threat to their national security. War broke out on a scale never seen before as European states formed a powerful coalition; first, against the massive French Republican armies that built their numbers by employing military conscription for the first time in history and second, against the even larger French armies of Napoleon Bonaparte. Warfare dominated the European continent up to Napoleon's final defeat at Waterloo in 1815. What emerged in his wake was the Congress of Vienna led by the influential Prince Metternich of Austria. Besides agreeing to restore monarchs to their thrones throughout the continent, the Congress set a new foreign policy tradition: the importance of maintaining the balance of power. It took a combination of nations, Austria, Prussia, Great Britain and Russia, to bring down Napoleon. From that day on, nations were prepared to band together again whenever a single nation might threaten the security of the others.

Napoleon's return from the island of Elba
Courtesy of the Library of Congress, Prints and Photographs Division
LC-DIG-pga-04089

With only some minor exceptions, this approach to foreign policy succeeded at maintaining a peaceful and orderly world for almost a century. The dawn of the 1900s, however, saw a shift from nations coming together to maintain the balance of power towards an international order where European nations joined an alliance for their own mutual protection. With tension building due to rising nationalism as well as competition over the desire to acquire overseas colonies, the world had become a powder keg waiting for a spark to ignite a massive explosion. That spark came in the summer of 1914 in the form of an assassination, and by the end of the summer the two major alliances were locked in a titanic struggle called the Great War. Later known as World War One, the bloody stalemate was not broken until November of 1918, and by that point, over 17 million soldiers and civilians were dead. The international order that had existed prior to 1914 had failed and something new would have to take its place.

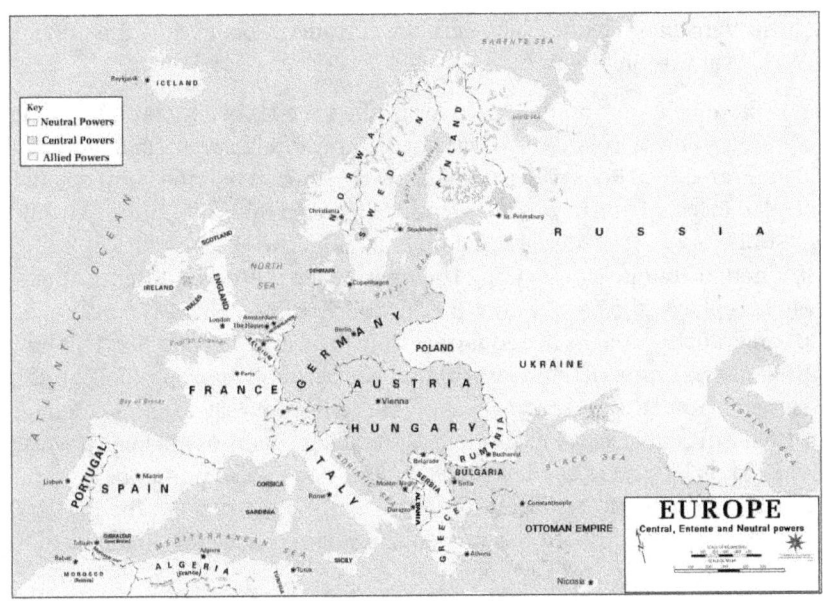

European alliances during the 1914-18 war
Courtesy of US Federal Government (PD-US Army)
https://commons.wikimedia.org/wiki/File:Europe_1914.jpg

In the Versailles Treaty that ended the First World War, President Wilson, representing the United States, had succeeded in creating a new international organization called the League of Nations. In principle, the League's member nations would be able to come together and meet face to face to resolve their problems peacefully. The launching of the League of Nations was marred from its inception by the fact that the United States failed to join. President Wilson may have possessed an idealistic vision of a future where peace would prevail over war, but the Senate was more concerned about U.S. national security. It voted not to ratify the treaty; therefore, the United States, which had emerged from the war as arguably the strongest, and certainly one of the wealthiest nations in the world, played no role in this new approach to international affairs. In the years that followed, as fascist governments came to power in Italy, Germany and Japan, and as these nations took steps that would lead to an even deadlier war, the United States was nowhere to be found. Any hope that the League of Nations might prevent a future war was probably dashed when America decided to return to its policy of isolationism. Twenty years after the writing of the Versailles Treaty, Nazi Germany invaded Poland and the Second World War was underway.

When the attack on Pearl Harbor pushed the United States into World War II, the end of isolationism was not the only foreign policy change. President Franklin D. Roosevelt immediately recognized that the United States needed to learn from its mistakes from the past, so this time, America would not only join a new international organization, the U.S. would play an instrumental role in its creation. The charter for the new United Nations, which replaced the League after the Second World War in 1945, was signed in San Francisco and its headquarters were to be in New York City. This new international approach to world affairs has certainly had its pitfalls, but it has lasted until the present, and as my students often say when we manage to hold a decent discussion about foreign policy, there has not been a World War Three. Of course, some of the students like to also point out that this may be due more to M.A.D. (Mutually Assured Destruction); the fact that nations are deterred from starting a world war because they do not want to be targeted by thousands of nuclear missiles.

In the realm of American history, as previously stated, foreign policy got its start with the advent of isolationism. While this approach of keeping to ourselves lasted in one form or another for about 150 years, there were plenty of exceptions. For example, in 1812, the United States went to war for a second time with Great Britain. While the first time was aimed at acquiring our independence, this War of 1812 was primarily over trade rights. The United States was caught in the middle between Napoleonic France and the British, and when English ships not only threw a blockade around the European continent, but even began to *"impress"* American sailors into their navy on the high seas, the United States had had enough and declared war. After a three-year stalemate and Napoleon's defeat, a treaty was signed between the United States and Great Britain with nothing gained and nothing lost. One result within the United States, however, was a major boost in American nationalism.

A few years later, with other new nations in the Western Hemisphere like Haiti and Mexico winning their independence, the United States decided to introduce another exception to isolationism. Known as the Monroe Doctrine, but primarily written by President James Monroe's secretary of state, John Quincy Adams; the document informed European powers that they should butt out of North and South America, thereby respecting the freedom of new countries that were emerging from what had previously been European-held colonies. It is doubtful that nations like Britain and

France took the Monroe Doctrine seriously when it was first issued, but over time, it has come to represent a major piece of U.S. foreign policy. This was particularly true when President Theodore Roosevelt added his infamous *"Corollary"* to the Monroe Doctrine in the first part of the 20th Century, stating that the United States would exercise *"international police power"* to put an end to European meddling and wrongdoing in the Western Hemisphere. The Corollary may have looked good on paper, but in reality, it was used numerous times to justify American meddling in the Western Hemisphere and has therefore stirred up a great deal of resentment in Latin America towards the United States.

America's westward expansion in the 19th century also created foreign policy issues for the United States. After Mexico gained its independence in 1821, land-hungry Americans had been invited to settle in a Mexican region called Texas. The Texans successfully revolted against Mexico in the 1830s and then promptly asked to be annexed by the United States. This was accomplished in the following decade, but on the pretext of a border dispute between Mexico and the newly acquired Republic of Texas, President James Polk convinced Congress to declare war on Mexico in 1846. Two years later, he added the territory stretching from Texas to the California coastline. Expansion was a theme that dominated most of the first century of American history, and much of this expansion came about due to a foreign policy that was not always consistent with the overarching policy of isolationism.

After the Civil War ended in 1865, American expansion began to look overseas. Alaska was purchased from Russia in 1867, and Hawaii had become an American territory by 1900. In addition, in order to join the European nations in their imperialistic quest to colonize most of Africa and the subcontinent of Asia, the United States picked a fight with the aging empire of Spain over the pretext of *"liberating"* Cuba, and fought the Spanish-American War in 1898. The result was a relatively easy victory over the Spanish. However, what followed was U.S. entry into the imperialist race to acquire an overseas empire. This included a bloody, two-year campaign to convert the Philippines from a Spanish colony to an American colony, the direct U.S. acquisition of Guam and Puerto Rico, and sixty years of America indirectly controlling the island of Cuba. Ironically, this was the same place that the war with Spain had been ostensibly fought to liberate. A short time later, President Theodore Roosevelt, who probably represented the epitome of American overseas imperialism, used questionable maneuvers to wrest Panama away from Columbia and then proceeded to sign a treaty with Panama that would lead to the construction of a canal allowing American ships to sail from the Atlantic to the Pacific. As the world approached the outset of the First World War in 1914, the United States was still *"isolated"*, but isolationism was hardy an absolute policy.

As stated earlier, all illusions of American isolationism finally ended the day Pearl Harbor was bombed. Then, when the Second World War came to an end in 1945, U.S. foreign policy was dominated by the Cold War that lasted until the fall of the Berlin Wall in 1989. For almost 45 years, America was almost obsessed with the goal of *"containing"* communism. Thanks to a nuclear arms race that at its apex saw the construction of 60,000 atomic weapons, the United States and the Soviet Union never fought a face-to-face war. Instead, the two superpowers frequently tested each other by going to the brink of a full-scale war before one would back down and the crisis was averted. Proxy wars were fought during this time period in nations like Korea and Vietnam; and to a lesser extent, in places like Berlin, Cuba and even outer space. However, the cataclysmic nightmare that would have resulted from a hot war between the United States and the Soviet Union was thankfully avoided.

During the Cold War, foreign policy was a relatively easy issue to understand. Most Americans agreed that communism needed to be contained and the only real issue was over the best way to accomplish this goal. One side, usually considered to be the liberal position, was more inclined to trust the Soviets and supported any negotiations designed to reduce the massive number of nuclear warheads. The other side, generally considered to be more conservative, did not trust the Soviets and therefore advocated the continued expansion of all weapons, conventional as well as nuclear. The two political parties sometimes split between themselves over this foreign policy issue. After all, it was President Lyndon B. Johnson, a Democrat, who sent hundreds of thousands of American troops to fight against communism in Vietnam. On the other hand, it was President Richard Nixon, a Republican, who visited China and normalized relations with that communist nation.

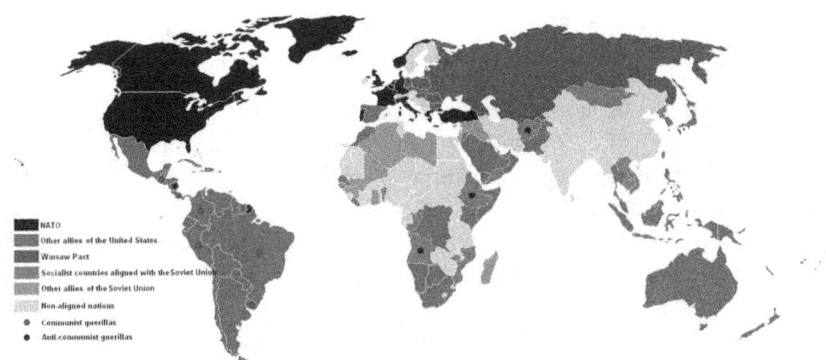

Cold War Map 1980
Courtesy of Aivazovsky (CC BY-SA-3.0)
https://en.wikipedia.org/wiki/File:Cold_War_Map_1980.png

When the Cold War ended, most Americans were thoroughly delighted. They watched with tears in their eyes as the events unfolded every night on the evening news: the breakup of the Soviet states, the free elections taking place in Russia and the nations of Eastern Europe, the signing of treaties significantly reducing the number of nuclear weapons and the tearing down of the Berlin Wall. In addition, most Americans thought that the end of the Cold War left the United States as the one remaining superpower without a major rival. Freedom and peace would prevail around the world, and foreign policy as a serious issue could become less important in the daily lives of most Americans. A deeper understanding of history, however, would reveal that the question of how nations should best get along would remain just as important as always, largely because it was still complicated by several key issues.

The first was the question of trust. For example, just like the Cold War divided those who were more inclined to trust adversaries from those who did not, recent circumstances in the Middle East brought the same issue to the surface. In the summer of 2015, for example, President Barak Obama and the United States signed off on a treaty that would remove trade sanctions against Iran in return for Iranian agreement to allow inspections of all facilities that might be used to enrich enough uranium to build a nuclear weapon. President Benjamin Netanyahu of Israel strongly criticized the deal on the grounds that Iran could not be trusted. President Obama said at one point in a press conference that *"this deal is not built on trust. It's built on verification."* However, most of the people opposed to the treaty would not agree with this statement. They have criticized secretary of state John Kerry and President Obama for being naïve and too trusting.

Yet seen in a broader context, trust has always been a divisive subject. Way back in 1946, for example, the United States was the only nation in the world with atomic bombs. In the hands of a different nation, successful attempts might have been made to take over or dominate the planet. The United States, however, made a much more surprising move. Knowing that it was only a matter of time before the Soviet Union had nuclear weapons of its own, the U.S. proposed a policy called *"Trust but Verify."* Under this proposal, the United States offered to destroy its atomic bombs and agree to not build any more if other nations would pledge not to build them and agree to inspections. At the heart of this idea was the question of trust. The U.S.S.R. refused to pledge anything unless America agreed to give up its bombs first. At the heart of their response was a lack of trust. Knowing how much to trust or not trust an adversarial opponent has always been an integral part of foreign policy.

A second foreign policy issue, dating back to the days of the Versailles Peace Conference of 1919, has involved the role played by international organizations. As stated earlier, the fear of not allowing American interests to be subverted to the desires of a majority of other nations kept the United States from ratifying the Versailles Treaty and joining the League of Nations that was created as a result. The twenty-twenty vision that comes from historical hindsight would probably reveal this to be a huge error of judgment. There are still many Americans today who harbor the same fear of America's membership in the United Nations. For example, they might point out that a vast majority of the nations that make up the U.N. General Assembly would probably like to force Israel to return all land taken in the 1967 Six Day War in order to create an independent Palestinian nation. Since the United States is the closest and most powerful ally that Israel has to help insure its survival as an independent Jewish state, these Americans would see that move as something that would violate U.S. interests. Fortunately for those Americans, the United States holds a permanent seat on the United Nations Security Council where it can veto any action by the United Nations that might actually force Israel to return this land. This use of a veto in the Security Council, which can be exercised not only by the United States, but also France, Great Britain, China or Russia, has greatly weakened the effectiveness of the United Nations. However, once again, those who are less inclined to trust adversarial nations also tend to be less inclined to trust international organizations. They would therefore not be too concerned about the ineffectiveness or even the demise of the United Nations.

Sharing the sandbox

Flags of the United Nations
Courtesy of the Library of Congress, Prints and Photographs Division
FSA/OWI Collection LC-DIG-fsa-8d26011

A third issue that might help to achieve a deeper understanding of how nations should best conduct foreign policy with each other might be labeled as *"self-interest"* versus *"altruism."* When the United States is confronted with a problem or crisis in another country, what should be the guiding norm: to do what is in America's best self-interest, or to do what is morally right? When Saddam Hussein led his nation of Iraq to invade the neighboring country of Kuwait on August 2, 1990, President George Herbert Walker Bush, with the support of the United Nations, chose to send American military forces to the Persian Gulf region to liberate Kuwait. At the time, he justified his decision by stating *"the acquisition of territory by force is unacceptable."* This may have implied a higher moral purpose to engage in what soon became the Persian Gulf War, but most Americans recognized the decision for what it was. At the time, much of the Western World's oil came from the Persian Gulf region and this oil played an essential role in the economies of the western nations. If Saddam Hussein could get away with grabbing Kuwait, what would be his next target, Saudi Arabia? The decision to send U.S. military forces to drive out the Iraqis was mostly about American self-interest. Those Americans, mainly Republicans who tended to side with the self-interest option, strongly supported President Bush's decision. The more liberal Democrats who tended to place a stronger value on altruistic reasons for getting involved in the affairs of other nations, were much more critical. The fact that the war turned out to be relatively brief and that there were few American casualties (although the same cannot be said about the Iraqis) helped to mitigate much of this criticism.

Four years later, insanity took over the nation of Rwanda. Over the course of one hundred days from April 6th to July 16th, 1994, the Hutu majority slaughtered an estimated 800,000 to one million Tutsis and some moderate Hutus, many by machete, in what came to be known as the Rwandan genocide. (A more recent report has estimated the total number to be closer to two million.) During this time, the United States did virtually nothing. That decision was defended partly on pragmatic considerations: everything happened too fast and Rwanda is a land-locked nation that was too inaccessible. But others pointed out that the real reason why the United States did so little was because there was nothing to be gained by getting involved. Some even brought up the subject of race. American military forces did play a role in the Bosnian civil war, but in a place where all of the victims were dark-skinned, we did nothing. In places like Rwanda, the Sudan or Somalia, where there may be no practical reason to justify American involvement through our own self-interest, many still argue the position taken by Elie Wiesel after the Nazi Holocaust, that *"We must take sides. Neutrality helps the oppressor, never the victim. Silence encourages the tormentor, never the tormented."* They might also agree with Spiderman at the end of the 2002 film when he stated *"with great power comes great responsibility."* Either way, the point is clear. Even if there is nothing in it for us, they feel the United States has a moral obligation to use its strength and its wealth to help others whenever the situation presents itself. This issue between self-interest and moral imperatives probably helps to define the subject of foreign policy better than any other.

Finally, there is one other foreign policy framework that might help to tie together all of the other issues. In 1994, former National Security Advisor and Secretary of State, Henry Kissinger, published a book called *Diplomacy*. In its sweeping history of international relations and the art of diplomacy, Kissinger devoted all of chapter two to what he called, *"The Hinge: Theodore*

Roosevelt or Woodrow Wilson." In this chapter, he presents Roosevelt as a pragmatic practitioner of the Realpolitik, a diplomacy primarily based on power and on practical and material factors or considerations. On the other hand, Wilson is presented as the idealist who possessed ideological notions or moral premises. Of course, it was Woodrow Wilson who visualized the creation of the League of Nations, which even though it later helped him win the Nobel Peace Prize, his own nation refused to join.

Henry Kissinger
Courtesy of the Library of Congress
Prints and Photographs Division LC-DIG-ds-01512

According to Kissinger, most foreign policy decisions, especially in the past couple of centuries, have involved a tug-of-war between these two positions. To deepen our understanding of history on the subject of foreign policy, almost any event or development involving two or more nations can be seen in this context. The Roosevelt position would be less likely to trust and would prefer a stronger, more secure military. The Wilson position would place greater emphasis on negotiations and trust rather than on being so quick to exercise the military option. The Roosevelt position would have less faith in international courts or organizations that might violate our national interests. Wilson's idealism felt that the League of Nations, or later, the United Nations, was the best hope for preventing the horrors of war. Clearly, Theodore Roosevelt, and for that matter, Henry Kissinger, believed American foreign policy should be guided by what was best for America; whether it be protecting national security, guarding our economic interests or effectively waging a war against modern terrorism. On the other hand, Woodrow Wilson would have preferred our foreign policy to be guided by a set of moral or ethical values.

As stated earlier, most efforts to explain these historical developments and foreign policy principles to high school students through a traditional, teacher-centered approach usually meets with glazed expressions and the sounds of gentle sawing. Socratic seminars are more effective, but if overused, these too can grow a bit tiresome. Fortunately, the subject of foreign policy lends itself to a class activity that never fails to raise the level of student interest and engagement: the simulation.

In a U.S. History class, it might be advisable to create a set of roles based upon the membership of the President's National Security Council. A class can be divided into groups of separate *"councils"* where each includes a President, a Vice-President, a Secretary of State, a Secretary of Defense, a Chairman of the Joint Chiefs of Staff, a Director of National Intelligence, a National Security Advisor and an Ambassador to the United Nations. Depending on the nature of the issue to be addressed, other roles can be included; such as the Director of National Drug Control Policy, the Attorney General, the Secretary of the Treasury and the Secretary of Homeland Security. Because the National Security Council includes a number of statutory and non-statutory roles, there is much discretion that can be used in determining its composition.

Once roles are assigned, students can research their respective positions. They not only should ascertain their political responsibilities within the government but can also research the actual person who held that position at a specific time. Of course, research on the foreign policy question or issue to be addressed must also be completed. These questions or issues can come from the past or the present. Over the years, I have conducted National Security Council simulations over the Berlin Crisis of 1948 that led to the Berlin Airlift, the Cuban Missile Crisis of 1962 and Iraq's invasion of Kuwait in 1990. I have also used them to address hypothetical situations, such as Russia increasing its military involvement in Ukraine, the successful testing of an ICBM by North Korea and an ISIS terrorist attack killing thousands on American soil. The goal of each group is to devise and defend a plan to handle the foreign policy crisis. By the end of the activity, students are usually much more interested in complicated foreign policy principles.

In World History classes, a mock United Nations conference usually meets with similar success. For years, another teacher and myself flipped a coin to determine whether our students would represent the Israelis or the Palestinians in a U.N. peace conference. After background research was completed, three students from each class came together to form a group of six. Their task was to try to hammer out a permanent peace treaty. Not only did the level of interest and engagement rise, but also the students often came up with creative solutions that might actually bring peace to the Middle East if only the real situation was not so clouded by decades of emotional hatred and animosity.

In another variation, each student was assigned his or her own nation and was then tasked with the responsibility of researching, writing and proposing a resolution for the U.N. General Assembly. After time was provided for debate, politicking and negotiations, the goal was to see how many of their resolutions could be passed. Similar approaches have been used to simulate the writing of treaties. For example, in teaching about the Versailles Conference at the end of World War One, I create groups of four where each student takes on the role of either President Wilson of the United States, the British Prime Minister David Lloyd George, French Premier Georges Clemenceau or Premier Vittorio Orlando of Italy. After researching their roles, each group must then wrestle with such questions as reparation payments, the transfer of land, the creation of new nations, military restrictions and plans to prevent future wars. The agreement written by each group is then compared to the real Versailles Treaty and much is learned from the ensuing discussion.

There are many variations of simulations that can be used in the classroom. Different teachers can tailor-make these activities to fit the unique needs of their students as well as their own particular strengths. The end result is that students will have a higher level of interest in the subject and will improve their critical thinking skills along the way. Most important, they will develop a deeper understanding of how foreign policy has been created in the past and how it should be made in the future. The main point is that foreign policy is far too important to be marginalized or ignored.

In the final analysis, this much is crystal clear. With just over 300,000,000 people in a world of 7.3 billion, the United States represents fewer than 5% of the world's population. And yet, the United States produces about 22% of the world's gross domestic product (wealth) and spends 34% of the world's military spending. In fact, not only does America spend more on its military than any other nation, it spends more than number two through number ten countries combined. And yet with all of that wealth and power, we have also learned that there are serious limitations to America's international muscle. The United States could have bombed Vietnam back into the Stone Age, but that would have defeated the purpose of protecting that nation from the tribulations of Communism. And over the past 15 years, America's war with terrorism has raised similar frustrations. Fires might be temporarily extinguished in places like Kabul or Bagdad, but with the rise of ISIS and the ensuing bombings taking place around the world, fear and paranoia are once again on the rise.

The United States still has giant oceans on its eastern and western borders, and friendly nations to its north and south, but as we quickly learned after the Japanese attack on Pearl Harbor, the planet has shrunk into a much smaller place. In a world where an intercontinental ballistic missile carrying a nuclear warhead 1000 times more powerful than the bomb dropped on Hiroshima can arrive in less than an hour after its launch, we can hardly expect those natural barriers to provide much protection in the future. Knowing that problems and issues such as foreign trade, global warming, Internet hacking, international terrorism and even thermonuclear war encompass the entire planet, most Americans would acknowledge that returning to the tortoise-like isolationism of the past is no longer an option. With the knowledge that the United States has so much wealth and power and that much of the world, regardless of what they may think about the United States, turns to America for international leadership, there is something to be said for the notion that *"with great power comes great responsibility."* The United States must play an active role in the world. The question remains, however, what should that role be? A deeper understanding of the essential question, how should nations best carry on foreign policy, might go a long way in helping to develop an intelligent answer.

Suggested Reading:

Carroll, Lauren. "Obama: US Spends More on Military than Next 8 Nations Combined." *Politifact.* January 13, 2016. http://www.politifact.com/truth-o-meter/statements/2016/jan/13/barack-obama/obama-us-spends-more-military-next-8-nations-combi/.

Kissinger, Henry. *Diplomacy.* New York: Simon and Schuster, 1994.

O'Neil, Patrick H. *Essentials of Comparative Politics.* New York: W.W. Norton and Company, 2013.

Pederson, Susan. *The Guardians: The League of Nations and the Crisis of Empire.* New York: Oxford University Press, 2015.

"The Rwandan Genocide." *History.com.* 2009. http://www.history.com/topics/rwandan-genocide.

Sexton, Jay. *The Monroe Doctrine: Empire and Nation in Nineteenth-Century America.* New York: Hill and Wang, 2011.

Wiesel, Elie. *And the Sea Is Never Full: Memoirs, 1969-.* New York: Alfred A. Knopf, 1999.

Chapter 9
This land is mine

Nelson Mandela with the members of the Congressional Black Caucus
Courtesy of the Library of Congress, Prints and Photographs Division
LC-DIG-ppmsca-38881

How should control of land best be determined?

The place is Victor Verster Prison in South Africa and the date is February 11th, 1990. A dark-skinned man walks slowly, hand-in-hand with his wife; both with a fist raised high in the air. Not yet 72 years old, with a head full of gray hair, the years of prison have taken their toll. Most would never guess that Nelson Mandela once stood six feet tall. On this day, his smile beams across the land and his image is being broadcast around the world. Driven to Cape Town's city hall through massive crowds, he gives a speech declaring his commitment to peace and reconciliation with the nation's white minority. In all, Mandela had been imprisoned for 27 years, 18 of those on Robben Island: a rock quarry off the coast of Cape Town. Now, change has come to a land that has been fighting for greater freedom for centuries.

Coming on the heels of the fall of the Berlin Wall, the release of Nelson Mandela is seen around the globe as another symbol that the world is becoming a better place to live. When I asked my students to explain the significance of this event, most said it meant that apartheid was on its way towards extinction. When pressed further, they indicated that this meant the end of one of the world's most notorious systems of racism and segregation. With a little bit of digging, they uncovered a few facts about the historical background of apartheid.

After the National Party gained power in South Africa in 1948, its all-white government immediately began enforcing policies of racial segregation under a system of legislation it officially called apartheid. According to this system, nonwhite South Africans were forced to live in separate areas from whites, use separate public facilities, and limit all contact between the two groups. It should be noted, however, that racial segregation and white supremacy had been central aspects of South African policy long before apartheid began.

For thousands of years, the land had belonged to the aboriginal Khoi and San civilizations. Most of the rest of South Africa's population can trace their history to later immigration. The darker skinned Africans are primarily the descendents of Bantu tribes that migrated southward from the central part of the African continent about 2000 years ago. Then, in 1488, Bartolomeu Dias and the Portuguese arrived while attempting to discover a trade route to the Far East via the southernmost cape of South Africa. The Portuguese were then followed by the Dutch, who over time, transformed themselves into a distinct culture called the Boers. The Boers established a republic in the mid 19th century that lasted as an independent and internationally recognized nation-state in southern Africa until 1902. At the end of the Second Boer War on May 31st of that year, the Boers became part of the ever-expanding British Empire.

Over the next few years, Great Britain set about unifying the Boer lands into one self-governed country named the Union of South Africa. The Union became an independent Dominion of the British Crown. By 1925, English and Dutch both became the official languages of the Union. During this period, the foundation for apartheid was laid by the passage of harsh segregationist laws, including denial of voting rights to black people. The Union, with its combination of English, Dutch/Boers and black Africans continued to live under a segregated lifestyle until October, 1960 when a majority of white South Africans voted in favor of unilateral withdrawal from the British Commonwealth and established a fully independent nation known as the Republic of South Africa. Meanwhile, despite the pretense of calling itself a democracy, the racist system of apartheid continued to flourish; and those who spoke out against the injustices, like Nelson Mandela, were killed off or imprisoned.

Map of South Africa
Courtesy of Amada44 (PD-self)
https://commons.wikimedia.org/wiki/File:Map_of_South_Africa.svg

While this historical background helps to explain the rigid system of racism in South Africa that would come to rival the similar scheme established in the American South from the dawn of Reconstruction up to the heyday of the modern U.S. Civil Rights Movement, there is an important distinction that must be made. There are counties in Mississippi and South Carolina that have African American majorities, but on the whole, African Americans are a numerical minority across the South. Throughout the nation, blacks in the 20th Century have never made up more than 13 percent of the U.S. population. In South Africa, blacks or nonwhites constituted 80 percent. Yet despite this overwhelming majority, they were not only denied the right to vote, but under the terms of the Native Lands' Act passed in 1913, received only eight per cent of South Africa's available land. White people, who constituted less than 20 percent of the population, held 90 percent of the land. This Land Act formed the cornerstone of apartheid for the next nine decades.

Racism has existed in a variety of ugly forms in many different times and many different places. There is no question that South Africa under apartheid is one of the most egregious examples of bigotry and segregation the world has ever known. That said, in addition to the racism with which most people around the planet are most familiar, South Africa has served as a prime example of the essential question: how should control of land best be determined? Even today, despite all of the reforms that have come to pass in South Africa with the ending of apartheid and the election of Nelson Mandela as the nation's first black president, land remains a major issue.

The government had previously set the goal of shifting one third of the country's land from white farmers to black residents, but this goal was recently postponed until 2025. According to Edward Lahiff, a senior lecturer at the Program for Land and Agrarian Studies at the University of Western Cape in South Africa, less than 7 per cent of the land has been redistributed to date. He claims that if current performance continues, there is no likelihood that the target of one third will be achieved by 2025. The basic problem is that white owners do not want to sell and blacks lack the resources to buy. The only prescription Lahiff sees as a solution is for the government to step in, as it did in Zimbabwe in the 1980s, and play a significantly more active role in facilitating the transfer of land. This is not likely to happen.

Just like the American South, de jure segregation (segregation enforced by law) might be removed, but the de facto segregation based on the economic fact that wealth is still unevenly distributed, continues. Nothing short of a socialist revolt that would drastically redefine property rights will change this reality anytime in the near future. Therefore, the blacks in South Africa, like those in the American South, continue to live with the legacy of prejudice. Racism and civil rights is an important subject that will be dealt with in a subsequent chapter, but it is directly tied to the question of land ownership. Furthermore, when one compares the situation in South

Africa to the plight of African Americans in the U.S., South Africa has always proven to be an exception to the rule that those who possess the greatest numbers control the land.

What set the stage for this land quandary in South Africa? For thousands of years, kingdoms and empires had come and gone. In such areas as Egypt and Mesopotamia, Greece and Rome, India and China, Mesoamerica and Japan, one nation had always expanded at the expense of a neighbor. For the most part, the question of boundaries between these early kingdoms was determined by natural barriers and by a combination of numbers and military might. Europeans placed their own imprint on this topic by the start of the Renaissance in the 15th Century when they created the modern nation-state with boundaries that often resulted from wars, their subsequent treaties, and the arbitrary lines drawn on a map. After all, these were highly literate societies that were making use of paper maps as much as they were beginning to rely on the books rolling off their recently invented printing presses. But while these developments were taking place in Europe, land in such areas as Africa, the Americas, Australia and Oceania was still allocated according to the traditional patterns that had been shaped by centuries of geography and customary land use patterns. The various determinants that had always shaped the distribution of land were now settling into two distinct camps, and the misunderstandings that would subsequently take place have caused major problems ever since.

What have been the determinants in deciding who should control the land? The first is simple; who was there first? The indigenous people who first came to North, Central and South America could use this point to claim that since their ancestors arrived after the last ice age fifteen to twenty thousand years ago, they should be entitled to receive all of the acreage stretching from the northern reaches of Canada to the Tierra del Fuego archipelago of southern Chile. The Aborigines of Australia or the Maori of New Zealand might make a similar claim. While gaining their land back is not likely to happen, the ongoing debate between Israel and the Palestinians often begins with the question, who was there first? Overall, it probably does not matter very much. The reality is that in the present, most people have never given much credence to who arrived first.

A second and rather obvious determinant over who gains the land has been a combination of numbers and force. The two do not always go together – after all, 500 Spaniards with horses, metal swords and guns were able to take all of the Mexican land away from an Aztec Empire consisting of millions. But more often than not, greater numbers and superior military forces are linked. Take the Louisiana Territory for example. Many are taught that Napoleon sold Louisiana to the United States because he needed some quick cash to fund his upcoming wars for conquest. While this is partially true, the fact that a large number of Americans had already trespassed into French Louisiana, and that everyone knew more were coming, was a significant factor in his decision to make a sale that doubled the size of the United States overnight. The same was true in the negotiations with the British over the Oregon Territory. Great Britain controlled all of Canada and held a claim to the land that would later become Washington, Oregon and Idaho. The fact that the Oregon Trail had already brought thousands of Americans to settle in the disputed area gave the United States a big edge in the negotiations. While American infiltration into parts of California also helped with U.S. expansion into the Southwest, numbers combined with military force in the Mexican-American War to bring in areas that would later become Arizona, Utah, Nevada and California. Either having superior numbers to occupy the land, or simply taking the land through superior military force have both been major determinants in deciding who will gain control over a particular area. That does not mean, however, that either is qualified to be the best way to determine who should control the land.

The next determinant is largely pragmatic, despite its Biblical origins. Who will make best use of the land? According to the Bible, the original Hebrews believed that Canaan was their destiny. They were the *"chosen people,"* the inheritors of God's covenant with Abraham, who had himself inherited God's promise to Adam, made on the first page of the first Book of the Bible, where God said, *"Let us make man... and let him have dominion over the ... earth...Be fruitful and multiply, and fill the earth and subdue it; and have dominion...over every living thing."* (Genesis 1:26-28) From this foundation, the early Pilgrims and Puritans came to America with similar ideas that just like the early Hebrews felt entitled to the land of Canaan, they were entitled to the wilds of North America. History generally teaches that the first settlers of New England were moral and religious people. The reality is that a pious people with virtually no military prowess populated the early settlements in Plymouth and Boston. How could they feel entitled to dominion over the Indians and their lands? From their maps, their laws, and most important, their actions, the earliest American settlers felt they had conquered the new lands simply by *"discovering"* them.

This Discovery Doctrine was soon supported by the Supreme Court decision, *Johnson v. McIntosh*. This case became the foundation for all United States law regarding indigenous people, and what it says is that by virtue of discovery, the Europeans/Americans have dominion and sovereignty over

Native peoples, lands and governments. The New World was seen as being legally *"vacant"* – terra nullius or vacuum domicilium in Latin. The discoverer thus held title to all Indian land, and the indigenous people were therefore subject to the overriding political sovereignty of the discoverer. How was this justified? In Chief Justice John Marshall's words, *"The character and religion of [the New World's] inhabitants afforded apology for considering them as a people over whom the superior genius of Europe might claim an ascendancy. To leave them in possession of their country was to leave the country a wilderness..."*

Chief Justice John Marshall
Courtesy of the Library of Congress, Prints and Photographs Division
LC-USZ62-54940

Though *Johnson v. McIntosh* was a judicial decision made by a secular government committed to the separation of church and state, the Supreme Court's adoption of the Discovery Doctrine was built on top of a long Judeo-Christian tradition found on the first page of the Bible. It was now being used to dispossess all of the indigenous peoples of the United States. In other words, Genesis had essentially told Adam and Abraham that a *"Chosen People"* who honored their one God through industry as well as faith were entitled to take the land they had *"discovered"* from any heathens not making full use of the bounty God had provided. This principle provided a platform for the development of Manifest Destiny within the United States as well as the rise of modern imperialism around much of the planet.

When John O'Sullivan said it was *"our manifest destiny to overspread the continent allotted by Providence for the free development of our yearly multiplying millions,"* he was simply echoing an idea that had been passed down for generations. Due to a combination of an open door to millions of immigrants and a high birth rate, America's population was exploding; therefore, it was only natural that people would seek western lands. The fact that many different native tribes, not to mention a large number of Mexicans in the Southwest, already populated the West was of no consequence. To most Americans, the land was *"empty"* and was not being used to its full potential. Therefore, after it was *"discovered"* by Americans like Meriwether Lewis or Zebulon Pike, it was free and available for the taking. Once settled as American states, resources could be put to their full potential; freedom and democracy would spread and *"civilized"* Christians would populate the land.

Similar thinking was reflected in Rudyard Kipling's poem "The White Man's Burden." Kipling's words, which became a rallying cry for British imperialism, called for England to *"take up the White Man's burden,"* and to *"go bind your sons to exile."* Why? In order to spread European civilization to *"your new-caught, sullen peoples, half-devil and half child."* This poem (which included six more stanzas all beginning with "Take up the White Man's burden") was originally written for Queen Victoria's Diamond Jubilee, but it was also intended to reflect the subject of American colonization of the Philippines, recently won from Spain in the Spanish-American War. The poem was published during the age of imperialism, a time when European powers were carving up whatever lands they could take. Their quest to overrun most of Africa, the subcontinent of Asia and much of Oceania was based on the same principles of *"discovery"* and *"utilization."* The Western powers that first *"discovered"* these underutilized but heavily populated lands were justified in taking them as colonies and controlling the land to best use it to its fullest potential. As a result, India, which had ten times the population of Great Britain, became the *"crown jewel"* of the British Empire. Cotton textiles were the first and one of the biggest industries in Great Britain. With India under its control to grow the cotton as well as to serve as an enormous market for English-made clothing, the exploitation of the Indian subcontinent was a terrific deal for the British.

Rudyard Kipling
Courtesy of the Library of Congress, Prints and Photographs Division
LC-DIG-pga-01742

The British established their control over the land of India through a combination of providing a centralized political bureaucracy, superior technology and more sophisticated weapons. One hundred years ago, the British rationalized their control over this land (as well as much of the planet) by saying they were making their colonies better places to live. However, imperialism was based on the often unspoken belief that the native people in these lands were culturally and racially inferior, and that in order for their souls to be saved, they needed to be converted to Christianity. The belief that one group of people is somehow better suited to take control over a land than the original inhabitants has played an enormous role in answering the question of how control of land should best be determined.

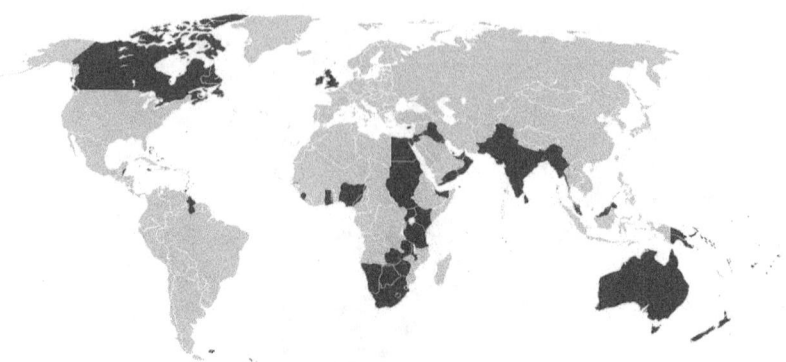

Map of the British Empire at its height, 1921
Courtesy of Vadac (PD-self)
https://commons.wikimedia.org/wiki/File:British_Empire_1921.png

In recent times, another more legal method has been used to settle the question over land control. Territory, ranging from small plots of land to millions of acres, is *"owned"* provided that first, the owner possesses a legal document in the form of a title or a deed, and second, the land has been surveyed so its exact boundaries are known. This allows land, the natural resources on or below the land, and any fixed structures on the property to be categorized as *"real"* property, or real estate. Real estate can then be legally sold, purchased or inherited. If there is any question regarding ownership, inheritance or boundary lines, courts are used to settle the issue. From one day to the next, this system seems to work well in our modern society.

Problems arise, however, when two societies that possess different concepts about land ownership come into contact with each other. If one society employs the *"legal"* approach, where land is owned by the possessor of a deed, and the other society uses a more traditional model based on a determinant like who was there first or customary land use patterns, conflict is bound to arise. The more legalistic approach will usually win, but in all likelihood, the documents and court decisions will almost always be backed up by superior military force. The classic example of this situation is North and South America. From the late 15th Century up through the 18th Century, most of this enormous land mass was transferred from the indigenous people who had occupied it for thousands of years to European settlers or their descendents. While this largely came about because the Europeans had the numbers and the guns, much of it was due to misunderstandings over who owned the land.

In much of British North America, settlers actually purchased the land from the natives. The hope was that buying the land would prevent conflict, but because Europeans and American natives had very different ideas about what it meant to buy and own land, these deals actually caused as much conflict as they prevented. The traditional view is that the Europeans tricked the Indians who failed to understand the consequences of their actions. For example, the Dutch allegedly bought Manhattan for $24 worth of beads and trinkets. In reality, the Indians often proved to be savvy negotiators, and most Europeans understood far less about Indian ideas concerning land ownership than the Indians understood about theirs. While the Europeans essentially viewed land as private property, Native Americans saw it as the sum of its uses and as a shared resource.

In the minds of most native cultures, an individual only owned what they made with their own two hands. A family might own the land on which its house stood, and women owned the land they farmed. But homes, agricultural fields and villages moved frequently, so land was only owned as long as it was being used. Villages collectively had rights to large territories that they used for hunting, fishing, gathering food, medicinal herbs, and raw materials for building or tools. Those rights, however, shifted depending on their use and the people using them. A village might claim exclusive hunting rights in a given territory, for example; but people from many different villages might share the use of a single river for fishing. What villages claimed, according to historian William Cronon, was *"not the land but the things that were on the land during various seasons of the year."*

While many native cultures farmed as well as engaged in hunting and gathering, their farms were relatively small and frequently changed location. Much larger areas were kept more primitive for hunting, and this became one of the first major sources for misunderstanding. In Europe, hunting was the sport of the wealthy, not a key source of food, and so to the European eye, the vast hunting grounds on which the Indians relied appeared uninhabited and unimproved. In other words, the Indians were not using the land; therefore, it was up for grabs. What may be surprising is that despite this point, the English still frequently purchased the land from the Indians rather than seizing it outright. However, when they bought the land, Europeans understood the deal to be a full transfer of rights. A settler who purchased a tract of land was understood to have the right to use it for any purpose, sell it to who ever he wished and forbid trespassers. By contrast,

Indians did not typically see themselves as signing away all rights to the land. They understood a land sale to mean that the colonists could live on the land in a native village's territory, but that all would continue to share hunting rights. These differing views inevitably led to conflicts.

In addition, Europeans, who were used to monarchy, often assumed wrongly that the chief of a village could sell land on behalf of his people, when in fact, his powers were much more limited. Europeans also assumed that every piece of land must either have a single owner or ruler or else it was not owned; when in fact, most land in America was shared in various ways. As a result, English colonists often paid for land only to find that other Indians did not recognize the sale. However, colonial courts generally supported colonial interests in most land disputes.

Another source of conflict rested over differing views concerning livestock. Colonists allowed farm animals like pigs to roam freely, then rounded them up in the fall and winter for slaughter. Since livestock could go anywhere, it was the responsibility of other farmers to fence in their crops and to fence out other people's animals. For the colonial settlers, letting their animals run free meant they did not have to feed them. Pigs in particular could find all the food and water they needed in the woods. And since pigs are fairly dirty animals, letting them roam the woods rather than keeping them penned together near a dwelling helped to keep disease down. On the other hand, the Indians, who did not raise animals for food and treated wild animals as a shared natural resource, did not like or recognize Europeans' ownership of wandering livestock. They saw the wandering pigs and cows trampling and rooting up undergrowth and eating new shoots of grasses and other plants, transforming native ecosystems, contributing to soil erosion and destroying the habitats and food sources of native animals. As a result, colonial settlers often complained that Indians stole cattle and hogs that the Indians saw as theirs to take.

In the end, the conflicts that resulted from these different understandings about land ownership took their toll. The European ideas of land ownership – backed by superior numbers, force of arms and a relentless legal system – were victorious. In the long run, the colonists and settlers won nearly every conflict over land ownership, if for no other reason, because there were more of them. Their numbers grew continually, while the native population dwindled from disease, warfare and slavery. The colonists, as they believed their God commanded, subdued the land. By parceling out and fencing off the land, they made native ways of life impossible to continue.

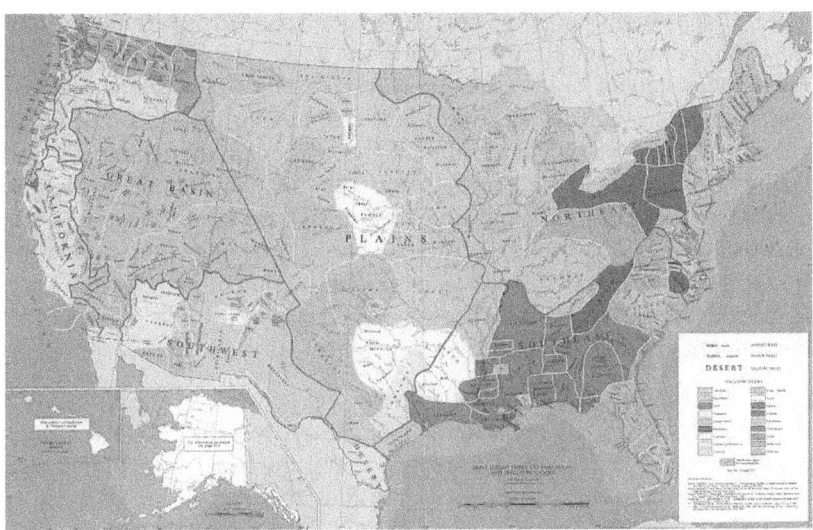

Early Indian tribes, cultural areas, and linguistic stocks
Courtesy of the U.S. Geological Survey (PD-USGS)
https://commons.wikimedia.org/wiki/File:Early_Localization_Native_Americans_USA.jpg

American history, particularly in the West, is filled with the same tragic tales. Some of the tribes, like the Sioux under Sitting Bull or the Apache under Geronimo, resisted with violence; but in the end, they all lost. Some, like the Cherokee under John Ross, resisted in the courts. Unfortunately, despite a victory in the U.S. Supreme Court, they were still forced to leave their lands in northern Georgia and eastern Tennessee. Hundreds died on the Trail of Tears while making their way to the Indian Territory in what is now Oklahoma. Some, like the Nez Perce under Chief Joseph, tried to flee to Canada, but after being stopped 40 miles short of the border, they were also sent to reservations in Oklahoma. Additionally, tribes like the Ute under Ouray the Arrow, or the Sioux under Chief Red Cloud, simply accepted their fate and agreed to give up their land. They too usually encountered carnage and extreme poverty. The question of how a people confronted with injustice should best react is an essential question deserving of its own chapter; but in the end, this was the only choice left to the indigenous people of the New World. All the advantages rested with the European settlers: larger numbers, better weapons, and in this situation, a better-established concept of land ownership. The Indians could debate among themselves as to the best way to react, but in the end, they still lost most of their land.

Of all the possible areas where the essential question regarding the control of land is most applicable, probably the best example is in and around the modern state of Israel. Lacking natural borders, this area has been the crossroads for attacking kingdoms and empires for thousands of years. Therefore, its history is filled with one group after another coming in and taking over. At one time or other, the Egyptians, the Babylonians, the Greeks, the Romans, the Turks and the British have all made a claim. It is also an area that has experienced human habitation longer than most other spots on the planet. Therefore, when the determinant of who was there first is applied, the answer is subject to debate. The Hebrews built Jerusalem after their arrival over 3000 years ago, but the land was already inhabited.

When examining the question of who would make best use of the land, the Israelis can proudly point to the many improvements they have made over the last seven decades. Under Jewish control, Israel has a democratic government, modern conveniences and the highest standard of living in the Middle East. Compared to what existed there prior to the First World War, when the Ottoman Turks controlled the area, modern-day Israel has considerably more agriculture and industry, not to mention better transportation, schools and hospitals. What is more, with economic and military support from the United States, Israel has not only defended itself effectively from surrounding Arab neighbors, but has in all likelihood, become a sophisticated, nuclear military power. There are few who would challenge the improvements that have been made in Israel since the land was partitioned by the newly created United Nations in 1947. Of course, no matter how many facts are brought in to support the argument that the Israelis are making the best use of the land, who is to say the Palestinians could not do the same if given the opportunity? Besides, many would see the point about making best use of the land as a rather spurious argument in determining who should control a given area.

As for *the "might makes right"* determinant, there is no question that Israel today possesses the superior military force. Not only did the Jewish people mount a successful defense in 1948, they did so again in 1956, 1967 and 1973. In the Six Day War of 1967, Israeli forces captured the Gaza Strip and the Sinai Peninsula from Egypt, the Golan Heights from Syria and the West Bank, plus the Old City of Jerusalem from Jordan. At the present, much of the world, including many Arabs in the Middle East, have come to accept that Israel has a right to exist as a Jewish nation. The more vexing question focuses on the lands captured in 1967 and whether at least some of this land could be used to create an independent Palestinian state. By definition, the Palestinians are a people that have occupied this same land for thousands of years. They trace their roots back to the Ancient Philistines; and when the Romans incorporated the area into their expanding empire, they called the province Palestine. Ever since, the people living there who are not Jewish consider themselves to be Palestinians. Some of them fled the area in 1948 and have been living in surrounding nations, even in refugee camps. Other Palestinians remained in Israel, but many claim that in a Jewish state, they are treated like second-class citizens. Without the military might to stand up to the Israeli army, backed up as it is by American money and weapons, the Palestinians remain a people without a land to call their own.

Map of Israel and the disputed territories
Courtesy of Jaakabou (PD-self)
https://commons.wikimedia.org/wiki/File:Israel_and_the_Disputed_Territories_map.png

While Israel may have a military advantage, the numbers tell a different story. By the end of 2014, Israel had a population of approximately 8.3 million inhabitants. Just over 6.2 million were Jewish, making up about 75% of the population. While the total number of Palestinians is estimated to be about 4.7 million, their growth rate is 33% higher than the Jewish rate of population growth. If one were to add in the population of the Arab nations surrounding Israel, the number of Jews in the area would be significantly dwarfed by the hundreds of millions of hostile neighbors that could potentially ally themselves with the cause of an independent Palestinian homeland.

Israel knows that numbers can be crucial in deciding who maintains future control of the land. They have therefore taken steps over the last several years to grow their population by encouraging a high birth rate as well as through immigration. What has been more contentious is the building of Jewish settlements in the West Bank of the Jordan River. Much of the world sees this development as something that will impede efforts to negotiate a settlement where land is exchanged for peace. The precedent for this expectation was established at Camp David, Maryland in 1978 when President Jimmy Carter brokered a deal where Israel returned the Sinai Peninsula to Egypt in exchange for official recognition and peace from the Egyptians. Just as its been a factor in so many places throughout history, many of the Jews in Israel know that increased numbers in the West Bank will help maintain Jewish control of this land.

So who should control Israel and its neighboring occupied territories? When asked, my students in all of their youthful idealism say that through some sort of compromise, the land should be shared. Even when told of Israel's concerns about secure borders and the desire by many Israelis to keep what was taken in war, the students still feel there is much land that did not originally belong to Israel and should therefore be used to create a fully independent Palestine. Remembering that this has been a hotly contested and emotional issue for at least three generations, that there have been many casualties on both sides, and that there is a multitude of details to consider, I usually point out to the students that their solution is not as easy as it sounds.

On the other hand, the students may have a point. Today, we have international law, the United Nations and a World Court. In most countries, there is a huge body of law governing the control and use of land. One wonders why a solution cannot be found in the Middle East. Who was there first? In this area, it was so long ago it probably does not matter. Who has the made best use of the land? Israel may have the advantage here, but again, it should probably not be the deciding factor. Military might? Numbers? Both have played a big role up to now, but should that continue? Or is there a better way to determine who should control the land?

As mentioned in the last chapter, my students have confronted the land control question in the Middle East by conducting a simulation of a United Nations peace conference. However, to bring focus to the essential question over how should control of land best be determined, I have used this as an opportunity to introduce students to the thinking skills employed in a structured debate. Working in teams of two, students are told to conduct research, develop arguments, provide opening statements, cross examination questions and conclusions. I typically invite in my school's debate coach as a guest speaker to review to the skills necessary for this project. In addition, I work with the debate coach to model these skills. Because of their competitive nature, debates tend to raise the level of student interest and engagement, and they have proven to be a wonderful tool in teaching higher level thinking skills.

As for the debate issues, these are taken directly from the essential question and are listed below. Agree or Disagree?

> *The South African government should purchase land from white farmers to be redistributed to black residents.*
>
> *The American government should provide enough money for Native Americans to fully compensate them for the land taken from their ancestors.*
>
> *Israel should return all land taken in wars since 1948 to be used for the creation of a fully autonomous Palestinian nation.*

The class as a whole votes on these issues before and after each debate to determine how successful the presentations are in helping students to make up their minds. Like any other activity designed to raise the level of student engagement, it is vital that each debate be thoroughly vetted by a class-wide discussion and that students individually write about each debate topic and its link to the essential question regarding the best way to establish the distribution of land. This can be done in the form of journaling, in-class essays or even blogging sites. While the essential question can be used as vehicle to deepen the students' understanding of the past, the debates and their subsequent activities are an effective means to better engage students with the question.

History is filled with examples of different groups that have competed for ownership or control of a particular piece of land. The Israeli-Palestinian conflict is probably the most deeply rooted; the situation in South Africa is unique due to its racial considerations; the story of the indigenous people in North America, South America, Australia and Oceania is arguably the most tragic. Each of these, along with countless other examples, has its own unique set of circumstances. What they all share in common is the ongoing disagreement over how to best answer a single essential question: how should control of land best be determined? The world would be a much more peaceful and stable place if a consensus could ever be reached over how to answer that question.

Suggested Reading:

Clark, Nancy L., and William H. Worger. *South Africa: The Rise and Fall of Apartheid.* New York: Pearson Education Limited, 2004.

Cronon, William. *Changes in the Land: Indians, Colonists, and the Ecology of New England.* New York: Hill and Wang, 1983.

Gelvin, James L. *The Israel-Palestine Conflict: One Hundred Years of War.* New York: Cambridge University Press, 2006.

Kipling, Rudyard. *Kipling: Poems,* Edited by Peter Washington. New York: Alfred A. Knopf, 2007.

Klein, Naomi. *The Shock Doctrine: The Rise of Disaster Capitalism.* New York: Picador, 2007.

"Land Reform in South Africa." *PBS.* July 6, 2010. http://www.pbs.org/pov/promisedland/land-reform-in-south-africa.

Miller, Robert J. *Native America, Discovered and Conquered: Thomas Jefferson, Lewis and Clark, and Manifest Destiny.* Lincoln: Bison Books, 2008.

Unger, Harlow Giles. *John Marshall: The Chief Justice Who Saved the Nation.* Boston: Da Capo Press, 2014.

Chapter 10
I pledge allegiance

Workmen parading at the 1937 Nazi Party rally
Courtesy of Bundesarchiv, Bild 146-1975-050-24A / (CC-BY-SA 3.0)
https://en.wikipedia.org/wiki/Festliches_N%C3%BCrnberg#/media/File:Bundesarchiv_Bild_146-1975-050-24A,_N%C3%BCrnberg,_RAD_beim_Reichsparteitag.jpg

How should nationalism be assessed in history?

The place is Nuremberg, Germany and the date is September 5th, 1934. For the Nazi Party, which had just come into power the year before, Nuremberg was a special place. Most religious movements and political dynasties throughout history have had one city that could be called the focal point, or heart of the movement: Rome, Jerusalem, or Constantinople. For the Nazis, the heart of their movement was the beautiful medieval city of Nuremburg that symbolized the link between Germany's Gothic past and its Nazi future, a future that was supposed to last one thousand years. Each September, a pilgrimage took place in which followers gathered from all over the Reich to participate in torchlight marches and solemn ceremonies paying homage to the spirit of German nationalism. There were also big military-style parades, and most important, a chance to see the Fuhrer in person.

Adolph Hitler was unexceptional in appearance. Born in Austria, he was a frustrated, marginally talented artist who as a young man, had been searching for meaning in his unexceptional life. In the First World War, he joined the army, and on the day of the Armistice, found himself as a corporal recovering from injuries sustained in a British gas attack. Over the next few years, Hitler drifted until he latched on to a small fringe party of extremists that called itself the National Socialist German Workers Party: the Nationalsozialistische Deutsche Arbeiterpartei, abbreviated NSDAP. In English, this group was better known as the Nazi Party. Discovering his skills as an organizer and speaker, Adolph Hitler quickly emerged as the party's leader. He had finally found meaning to his life, and despite his ordinary appearance and a silly mustache, Hitler's intensity gave him the kind of charisma that drew notice whenever he walked into a crowded room.

In 1923, after a failed attempt to take over the German government in Munich, Hitler was jailed for five years for high treason. Even though he served less than a year, it gave him time to write a book called *Mein Kampf*, or *My Struggle*, where he outlined his long term plans for a Nazi Germany. The Fatherland under Hitler would be a nation that would significantly expand eastward in order to acquire more land for his *"master race."* Scattered throughout the book was Hitler's belief that Germany was the greatest nation in the world, that the German people were the greatest race in the world and that the only barrier holding the German master race back was the corruption introduced into German blood by certain undesirable elements; particularly the Jews. This emphasis on race and space was at the heart of Nazi dogma, and the foundation for this creed was extreme German nationalism.

Due to bank closures and high unemployment that had entered Germany with the start of the Great Depression, combined with the Nazi messages about getting even for losing World War One, and the desire to overturn the punitive measures of the Versailles Treaty, larger and larger numbers of voters had been turning out to support the Nazi Party in Germany's elections. By 1933, Hitler's charisma and speaking ability helped to win over 33% of the Reichstag vote, more than any other party. Hitler was chosen to be chancellor, and soon after, his storm troopers, using strong-arm tactics, terrified all opposition into submission. Hitler assumed dictatorial powers and set up a terrifying fascist state. Freedom and individual rights disappeared, but few complained because most were delighted with the positive economic and military direction the nation had taken. The Great Depression ended almost overnight, and as Hitler ignored the Versailles Treaty by building up the nation's military might, the German people could once again hold their heads up high.

In September of 1934, American journalist William L. Shirer had just arrived in Germany to work as a reporter for the Hearst Company. He proceeded to keep a diary of the entire seven years he spent reporting from inside Hitler's Reich. (In fact, these notes proved useful years later when Shirer published his most famous book, *The Rise and Fall of the Third Reich*.) Shirer thought it would be a good idea to attend the 1934 Nuremberg Rally to better understand the Nazi phenomenon. He wrote in his diary that he was shocked by the looks on the faces in the crowd; that they reminded him of the crazed expressions he once saw on the faces of *"some holy rollers in the backcountry of Louisiana."* He stated, *"They looked up at him* (Hitler) *as if he were a Messiah, their faces transformed into something positively inhuman."*

To Shirer, the intoxicating atmosphere inside the hall was such that *"every word dropped by Hitler seemed like an inspired word from on high."* It was during this opening meeting that Hitler's victorious proclamation was read: *"The German form of life is definitely determined for the next thousand years."* In 1934, over a million Germans participated in the hugely successful Nuremberg Rally. The gatherings grew even larger in subsequent years.

Why did Hitler and his Nazi Party have such magnetic appeal? So much has been expended trying to answer this question. In class, my students have been very excited to explore potential answers. Over the years, they have analyzed Stanley Milgram's controversial research where so many ordinary Americans administered what they thought were potentially lethal doses of electricity to participants in the experiment simply because an authority wearing a while lab coat told them to do so. They have discussed the Stanford Prison Experiment where college students playing guards went so crazy with the power they held over the *"inmates"* that a two-week experiment had to be suspended after just six days. But most of all, they have been intrigued by Todd Strasser's book, *The Wave*. This is probably because the subjects of this simulation were high school students in a history class much like their own. In *The Wave*, the teacher, in order to educate his students about the appeal of nationalism, created a set of rules and procedures that gradually turned his students into fascist drones. The main idea from all of these social psychology experiments and simulations is that anyone, not just Italians or Germans, can be susceptible to the appeal of nationalism under certain circumstances. In fact, a simple formula is that if extreme nationalism is added to a totalitarian dictatorship, the sum total is fascism.

Stanley Milgram experiment
Courtesy of https://www.flickr.com/photos/nearnearfuture/871926172(CC BY-SA 2.0)

Before going further, the term nationalism should be defined. A good source might be George Orwell, the British dystopian writer. Orwell described patriotism as the *"devotion to a particular place and a particular way of life, which one believes to be the best in the world but has no wish to force on other people."* Conversely, he described nationalism as the feeling that your way of life, country, or ethnic group is superior to others and warned that this feeling can lead a group to impose their way of life on others. In other words, patriotism can be good, but since nationalism is a form of patriotism on steroids, it is potentially dangerous and can lead to war. The juxtaposition between patriotism and nationalism came to the surface in the days following September 11, 2001. Initially, there were American flags sprouting everywhere and plenty of spontaneous patriotic singing. However, within just two days after the attack on the World Trade Center, a practitioner of the Sikh faith wearing a turban to express his beliefs was run off the road in his car and punched in the face without explanation. He was not even a Muslim, but his Middle Eastern appearance made him a target. According to the FBI, hate crimes against people of Middle Eastern origin or descent increased from 354 attacks in 2000 to 1,501 in 2001. Based on Orwell's descriptions, none of these could be justified as patriotism. They were more a product of blind nationalism.

When viewed through a historical lens, however, the dichotomy between the good patriotism and the bad nationalism is not so simple. Where should the line be drawn distinguishing between the two? At what point does the love for one's country devolve into a destructive force? To help students better understand the distinction between the two, I have frequently asked them to explain where they would fall on the following 1 to 6 spectrum. The result has led to some engaging discussions.

1. Nations do not matter. We are all citizens of the planet Earth.
2. It is human nature for people to group themselves into nation-states, but countries themselves are not deserving of significant loyalty.
3. Citizens of a nation should demonstrate a reasonable sense of patriotism, but this should be mostly through symbols such as flags and anthems.
4. The citizens of a nation should be prepared to fight, kill and die for their country if it comes under a major military attack.
5. The citizens of a nation should be prepared to fight, kill and die for their country anytime there is an opportunity to make it bigger, richer or more powerful.
6. The citizens of one nation should consistently view themselves as superior to those of all other countries.

Some of the statements on this spectrum are typically clarified with examples. The Japanese attack on Pearl Harbor in 1941 is used for number 4 and the U.S. wars against Mexico in 1846 and with Spain in 1898 are plugged into number 5. Most students admit by the end of the discussion that both patriotism and nationalism have been powerful forces in recent world history, and that nationalism hit its apex with the rise of Hitler and the enormous role he played in the Second World War. It is therefore a major surprise to my students when they learn that neither existed as we understand them prior to the end of the 18th Century.

For thousands of years, people felt a love and loyalty towards someone or something beyond themselves; but more often than not, this devotion was not towards the nation where they lived. Instead, it was focused on a monarch or a religious leader. There were many times when professional soldiers employed by the king of France would wage war against professional soldiers sent by the king of England. Meanwhile, Englishmen would visit Paris as tourists with little regard to the battles taking place around them. A Frenchman could feel loyal to his king and devoted to his Pope in Rome without ever feeling any sense of loyalty to the nation of France. This all began to change due to two revolutions that occurred in the late 18th Century.

When the American Revolution first began in 1775, it has been estimated that only about one third of the population were *"Patriots,"* while another third remained loyal to the king of England and the final third sat on the fence in between. In order for the Patriots to recruit thousands of Loyalists or those stuck in the middle to a movement where they would no longer feel devotion to their king, something would have to arise to take his place. And keep in mind they were not just seeking a vote. They badly needed soldiers who would be willing to fight, kill and die if necessary, but for what? Since the thirteen British colonies were not looking to replace King George III with another monarch, and since the ragtag group of representatives meeting in Philadelphia would not fit the bill either, that something would have to be the new nation itself.

Modern patriotism and/or nationalism came into the world accompanied by the birth of the United States. Patrick Henry made this point when he said, *"The distinctions between Virginians, Pennsylvanians, New Yorkers, and New Englanders are no more. I am Not a Virginian, But an American!"* Benjamin Rush spoke directly to this point when he wrote, *"Patriotism is as much a virtue as justice, and is as necessary for the support of societies as natural affection is for the support of families."* And Thomas Paine did the same when he said *"The summer soldier and the sunshine patriot will, in this crisis, shrink from the service of their country; but he that stands it now, deserves the love and thanks of man and woman."*

Worldwide, the French Revolution of 1789 played an even larger role. When Louis XVI and his wife, Marie Antoinette, were beheaded in January of 1793, it sent shivers down the spines of European nobles and monarchs. There was soon a coalition of armies invading France intent on putting a stop to the viral disease of revolution. In order to defend the nation against the rest of the continent, French soldiers were not just recruited, but for the first time in history, were drafted. How could a typical French peasant be expected to lay down his life for this cause? His king was dead and his Church was under attack by the new regime, so something would have to arise to command his loyalties. Once again, that something would be the modern nation-state of France. In both America and France, soldiers marched onto the battlefields under new flags, singing new patriotic songs and looking forward to the new freedom and opportunities that their nations would soon provide. The French went on to fight for the next 25 years. Even after the defeat of Napoleon in 1815, nationalism did not disappear. Instead, while the Congress of Vienna tried to restore monarchs to the thrones of Europe, nationalism continued to spread like a contagious disease.

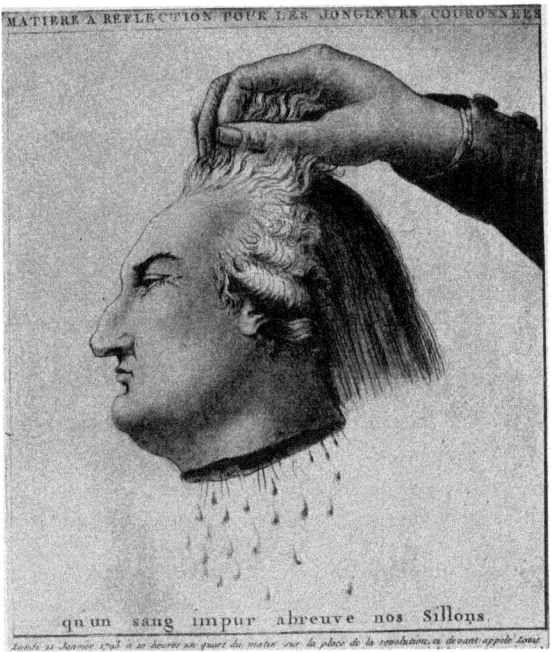

Symbol and Satire in the French Revolution
Courtesy of https://www.flickr.com/photos/internetarchive-bookimages/14782835102/

In the United States, it took another war with our former mother country, the War of 1812, to solidify the establishment of American nationalism.

Victory against the British was hardly achieved, but just the knowledge that our new nation held its own and was not defeated helped to spread a surge of American patriotism to the western frontier and beyond. In addition, the United States experienced a strong desire to break from the European continent in such areas as music, art, literature and architecture. In the years following the War of 1812, writers like Whitman, Thoreau and Hawthorne began to develop a form of literature that was not just European culture transplanted across the Atlantic Ocean. The Hudson River School of Art would serve the same purpose. It should come as no surprise that our national anthem, "The Star Spangled Banner", was written during the War of 1812. Americans had decided not to be ruled by a king, and their First Amendment had divorced religion from the public realm. Instead, patriotic music, the flag and the nation itself would have to suffice.

By the middle of the 19th Century, nationalism had grown into such a powerful force that it almost split the United States in half. Geographically, America was a large nation that from the beginning divided itself into different regions. The differentiation between north and south as well as between east and west was largely based not only on the various cultural backgrounds of the earliest settlers to the region but also on economic factors. Simultaneous to the growth of American nationalism after the War of 1812 was the rise of slavery in the southern states.

By the 1840s, someone traveling from Boston to Chicago would have seen mills, mines, a few early factories and a large number of family-owned farms growing corn, wheat, chickens or cows. On the other hand, if one traveled from Richmond to New Orleans, he would see small farms squeezed between enormous cotton plantations. Cheap immigrant labor provided most of the muscle in the North while slavery reigned in the South. The differences between the two regions were becoming increasingly apparent every year and the rise of nationalism only exacerbated the situation.

When Congress passed a tariff in 1828 that was so high it was known as the Tariff of Abominations, South Carolina threatened to secede from the Union. Military saber rattling by President Andrew Jackson threw gasoline on the fire, and only a last minute compromise by Senator Henry Clay managed to prevent the Civil War from beginning 30 years earlier than it did. The craze of nationalism had taken root in the South, and combined with the growing differences between the North and the South, it was only a matter of time before something would ignite the most deadly war in American history. That something was pushed to a front burner after the United

States won the Mexican-American War in 1848. The burning question that arose was whether slavery should be allowed to spread to the land recently acquired from Mexico, the territory stretching from Texas to the California coastline.

Tension continued to grow over the next decade, and the final straw came in November of 1860 when the nation elected Lincoln as its new president with only 40% of the popular vote. (There were three other candidates who ran for president that year.) It was no surprise that the first southern state to react was South Carolina, which seceded from the Union the following month. Five other states quickly followed and within months, a new nation was born. The CSA, or Confederate States of America, soon had its own Constitution, its own Congress, its own President, and the stars and bars on its own new flag. When South Carolina fired on Fort Sumter, the federal citadel in Charleston Harbor in April of 1861, five other states soon seceded to join the Confederacy and the Civil War was underway.

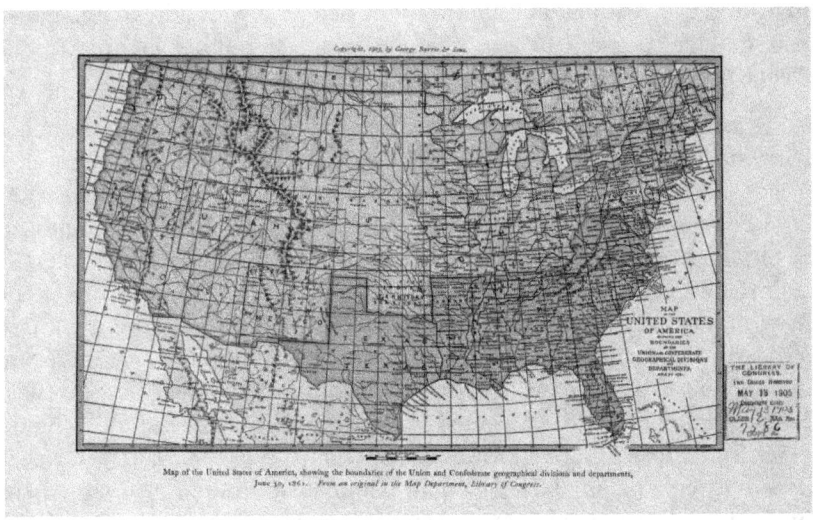

Map of the United States of America showing the boundaries of the Union and Confederate geographical divisions and departments, June 30, 1861.
Courtesy of George Barrie and Sons(1905), Library of Congress Geography and Map Division
https://www.loc.gov/item/99447006

It has taken over a century to correct some of the misperceptions about why the Civil War was actually fought. Was it over states rights as many in the South have maintained, or was slavery the real issue? President Lincoln's goal when he called for 75,000 recruits to expand the army after the firing on Fort Sumter was simply to preserve the Union. He had never been an Abolitionist, and when the Civil War first began, he did not intend to free four million slaves. After seeing the horrible carnage generated by the war in just its first year, Lincoln had a change of heart and by January 1, 1863, his Emancipation Proclamation went into effect. The South seceded from the Union to preserve slavery and by the time the war ended in April of 1865, the 13th Amendment freeing the slaves for all time had been passed. The Civil War was fought over slavery, and it is disingenuous to say otherwise. However, like so many events in history, the more obvious causes and events rest on a more unseen foundation. If nationalism had not taken root in the South in the years leading up to the Civil War, it is doubtful that this cataclysmic event would ever have taken place. Nationalism has acted like such a potent narcotic over the last two centuries. It has prompted people to fight in wars without question, to deny people their fundamental rights, and to die for patriotic causes. There is no question it helped drive in the wedge that almost destroyed the United States.

Before dismissing nationalism as one of the pathological causes underlying the American Civil War, it should be noted that some historians see a bright side to America's rising patriotism. Historian Mark E. Neely Jr., in his 2011 book *Lincoln and the Triumph of the Nation: Constitutional Conflicts in the American Civil War*, stated that nationalism played a positive role. He claims it was stabilizing, peaceful, and unifying; ultimately, it was an effective lubricant that kept both the Union and the Confederacy from self-destructing. For example, he points out the willingness of both sides to resort to nationalism as a means to support the conscription of soldiers for their armies. Nationalism acted a glue to keep both the Union and the Confederacy from further fragmenting once the conflict had begun. In fact, Neely does not see anything adverse about nationalism in the 19th Century. He only sees it developing as a negative force a century later, when it evolved with the growing tendency of the modernizing nation-state to rely on coercion and even violence to sustain itself.

Nevertheless, since its inception over 200 years ago, nationalism has been a divisive force all over the world. In the last century, it has played a role in dissolving the Soviet Union, splitting apart nations like Korea, Czechoslovakia and the Sudan and creating havoc in much of the Middle East. Probably the best example of nationalism splitting a nation apart was in the Balkan Peninsula. After the end of the First World War, a decision had to be made about the different ethnic groups that had formerly belonged to the Austro-Hungarian and Ottoman Empires. Fueled by nationalism, each of these groups was delighted to be free from outside control and looked forward to creating independent nation-states of their own.

Since the Balkan Peninsula is characterized by mountainous terrain and an extremely jagged coastline, it has always been a region were the residents were more divided than not. In fact, the term balkanize has come to mean to divide into smaller mutually hostile states or groups. The problem is that if each group formed a nation of their own after World War One, most of southeastern Europe would consist of dozens of tiny principalities, some which might never be seen on a world map. Therefore, the solution after the war was to unite several of them into one nation called Yugoslavia. Many were not happy with this compromise, but the leadership of Marshal Tito, particularly in driving out the Nazis during the Second World War, provided the adhesive that held the nation together. This all changed in 1980 when Tito died. After several years of bloody warfare, atrocities and *"ethnic cleansing,"* the result was that what had been the nation of Yugoslavia became Slovenia, Croatia, Serbia, Montenegro, Macedonia and Bosnia-Herzegovina.

Surprisingly, nationalism can also have the opposite effect; it can unite just as easily as it can divide. The consummate example of this magnetic attraction was the unification of Italy and Germany in the second half of the 19th Century. Prior to the 1870's, Italy and Germany were not the Italy and Germany of today. Instead, both were a collection of smaller states that shared a common language, culture and heritage, but not a unified nation. The specific names, events, wars and other details that led to the fusion of the Italian and German states can be found in any world history textbook, but the bottom line is that the dream of Italian and German unification that had festered for hundreds of years was finally achieved by 1871. Modern Italy might look up to names like Giuseppe Garibaldi and Camillo Benso Cavour, and there is no question about the role played by Otto von Bismarck in Germany, but the real foundation for the unification of both nations was nationalism.

Ever since its inception in the French Revolution, the appeal of forming and belonging to a unified nation had spread like wildfire across the European continent. If one already lived in an independent nation-state, the goal then became to make that country stronger, richer or more powerful. This included the design of a colorful flag and the placement of that flag in as many different colonies as possible around the planet. As stated before, the British Empire had grown so large by the end of the 19th Century that it was rightfully said, *"the sun never set on the British flag."* On the other hand, if one lived in one of many separate areas that shared a common national bond, then nationalism infused all of these regions with the dream of unification. That dream had finally come true for Italy and Germany by the 1870's, and as the new kids on the block, both had plenty to prove.

Over the next 45 years, both Italy and Germany took steps to modernize their industries, build up advanced militaries, and acquired an overseas colonial empire. Italy was checked a bit by its enormous regional differences between North and South, and as a result, did not make as much progress as its German neighbor; but each of these new nations soon became diplomatically, economically and militarily aggressive. The disease of modern nationalism had clearly infected both. This in turn led to intense rivalries with other nations in the race to secure colonies, particularly in Africa. It also brought about the formation of alliances to protect national security as well as a rapid military arms race. By 1914, the powder keg created by these developments only needed a spark to ignite an enormous explosion, and when the heir to the throne of the Austro-Hungarian Empire was assassinated that summer in Serbia, Europe soon detonated into world war. The nationalism that had united Italy and Germany by 1871 had pushed the first domino that led to the start of World War One.

Germany lay defeated and ruined by the fall of 1918, but that did nothing to diminish German nationalism. In just a few years, Adolph Hitler and the Nazis came to power in Germany riding a resurging tsunami of nationalism, and 20 years after Germany's defeat in the First World War, it all started over again. Thanks to the new developments in modern warfare that emerged in World War Two, particularly the use of indiscriminant air bombings of urban civilian areas, Germany in 1945 was in even worse shape that in 1918. In addition, due to the Cold War between the United States and the Soviet Union that emerged even before the final shots of the Second World War were fired, Germany was split between East and West, as was its capital and largest city, Berlin. More than anything, the end of the Cold War was marked and symbolized by the tearing down of the Berlin Wall in 1989. This once again led to the reunification of Germany, and the looks of exhilaration on the faces of thousands of German people when this momentous event occurred also reflected the underlying German nationalism of the past.

In today's world, it might be tempting to argue that nationalism has lost its appeal. Before rushing to this conclusion, one more example should be examined. Ukraine was originally one of the 15 republics that constituted the Union of Soviet Socialist Republics back in the 20th Century. The modern nation of Ukraine came about with the demise of the USSR in 1990. Sandwiched between Russia to the east and the rest of Europe to the west, the Ukrainian population was always split in their loyalties.

In 2013, Viktor Yanukovych, Ukraine's president began to shy away from an association agreement that had been in the works with the European Union and instead chose to establish closer ties with the Russian Federation. Some Ukrainians then took to the streets to show their support for closer ties with Europe. Meanwhile, in the predominantly Russian-speaking east, a large portion of the population opposed these protests, instead supporting the Yanukovych government. The protests and counter demonstrations soon escalated into violence. Anti-government demonstrators then occupied buildings in the center of Kiev, including the Justice Ministry building, and riots left 98 dead with approximately 15,000 injured and 100 considered missing.

Ukraine
Courtesy of the United States Central Intelligence Agency
Retrieved from the Library of Congress, Geography and Map Division
https://www.loc.gov/item/2005626463

For better or worse, nationalism had once again created enlarged headlines around the world. The political loyalties of the Ukrainian population were drawn in opposite directions, and the result was violence. After the fall of Yanukovych's pro-Russian government, Vladimir Putin, Russia's President, began preparations to annex a part of Ukraine heavily populated by ethnic Russians called Crimea. He directed Russian troops and intelligence agents to disarm Ukrainian forces and take control. The people of this peninsula then voted in a hastily organized referendum and a majority voted to join Russia. Although the UN General Assembly responded by passing a resolution stating that this referendum was invalid, a treaty was quickly signed giving Crimea to Russia. Infected by the lure of Russian nationalism, armed men in eastern regions of Ukraine, declaring themselves as local militia, then seized government buildings and police stations in several cities of the region and held unrecognized referendums of their own.

Vladamir Putin
Courtesy of Kremlin.ru(CC BY 4.0)
https://commons.wikimedia.org/wiki/File:Vladimir_Putin_12023_%28cropped%29.jpg

Meanwhile, the Ukrainian government has continued military operations to end the armed insurgency. More than 6000 people have been killed in this military campaign. According to the United Nations, 730,000 Ukrainian refugees have fled to Russia since the beginning of 2014 and 117,000 more have fled to other parts of Ukraine. In July of 2014, a Malaysian Airlines jetliner flying from Amsterdam to Kuala Lumpur, while traveling over the conflict-hit region, was shot down. A total of 283 passengers, including 80 children, and 15 crewmembers were all killed. The Ukrainian government and several Western officials said a Russian-made Buk missile launched from the rebel-held part of Ukraine took down the aircraft.

A ceasefire with the separatist troops was negotiated in February 2015. However, Crimea has yet to be returned and there is still much tension in the area. The United States and its western allies have clearly sided with the

Ukrainian government while Putin and the Russians are still angling to add more Ukrainian territory to what has already been gained. The Cold War may have ended over 25 years ago, but rising tension between Russia and America, both of which still possess thousands of nuclear warheads, is never a healthy situation. And what is ultimately the source of this tension? The same force that was behind the U.S. Civil War, World War One and the Second World War: nationalism.

So how should nationalism be assessed? There may be a few people today who see themselves strictly as citizens of the planet, but most of the world's seven billion humans proudly count themselves as citizens of the nation wherein they reside. Most see nothing wrong with the emotional feelings of patriotism that give them a sense of belonging and self-worth. Human nature dictates that if people share a common language and a common heritage, as well as a core set of values and traditions, it is only natural they would feel a strong affinity towards each other. Whatever it is about people that promote a desire to belong to a larger group and to feel a sense of loyalty towards that group is the reason why there are 196 nations in the world today. Some people may be quicker than others to rise upon hearing their national anthem or to feel a lump in their throat when seeing their flag raised after winning an Olympic medal, but most people see loyalty towards their country the same way that most people have faith in their respective religion. Both are perceived as positive values that contribute to the overall quality of their lives.

The more important question is at what point does patriotism evolve into the perils of nationalism? When Ukrainian patriots broke from the Soviet Union in 1990, wrote a democratic constitution and celebrated their collective sense of unity, did they ever anticipate the civil war that would break out 24 years later? The same question might be raised with American patriots after 1776. Where should the line be drawn between patriotism and nationalism? Like other essential questions, this one does not have a definitive answer. However, it is imperative that people have at least a well-grounded understanding of the question.

Suggested Reading:

Anderson, Benedict. *Imagined Communities: Reflections on the Origin and Spread of Nationalism*, rev.ed. New York: Verso, 2006.

"Hate Crime Reporting." *FBI.* 2001. http:www.fbi.gov/about-us/cjis/ucr/hate-crime/2001/hatecrime01.pdf.

Middlekauff, Robert. *The Glorious Cause: The American Revolution, 1763-1789.* New York: Oxford University Press, 1982.

Neely, Mark E. *Lincoln and the Triumph of the Nation: Constitutional Conflict in the American Civil War.* Chapel Hill: University of North Carolina Press, 2011.

Orwell, George. *A Collection of Essays.* New York: Mariner, 1970.

Schama, Simon. *Citizens: A Chronicle of the French Revolution.* New York: First Vintage Books, 1990.

Shirer, William L. *The Rise and Fall of the Third Reich: A History of Nazi Germany.* New York: Touchstone, 1959.

Strasser, Todd. *The Wave.* New York: Dell Laurel-Leaf, 1981.

"Ukraine Death Toll Hits 6,000 Amid Ongoing Fighting." *UN News Centre.* March 2, 2015. http://www.un.org/apps/news/story.asp?NewsID=50215#.VvP573DdgVI.

Chapter 11
Let the ruling classes tremble

The Peasants' Revolt
Courtesy of https://commons.wikimedia.org/wiki/File:Bund-
schuhfahne_Holzschnitt_1539_Petrarcas_Trostspiegel.jpg(PD-old-100)

When, if ever, is a rebellion justified?

The place is London, England and the date is June 13th, 1381. A mob of peasants has just entered the city and they, in addition to many local townsfolk, have attacked the jails, destroyed the Savoy Palace, set fire to law books and buildings in the Temple, and killed anyone associated with the royal government. The following day, King Richard II, then only 14 years old, met the rebels at Mile End and acceded to most of their demands; including the abolition of serfdom. Meanwhile, other rebels entered the Tower of London, killing the Lord Chancellor and the Lord High Treasurer, whom they found inside. Thus began the Peasants' Revolt of 1381, also known at the Great Rising.

The Peasants' Revolt was a major uprising across large parts of England. The revolt had various causes, including the socio-economic and political tensions generated by the Black Death in the 1340s, the high taxes resulting from the conflict with France during the Hundred Years' War and the instability within the local leadership of London. The final trigger for the revolt was the attempt by a royal official, John Bamptom, on May 30th, to collect unpaid poll taxes in Brentwood. This soon led to a violent confrontation that rapidly spread across the southeast of the country. A wide spectrum of rural society, including many local artisans and village officials, rose up in protest, burning court records and opening the local jails. The rebels sought a reduction in taxation, an end to the system of serfdom and the removal of the King's senior officials and law courts.

On June 15th, Richard left the city to meet with the rebels at Smithfield. Violence broke out and the rebel leader was killed. Richard diffused the situation long enough for London's mayor to gather a militia from the city and disperse the rebels. Unrest continued until a rebel army was finally defeated at the Battle of North Walsham on June 26th. Richard then mobilized 4,000 additional soldiers to restore order. Most of the rebel leaders were tracked down and executed. By November, at least 1,500 rebels had been killed.

The Peasant's Revolt has been widely studied by academics over the last two centuries. Interpretations of the revolt have shifted over the years. It was once seen as a defining moment in English history, but modern historians are less certain of its impact on subsequent social and economic history. While the revolt heavily influenced the course of the Hundred Years' War by deterring later Parliaments from raising additional taxes to pay for military campaigns in France, the bottom line is that the revolt was a failure. It is worth noting, however, that the Peasants' Revolt has been widely used in socialist literature and remains a potent symbol for the political left. In my classroom, we have often discussed the revolt as an example where the poor serfs, laboring from sunrise to sunset on feudal manors in the service of lords who had complete control over their lives, actually fought back. Two major institutions dominated their lives during the middle ages: the Roman Catholic Church and feudalism. For centuries, serfs had provided long hours of labor in return for protection and security at a time when there was no strongly centralized government. But while lords and their vassals enjoyed the relative comforts of their castles, serfs lived miserable lives in dirt floor huts and most were kept entirely uneducated. Now, for one of the few times in this dark chapter of history, the exploited masses had fomented a rebellion.

So why did their insurrection fail? And more important, why were there so few other efforts to overthrow a system that was so blatantly unfair by our modern standards? Part of the answer lies in the fact that while the masses generally have the numbers on their side, they are usually lacking in weapons, experience and organization. A betting person would say the odds are against them. However, prior to the late 1600s, there was another factor detrimental to their cause. They were lacking focus. The peasants knew they were not happy with their status as serfs or the unfair taxes they were forced to pay for a war with which they had little interest. They had natural leaders to provide inspiration and at least some direction. What they lacked was a theoretical framework to serve as a solid foundation for their rebellion. A state of unhappiness may be enough to start a revolution, but it usually takes a set of philosophical values to sustain it for the long haul. In order to answer the essential question *"what, if anything, justifies a rebellion,"* the theoretical underpinning of our modern revolutions must be examined. Unfortunately for the rebels in 1381, the abstract justification for modern revolts did not start until 1651 when an Englishman named Thomas Hobbes published a book called *Leviathan*.

Thomas Hobbes
Courtesy of https://www.flickr.com/photos/63794459@N07/6239384009/ (CC BY 2.0)

Leviathan provided much of the foundation for the Western political philosophy that has followed ever since. The work concerns the structure of society and government, and is regarded as one of the earliest and most influential examples of social contract theory. Written during the chaos of the English Civil War between 1642 and 1651, *Leviathan* argues for a social contract between an absolute sovereign and his or her subjects. It must be noted, however, that Hobbes argued that civil war and the anarchy found in a *"state of nature"* can only be avoided through a strong, undivided government. After all, during the English Civil War, King Charles I was beheaded and for a few brief years, England had no one on the throne to provide a sense of traditional order. There was a reasonable amount of stability during the *"Commonwealth"* years under the leadership of Oliver Cromwell. However, after Cromwell's death, a fear spread across the land so profound that in 1660, the decision was made to restore Charles II to the throne. It was during this period that Hobbes developed his idea that while society would enjoy the most order and stability when a monarch possessed absolute power, the king or queen was obligated through a social contract to provide good government to his or her subjects. The implication was that if the monarch violated the contract, a rebellion might be justified.

John Locke developed the principle of the social contract even further when he published his *Two Treatises of Government* in 1690. Like Hobbes, Locke was heavily influenced by events taking place all around him. Much of the English populace was deeply concerned when King James II produced a son to be his heir to the throne. James was a Roman Catholic in a nation that had turned to Protestantism more than 150 years before, so the fact that he now had a Catholic male heir proved to be problematic. Fearing the bloodshed and carnage that had occurred 50 years earlier in the civil war, a decision was made by leaders in Parliament to simply ask James to step down and flee the country, and to invite a distant relative, William of Orange, to assume the throne. England would remain a monarchy, but if Parliament now possessed the power to replace one king with another, England from that day on would be considered a constitutional, or limited, monarchy. The fact that this change was achieved without a single drop of blood is arguably the best reason why the Glorious Revolution was truly glorious.

Locke's ideas reflected all of these developments. According to John Locke, we are all born into a state of nature, and from the time of birth, we possess three natural rights: *"life, liberty and estate."* When hearing this, my students quickly make the link between these three natural rights and the rights to *"life, liberty and the pursuit of happiness"* mentioned in Thomas Jefferson's Declaration of Independence. It is always interesting to hear them speculate on why *"estate"* or *"property"* in 1690 became *"happiness"* in 1776, but the point here is that Locke, like Jefferson, felt these natural rights were sacred and should never be violated. Applying Hobbes' principle of the social contract, Locke argued that since there was the need for a government to guard these natural rights, the people should be able to create one based on a contract that the government would protect our natural rights and do nothing more. If the established government did anything to violate the rights of the people, then the people were justified in overthrowing the government and replacing it with another. In other words, Locke had found a way to legitimize a rebellion, even a violent revolution. This was truly revolutionary. It has been used to validate rebellions ever since and has become the cornerstone of modern liberalism.

Over the next century, other political philosophers, particularly French thinkers like Voltaire, Montesquieu and Rousseau, continued to add to this theoretical framework. The entire age was characterized by their logical and pragmatic approach to science, government, religion, art and most other areas of human life. This was the Age of Enlightenment, and it is doubtful that the revolutions which occurred in 1776, 1789 or ever since could have ever enjoyed much success without the ideas churned out during this period. When people are unhappy, they will take steps to ease their pain. However, when given a higher moral purpose to justify their efforts, they will unite, organize, fight, kill and die if necessary to overthrow the existing order.

This idea can be clearly seen in the thirteen British colonies between 1763 and 1776, and the ensuing results would dramatically change the world. Some historians have argued that the people who resided in the colonies that stretched from New Hampshire to Georgia enjoyed more freedom and a higher standard of living than anyone else on the planet at that time. For example, according to University of Toronto historian, James T. Lemon, the 13 colonies enjoyed a relatively low death rate due to its healthy population. They had more than enough food, a diverse and excellent diet, adequate clothing, an abundance of wood for winter fuel, low levels of communicable diseases with only occasional epidemics in rural areas (where most Americans at the time lived) and modest working hours for much of the year. This all helped to keep premature death largely from the door. In addition, according to Lemon, the per capita annual income of 13 pounds ($845 in 1980 terms) was the highest in the world.

True, only white, male property owners could vote; but nonetheless, each colony had an elected assembly to make its laws. In addition, with over a century in most cases to grow and mature, the colonies had gone far beyond the primitive conditions that characterized life in Puritan Boston or Colonial Jamestown in the first half of the 17th Century. By 1776, the colonies enjoyed more land, greater natural resources and superior economic opportunities than their brethren did back in England. Life was good, why would they want to revolt? More important, how could radical patriots like Samuel Adams, James Otis or Thomas Paine theoretically justify a violent revolution against our mother country?

The roots of this insurrection extend back to 1763; the year victory was achieved by the British against France in the French and Indian War, better known around the world as the Seven Years War. Most of the indigenous tribes that had sided with the French were not happy about their loss and many feared it would open up the floodgates to American settlement on their lands west of the Appalachian Mountains. Led by Chief Pontiac, they pursued their own rebellion against the British and the American colonies.

After much effort, the English put down this insurrection, but then, in a fit of surprising moral wisdom way ahead of its time, issued the Proclamation of 1763, telling the Americans they could no longer advance through the Appalachian Mountains to settle on Indian lands. The indigenous tribes were delighted by this development and the American colonials were outraged.

Even more anger was provoked by the British decision to start enforcing Navigation Acts that had been on the books for decades but had been largely ignored. Americans had grown so used to the benefits of widespread smuggling they were indignant over the thought that the English now intended to enforce the law. To top it off, the English also had the audacity to expect the Americans to start paying for the protection afforded by being a part of the British Empire. From 1765 to 1775, taxes were placed on the stamps that were fixed on all legal documents, on tea and on the sugar used to sweeten that tea. Compared to the taxes paid back in England, these new taxes on the American colonies were more than fair. The Americans tried to get around this point by arguing they had no say in creating these taxes, calling it *"taxation without representation."* When the British argued that the members of Parliament *"virtually"* represented everyone throughout the empire, the American rebuttal was to demand *"actual"* representation. Granted, in the 18th Century, travel across the Atlantic was arduous and time-consuming, so pragmatically speaking, the British were probably correct to argue against allowing American representation in Parliament. Regardless, is a violent revolution justified by a restriction on land settlement, stricter enforcement of trade laws and *"taxation without representation?"* Or, as I ask my students, would this be enough for you to join a cause where you would be expected to fight, kill or die?

Put this way, one might assume most of my students would come to the conclusion the American Revolution was not justified. Yet, surprisingly, most say it was. The principles contained within the Declaration of Independence have been so driven into them starting with their early primary years that by the time they reach high school, words like *"patriot"*, *"liberty"* and *"protection of individual rights"* roll right off their tongues. Right or wrong, they see the American Revolution as standing for something more than just being able to send representatives to Parliament. They truly believe Lexington, Concord and Bunker Hill represented the birth of a new way of life; one based on the belief that no ruler or government should tread on the rights of the people. This is the reason why many say they would have been Patriots. They may or may not understand the details of what was taking place prior to 1776, but the reality is most can at least paraphrase from heart these words from the Declaration of Independence:

> *We hold these truths to be self-evident, that all men are created equal, that they are Endowed by their Creator with certain unalienable Rights, that among these are Life, Liberty and the pursuit of Happiness. That to secure these rights, Governments are Instituted among Men, deriving their just powers from the consent of the governed. That whenever any Form of Government becomes destructive of these ends, it is the Right of the People to alter or abolish it, and to institute new Government...*

With only minor changes, these are essentially the words and ideas of John Locke. More than 300 years later, they still live on in the minds of millions of American citizens, including the students I have taught over the last three decades. The reality of the situation in the years leading up to the American Revolution may not have justified a violent rebellion, but the perception, both at the time and certainly today, is that Thomas Jefferson's words did validate the taking up of arms against the British. In other words, in this case, the rationale for a revolution may have actually outweighed the specific circumstances.

Thomas Jefferson
Courtesy of the Library of Congress, Prints and Photographs Division
LC-DIG-pga-07205

These ideas soon became infectious, and combined with the success of the American Revolution, particularly with significant help from the French; it was only a matter of time before a similar event took place in the nation of France. While there is little question that the American Revolution directly influenced the events that took place in Paris in 1789, there are some rather obvious differences. First, the French were not fighting to establish a new nation. Second, the French Revolution turned into much more of a class struggle. Finally, the French Revolution went on to become arguably more influential, particularly throughout Europe. The French Revolution was bloodier and because of the threat it posed to monarchs throughout Europe, brought about warfare on an unprecedented scale. The Revolution in France was also messier in other ways. It was filled with periods dominated by chaos and confusion, and rather than leading to a democratic government in place of an absolute monarchy, Napoleon Bonaparte ended up crowning himself as an emperor just 10 years after the start of the Revolution. There would be other revolutions in France throughout much of the 19th Century and it really was not until the 20th Century that France settled down to become the constitutional democracy it is today.

With this in mind, the fuel that energized the French Revolution was very similar to what had produced the revolt in the American colonies just 13 years before. Like the Americans, the French were well versed in the writings and ideas being generated by the Enlightenment. In fact, a significant number of Enlightenment thinkers were French, and principles about limited government, individual rights and checks and balances had been discussed in the salons of Paris long before 1789. Also like the Americans, the French perceived themselves as victims of an absolute monarch. They viewed the arbitrary power of Louis XVI in a manner similar to the way Americans had complained about the oppressive rule of George III. In both cases, the imposition of what was perceived as unfair taxes had set off the start of each revolt.

Probably the greatest difference between the two revolutions was economic. By the end of the American Revolution, wealthy landowners remained wealthy landowners. The instability of the early years of the Articles of Confederation had scared the upper class in the United States, and led to the writing of the Constitution. In *An Economic Interpretation of the Constitution of the United States*, a book published by historian Charles Beard, it is argued that the writing of the Constitution was motivated primarily by the personal financial interests of the Founding Fathers. More specifically, Beard contends that a *"cohesive"* elite seeking to protect its personal property and economic standing attended the Constitutional Convention held in Philadelphia in the summer of 1787. In terms of the distribution of wealth, not much changed between 1775 and 1800, and so in that respect, the American Revolution was not really that revolutionary.

Execution of Louis XVI, King of France, January 21, 1793
Courtesy of the Library of Congress, Prints and Photographs Division
LC-DIG-ppmsca-10742

On the other hand, the French Revolution pitted hungry city workers and desperate rural peasants against hereditary nobles almost from the beginning. Shortly after the taking of the Bastille, which today is celebrated as the equivalent of Independence Day in France, the Great Fear spread across the countryside; and for their safety, many French nobles fled the nation. Although the term, *"socialism,"* was not being batted around yet, there was much talk of a significant redistribution of wealth in France during the heydays of the Revolution. The closure point taught for years in my World History classes is that three *"isms"* emerged out of the French Revolution: liberalism, nationalism and socialism. This point about socialism brings up yet another potential reason to legitimize a rebellion: economic equality.

The Industrial Revolution, which began in Great Britain during the 18th Century, soon spread to other nations during the 19th Century, including the United States, France, Germany and Japan. This radical change in how goods were produced and distributed not only involved the use of machines taking the place of human hands, it also meant a radical alteration in lifestyles. An industrialized nation was much more urban, much more polluted, and in the long run, much more likely to enjoy a substantially higher standard of living. In the short term, however, industrialization meant that the rich grew richer, especially since there were now new ways beyond land ownership to acquire wealth; and the poor grew poorer. In fact, unlike the humble peasants of the past who at least could enjoy fresh air and sunshine when they labored on their few acres of land, the factory workers had to punch an impersonal clock, work with dangerous and loud machinery, and received an hourly wage that could not even begin to support a family.

It was in this environment that Karl Marx entered the world stage. Born a German, Marx was soon forced to flee Germany because of his radical views. Writing in the slums of London, Marx went on to write books like *Das Kapital* and pamphlets like *The Communist Manifesto*. Karl Marx did not invent the doctrine of socialism; he simply took it a radically violent step further. Based on a deterministic view of history, Marx felt that in every period of the past, those with wealth and power have found ways to control those who did not. According to Marx, industrialization represented the highest stage of economic development, but it also accentuated the differences between the factory owners-the Bourgeoisie, and the factory workers-the Proletariat. Following this same deterministic line of thinking, Marx predicted the day was soon at hand for a violent revolution by the Proletariat. He wrote *"the Communists distain to conceal their views and aims. They openly declare that their ends can be attained only by the forcible overthrow of all existing social conditions. Let the ruling classes tremble at a Communist revolution. The proletarians have nothing to lose but their chains. They have a world to win. Working men of all countries, unite!"*

Karl Marx
Courtesy of the Library of Congress Prints and Photographs Division
LC-USZ62-16530

Marx went on to devote the remainder of his life to writing and organizing for the day of his predicted workers' revolution. Like Hobbes, Locke, and the Enlightenment thinkers a century or two before, Marx provided a theoretical framework for revolutions to come. The revolution led by Vladimir Lenin in Russia in 1918 was a Marxist Revolution. So were the subsequent communist revolutions and takeovers in China, Korea, Vietnam, Cuba and much of Eastern Europe. While it can be argued that communism is on the way out in most of those nations, there is no denying the profound influence of Marx and the other socialist thinkers in bringing about a massive redistribution of wealth around much of the world. Even in the United States, the wealthiest billionaires are supposed to pay considerably more in taxes than the rest of us; and the poorest Americans should in theory, have a roof over their heads, food on the table, access to decent health care and educational opportunities for their children. Democrats and Republicans endlessly debate over how big a role the government should play in seeking a fairer distribution of wealth, but few can argue that the poor today have it worse than they did in the late 19th Century. Most of my students look at me cock-eyed when I ask them if they would be willing to join a revolution motivated by the desire to bring about a fairer allocation of property, but when I remind them of the millions of Americans who were homeless and could not feed their children during the Great Depression of the 1930s, many acknowledge how this could have led to a rebellion.

Like usual, the essential question *"what, if anything, will justify a rebellion"* has contemporary applications. The other day, I was meeting with Trevor, a former student now in his mid twenties. Since we are both residents of St. Louis, the subject of the Black Lives Matter Movement that began in Ferguson, Missouri in the late summer of 2014 came up. Trevor asked if a rebellion might be warranted if it would bring more national attention to the cause of African Americans in their daily dealings with the police and the courts. When I asked if this was the only grievance of most African Americans in the United States, we quickly agreed that the problem is really much larger. On the whole, African Americans, and for that matter, Hispanics and other minorities, have less political power and a substantially smaller piece of the economic pie than the white, middle class majority. We also agreed that racism is deeply rooted and still exists in a more subtle form throughout much of our society.

Trevor raised an excellent question; one that took the essential question about what justifies a rebellion and applied it to the present. Do the political, economic and social problems faced by African Americans in St. Louis and most other urban areas justify any kind of revolution? At the present, a shooting of a black resident in St. Louis or the surrounding suburbs, particularly by a white police officer, is more than likely to touch off demonstrations, protests, and quite possibly, violence. Over the past year, Ferguson in particular has seen more than its fair share of protests that have ignited acts of arson, looting and gun shootings. The situation has become combustible, and it has spread to other cities; including New York, Baltimore and Cleveland.

Black Lives Matter protest in Oakland
Courtesy of https://www.flickr.com/photos/82417691@N00/16022084905/ (CC BY-SA 2.0)

My response to Trevor was to ask about whether the current *"rebellion"* is focused on any type of theoretical framework. In the late summer of 1963, Dr. Martin Luther King addressed 250,000 people from the steps of the Lincoln Memorial in Washington, DC. In his now famous "I Have a Dream" speech, he stated

> *I have a dream that one day this nation will rise up and live out the true meaning of its creed: "We hold these truths to be self-evident, that all men are created equal." I have a dream that one day on the red hills of Georgia, the sons of former slaves and the sons of former slave owners will be able to sit down together at the table of brotherhood.*

The source of these words is more than clear. King was deliberately quoting Thomas Jefferson from the Declaration of Independence and indirectly referencing Thomas Hobbes and John Locke. No moment in history exists in a vacuum; they all are interconnected with other moments from the past. In order to justify the non-violent rebellion that took place in the 1950s and 1960s, Dr. King understood the need to provide a theoretical framework. The Civil Rights Movement was most effective and successful when it was focused on these higher ideals of liberty and brotherhood. The question for Trevor and for everyone else following the events in Ferguson and beyond is whether there is currently enough of a theoretical foundation to support a rebellion at the present. One shooting incident might ignite protests and even riots, but by itself, it will not be enough to sustain a true rebellion. History has shown over and over again a theoretical scaffold that will effectively unite the rebels is necessary to nourish a meaningful rebellion.

To personalize this point for students, I have frequently asked them to consider their own student government. First, I ask if there is a student council constitution, and when most admit they have no idea, I provide them with a copy. After looking it over, they quickly realize that it mostly speaks to structural details such as the composition of the council and the election of officers. Since the constitution says little about the actual powers of their government, the students are usually forced to admit that while their elected leaders hold annual fundraisers, organize the homecoming activities and sponsor community service events, they have little power in making the larger decisions that have a significant impact on the school.

I then explain about the *Tinker v. Des Moines* Supreme Court decision handed down in 1969. In this case, students were suspended for wearing black armbands to school as a form of symbolic protest against the war in Vietnam, and the court handed down a 7-2 judgment in favor of the students' First Amendment rights. The court observed, "*It can hardly be argued that either students or teachers shed their constitutional rights to freedom of speech or expression at the schoolhouse gate.*" After some discussion about the long term significance of this case, I ask the students if they would hypothetically support a rebellion that would lead to a new student council constitution giving a meaningful voice to the student body whenever big decisions are made. This almost always leads to a very animated and sometimes heated discussion.

One year, these conversations led to action. When students began the school year, they learned about a new rule that had been enacted over the summer forbidding them to listen to music on personal headphones. While acknowledging that the new rule did not justify a "*rebellion*", some of the student leaders declared that it violated a more important principle: students having a voice in the decision-making process. This soon led to meetings with the principal, the circulation of a petition, and even a "*brownbag*" strike; where for a few days, students refused to buy cafeteria lunches and instead brought in their own food. The protest soon collapsed, especially after student leaders learned that the provision of lunch was contracted to a private business. However, by the end of the year, the principal agreed to the formation of a larger, more representative student body that would meet with her on a regular basis.

In the end, the students who participated in that year's *"rebellion"* felt a rare sense of victory. In the follow-up discussion, they recognized that these types of revolts go on everyday around the country. They usually do not involve violence or bloodshed, but to those involved, they are still important. Labor unions strike against their employers, college students protest against perceived racism on campus, and there can even be small-scale rebellions by teenagers against their parents. Those involved will have to make tough choices based on the circumstances; but in a healthy democratic society, they will be in a better position to decide if they have had the opportunity to thoroughly consider the essential question of when, if ever, a rebellion is justified.

Suggested Reading:

Barker, Juliet. *1381: The Year of the Peasants' Revolt.* Cambridge: First Harvard University Press, 2014.

Beard, Charles A. *An Economic Interpretation of the Constitution of the United States.* New York: Dover Publications, 2004.

Dierenfield, Bruce J. *The Civil Rights Movement: Revised edition.* New York: Routledge, 2013.

Fitzpatrick, Sheila. *The Russian Revolution.* New York: Oxford Univesity Press, 2008.

Hobbes, Thomas. *Leviathan.* Introduction by C.B. MacPherson. New York: Penguin Classics, 1982.

Kramnick, Isaac. *The Portable Enlightenment Reader.* New York: Penguin Books, 1995.

Lemmon, James T. *Liberal Dreams and Nature's Limits: Great Cities of North America Since 1600.* Oxford: Oxford University Press, 1997.

Marx, Karl. *Das Kapital.* Translated by Samuel Moore. Seattle: Pacific Publishing Studio, 2010.

Chapter 12
War, what is it good for?

USS Maddox (DD-731)
Courtesy of the US Navy, Naval Historical Center Collection (PD-USGov-Military-Navy). https://commons.wikimedia.org/wiki/File:USS_Maddox_(DD-731).jpg

When, if ever, should a nation go to war?

The place is onboard the USS destroyer *Maddox* sailing in the Gulf of Tonkin off the coast of Vietnam and the date is August 2, 1964. Vietnam, which was divided between the North and the South, has been engaged in a bloody civil war for the last several years and the United States had been providing money, weapons and military advisors to the South Vietnamese government of Saigon. Since this was the height of the Cold War, it was only natural for the U.S. government to back any nation attempting to resist the spread of communism. Earlier in the evening, South Vietnamese gunboats had conducted a clandestine raid on the North Vietnamese coast, and the destroyer *Maddox* had been engaged in electronic espionage nearby. It was now time for North Vietnamese payback. In the dark waters, the *Maddox* was fired on by North Vietnamese torpedo boats. Two days later, in the same vicinity, the *Maddox* and another destroyer were again under attack.

It is worth noting that no one was killed in these attacks; no one was even injured.

Although the veracity of these attacks has been seriously questioned in recent years, President Johnson quickly proceeded to authorize retaliatory air strikes against North Vietnam. The next day, he gathered congressional leaders and without divulging the circumstances that might have provoked the torpedo attack, accused North Vietnam of *"open aggression on the high seas."* He then submitted to the Senate a resolution that would authorize him to take *"all necessary measures to repel any armed attack against the forces of the United States and to prevent further aggression."* The resolution was quickly approved by Congress; only two senators voted in opposition.

Much later, when more information about the Tonkin incident became available, it appeared that President Johnson and his advisors misled Congress into supporting the expansion of the war. Gareth Porter in his book, *Perils of Dominance: Imbalance of Power and the Road to War in Vietnam*, claimed that it was the Secretary of Defense, Robert McNamara who deliberately deceived the president. Government documents available for decades in the LBJ Library clearly show that McNamara failed to inform Johnson that the U.S. naval task group commander in the Tonkin Gulf, Captain John J. Herrick, had changed his mind about the alleged North Vietnamese torpedo attack on the U.S. warships he had reported earlier that day. By early afternoon Washington time, Herrick had reported to the Pacific Commander in Chief in Honolulu that *"freak weather effects"* on the ship's radar had made such an attack questionable. In fact, Herrick went on to say, in a message sent at 1:27 pm Washington time, that no North Vietnamese patrol boats had actually been sighted. Herrick then proposed a *"complete evaluation before any further action was taken."*

Nevertheless, the Gulf of Tonkin Resolution was passed on August 7, 1964. It gave broad approval for expansion of the Vietnam War. During the previous spring, military planners had developed a detailed strategy for major attacks on the North, but at the time, President Johnson and his advisors feared that the public would not support an expansion of the war. By the summer, however, rebel forces allied with the communist government of North Vietnam had established control over nearly half of South Vietnam; and Senator Barry Goldwater, the Republican nominee for president in 1964, was criticizing the Johnson Administration for not pursuing the war in Southeast Asia more aggressively. Polls indicated that a majority of the public agreed with Goldwater, and so President Johnson was on the lookout for any cause that would enable him to take this hot political issue away from his opponent. In the end, Congress gave him the green light to send as many American combat troops to Southeast Asia as he wanted for the purpose of protecting U.S. national security interests in that part of the world. Three months later, an overwhelming majority elected Lyndon B. Johnson president over Barry Goldwater. Since combat forces were now making their way in large numbers to Vietnam, most historians would say this marked the official start of the Vietnam War for the United States.

The war went on to last another nine years. Among all the wars the United States has fought, the Vietnam War is ranked fourth in casualties. Only the Civil War and the two World Wars were deadlier for U.S. troops. Out of the 2,594,000 personnel who served in Vietnam, there were more than 58,220 American dead and another 153,303 wounded. More than 23,214 soldiers were one hundred percent disabled. Even when it had ended, the Vietnam War continued to cost many American lives. Somewhere between 70,000 and 300,000 Vietnam veterans have committed suicide and around 700,000 have suffered psychological trauma.

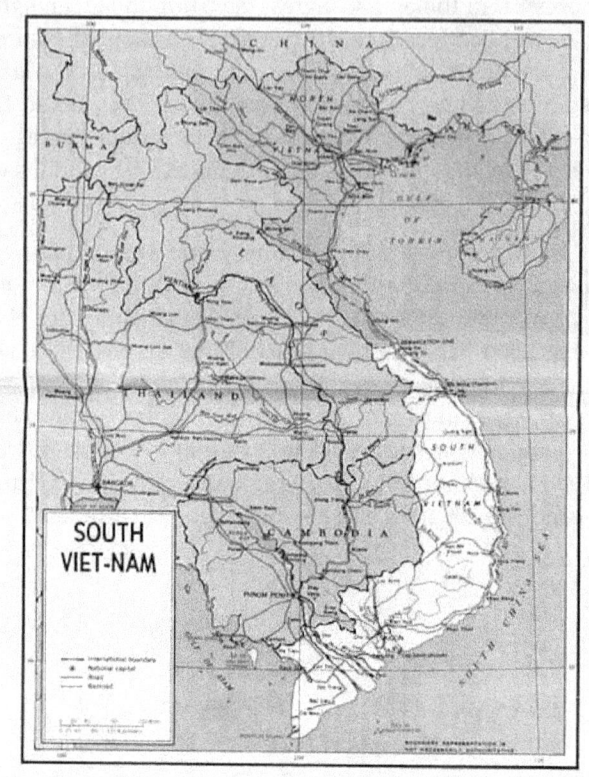

Map of partitioned Vietnam
Courtesy of Bureau of Public Affairs
US Government Printing Office(PD-USGov)
https://commons.wikimedia.org/wiki/File:North_and_south_vietnam_map.jpg

Then there is the economic cost. In the entire war, the United States spent about $140 billion, worth around one trillion dollars today. Another $25 billion went for economic and military aid to the Saigon regime. At that rate, the United States spent approximately $140,000 for each enemy killed. However, $140 billion was only the direct cost. According to Indochina Newsletter of the Asia Resource Center, the United States spent approximately $350 billion to $900 billion in total, including veterans' benefits and interest. Military funds spent overseas also led to budget deficits that caused a weaker dollar, higher inflation and increasing interest rates. Because of the war in Vietnam, the American economy was brought down from the growth it had sustained for the 20 years following World War Two. The economy would be in a state of crisis by the 1970s. In addition, for every dollar President Johnson's Great Society had spent in its *"War on Poverty,"* another ten dollars was spent in Vietnam. Whatever hopes the Democrats had that programs like Medicaid, Food Stamps and Project Head Start might significantly reduce poverty in the world's richest nation were dashed by U.S. involvement in the Vietnam War.

Towards the end, the United States gradually brought home more and more of its soldiers based on the idea that South Vietnamese troops had been adequately trained and equipped to defend themselves. The final end came in 1975 and would live on in the American consciousness for many years as a national humiliation. According to Christian Gerard Appy, Professor of History at the University of Massachusetts and author of *American Reckoning: The Vietnam War and Our National Identity*, Vietnam screamed back into the headlines in early 1975. By this point, 14 North Vietnamese divisions were racing toward Saigon, virtually unopposed. Tens of thousands of South Vietnamese troops stripped off their military uniforms, abandoned their American equipment, and fled. According to Appy, with the massive U.S. military presence gone, what had once been a brutal stalemate was now an overwhelming defeat, stunning evidence that *"nation-building"* by the U.S. military in South Vietnam had utterly failed. The longest war that the United States had waged up to that time was also the only one that had failed to achieve its objective.

Even if the U.S. could have kept communism out of South Vietnam as it did a decade earlier in Korea, the question might be asked: was this enough to justify fighting this war? Before examining this question and then applying it to other wars waged throughout history, a key point must be made. The cause(s) of a war must always be distinguished from the event(s) that trigger its start.

In Vietnam, the background cause was the Cold War. The United States was convinced that the spread of communism threatened America's long-term national security. It was President Eisenhower in the 1950s that first sent military advisors to Vietnam, and it was Ike who first coined the term, *"Domino Principle"* to justify his decision. According to Eisenhower, if nothing were done to check the spread of communism from China and/or the Soviet Union to nations like Korea, Vietnam, Laos, Cambodia, Thailand, Indonesia, Malaysia and the Philippines, it would soon proliferate as quickly as the tumbling of lined up dominoes. The situation was exacerbated in Southeast Asia because in 1954, this region had just succeeded in winning its independence from France. Now there was mounting concern that an independent Vietnam emerging from this former colony would soon become a communist nation just like its Chinese neighbor to the north.

A conference held in Geneva temporarily divided Vietnam between a communist North and a noncommunist South until elections could be held to reunify the country. A short time later, when it became evident that Ho Chi Minh and the communist government in Hanoi would clearly win a big majority, the decision was made to cancel the election. Civil war soon broke out, and the United States promptly gave financial, military and economic support to the government in the South. Even though it was wracked by corruption and inefficiency, it at least was not communist. U.S. support continued to grow in the early 1960's under the Kennedy Administration to the tune of about 17,000 "military advisors." In light of the fact that America had resisted communism in such far-flung places as Berlin, Cuba, Korea and even outer space, Vietnam was seen as just another battle in the over-arching Cold War. At the risk of an oversimplification, the cause of the Vietnam War was America's effort to stem the spread of communism. The alleged attack in the Gulf of Tonkin was the immediate trigger that began U.S. combat involvement, but it was not the real cause. In fact, in this case, it was more of a made up excuse.

The same point about distinguishing between cause(s) and actual triggers can be made about most of the wars fought throughout history. When the Athenians attempted to help Greek city-states in Asia Minor that had rebelled against the Persian Empire, the Persians used this as a pretext to invade Greece. The real cause was that the Persians simply wanted to expand their empire westward. The Romans built their enormous empire in a similar manner. One area under attack from a neighbor would invite in the Romans to render aid, but when the fighting ended, the Romans never left. Slavery, or at least the spread of slavery, served as the actual cause of the American Civil War. However, armies were not recruited and did not engage in combat until the South Carolinians, who had seceded from the Union just months before, fired upon Fort Sumter in order to drive Federal troops off *"their soil."* And probably the most notorious example of this background causes versus immediate trigger scenario was World War One.

Year after year, I have taught the same lesson as thousands of other history teachers in order to explain the reasons why the First World War was fought. By 1914, Europe had become a *"powder keg"* just waiting to be ignited by a single spark. There had not been a major war fought on European soil in 99 years, so many Europeans were almost giddy by the prospect of a war that would clear the air over a host of issues. During those years, European nations had experienced nationalism on an unprecedented scale, and this had prompted rivalries and confrontations as these countries competed with each other to acquire overseas colonies in places like Africa and Southern Asia. This rise in nationalism and imperialism then led to the creation of a system of alliances, a military arms race and a rising premium placed on militarism in general. It had reached the point in Germany that the best way for a young man to earn the respect of his father was to make a career in the military rather than in medicine or politics. By the spring of 1914, millions of young men in nations like Austria, Germany, Italy, Russia, France and Great Britain were excited by the prospects of going to war. They were convinced they would all be home by Christmas with medals pinned to their chests and great stories to tell their grandchildren. When the Archduke Franz Ferdinand, the heir to the throne of the Austro-Hungarian Empire, was assassinated in neighboring Serbia on June 28, 1914, it immediately set off a chain reaction of events that led to the outbreak of world war by August. We know today that the result was the first modern war in history with 17 million deaths and another 20 million injured, but at the time, much of the European continent was delighted. The immediate trigger for one of the deadliest wars of all time was the assassination of one man, but the real causes went much deeper.

Franz Ferdinand
Courtesy of the Library of Congress
Prints and Photographs Division
LC-DIG-ggbain-07650

With the understanding that the background causes are much more relevant to the essential question: *"When, if ever, should a nation go to war?"* an examination of these causes might be placed on a spectrum. Below is the one I have used in my classes for many years:

1. Pacificism
2. Self-Defense
3. National Security
4. Protect Allies
5. Trade & Economic Interests
6. Expansion

At the far left of the spectrum are the pacifists, the people who believe there is nothing that will ever justify going to war. While their ideas are generally predicated on strong moral convictions, most are also quick to say they would never support bending to the will of a tyrant or an oppressive dictator. Taking their stratagem from Henry David Thoreau's *Civil Disobedience* and from the teachings of Mohandas Gandhi in his drive to achieve Indian independence from British rule, they employ a method of nonviolent noncooperation. To help students better understand all of the nuances of this tactic, I usually show them the Salt March scene from the film, *Gandhi*.

The year was 1930, and Britain's Salt Acts prohibited Indians from collecting or selling salt: a necessary staple in the Indian diet. The people of India not only had to buy their salt from the British monopoly, they also had to pay a heavy tax on the mineral. Americans today tend to consume too much salt in the processed foods we eat, but in India, salt was required to live, and the Indians had no choice but to buy British-made salt and pay the tax. Defying the Salt Acts, Gandhi reasoned, would be an ingenious way for Indians to break British law nonviolently. Gandhi declared resistance to British salt policies to be the unifying theme for his new campaign of *"satyagraha"* or mass civil disobedience. On March 12, Gandhi set out from his ashram with several dozen followers on a trek of 240 miles to the coastal town of Dandi on the Arabian Sea. There, Gandhi and his supporters planned to defy British policy by making salt from seawater.

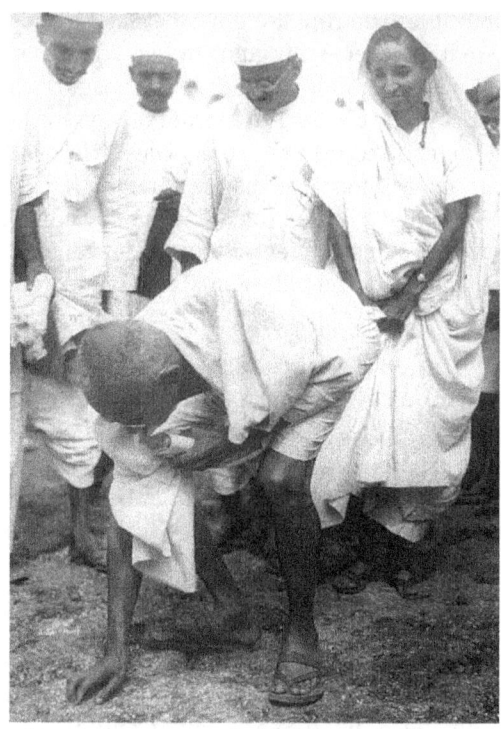

Mohandas Gandhi in 1930 Salt March
(PD-India, PD-1996)
https://commons.wikimedia.org/wiki/File:Salt_March.jpg

All along the way, Gandhi addressed large crowds, and with each passing day, an increasing number of people joined the salt satyagraha. By the time they reached Dandi on April 5, Gandhi led a crowd of tens of thousands. He spoke and led prayers and early the next morning, walked down to the sea to make salt. He had planned to work the salt flats on the beach, encrusted with crystallized sea salt at every high tide, but the police had forestalled him by crushing the salt deposits into the mud. Nevertheless, Gandhi reached down and picked up a small lump of natural salt out of the mud and British law had been defied. Thousands more followed his lead, and in the coastal cities of Bombay (now called Mumbai) and Karachi, Indian nationalists led crowds of citizens in making salt. Civil disobedience broke out all across India; soon involving millions of Indians, and British authorities arrested more than 60,000 people. Gandhi himself was arrested on May 5, but the satyagraha continued without him.

On May 21, 2,500 of the satyagraha's followers marched on the Dharasana Salt Works, some 150 miles north of Bombay. The movie does such a terrific job of building up the suspense in this scene that most students are now at the edge of their seats. Hundreds of British-led Indian policemen are standing in front of the entranceway to the Salt Works. When a line of marchers takes a step forward, they are viciously beaten. The incident, recorded by American journalist Webb Miller, prompted an international outcry against British policy in India. It would still take almost twenty more years and hundreds of additional acts of civil disobedience before the British finally agreed to leave India, but when they did, it was without any major outbreaks of violence. Most of the students usually grimace during the scene where the protesters are beaten by heavy clubs, but upon further reflection, they come to realize that casualties would probably be much heavier if a violent assault was employed. In addition, the pacifists in the class love to point out that the Indians have now occupied the higher moral ground. By refusing to use violence in the face of violence, the British are perceived as the villains and there is a great outpouring of international sympathy for the Indians and their cause. In most of my classes, the pacifism option usually has the least support initially, but their numbers tend to grow upon completion of a classroom Socratic seminar examining the question about when to go to war.

Many students who tend to share some of the same *"dovish"* values of the pacifists like option number two on the spectrum, which is the belief that we should only go to war for self-defense. The obvious question they throw at the pacifists is what should we have done the day after the Japanese bombed Pearl Harbor in December of 1941. Or better yet, should the United States just sit back and watch as the Nazis slaughtered millions of Jews and other *"undesirables"* in their Holocaust death camps? Their point is that there have been many occasions in the past where an evil form of violence can only be suppressed by the judicious use of violence. At this point, one of the more astute pacifists in class usually quotes Gandhi when he was basically asked the same question: *"Remember that all through history, there have been tyrants and murderers, and for a time, they seem invincible. But in the end, they always fall. Always."* While this point is morally compelling, the rebuttal from the self-defense advocates usually involves time. How long, they ask, did Gandhi have to wait before the British agreed to leave India? What about Dr. King's patience before civil rights legislation was finally passed? How many more Jews would have died had England and France not declared war on Germany after the Nazi invasion of Poland in 1939?

Another good opportunity to raise the point about self-defense is with the American Revolution. Assuming the rebellion against the British was justified in 1776, was open warfare also necessary? Australia, South Africa, Canada, even India managed to gradually gain their independence from Great Britain without going to war. Why not the same approach by the 13 American colonies? Besides the obvious fact that the principles of nonviolent noncooperation had not yet been formulated, the self-defense advocates generally point out that in 1776, British troops had closed Boston's harbor and were occupying a number of American cities and towns. It is for this reason that the Revolutionary War is usually cited by the defenders of self-defense along with the U.S. decision to enter World War Two after the Japanese attack on Pearl Harbor.

Related to self-defense is option number three: the principle that war is justified by the need to guard national security. This belief takes the need to protect American soil by extending it to foreign territory. After Islamic fanatics hijacked jet liners and flew them into the World Trade Center in New York City and the Pentagon on the outskirts of Washington, DC on September 11, 2001, President George W. Bush called for a war on terrorism. This soon led to an American invasion of Afghanistan with the intent to root out the Taliban for its support of Al Qaeda; the terrorists responsible for the attacks on 9/11. Shortly afterwards, President Bush then called for an attack on Iraq and its leader, Saddam Hussein; who was suspected not only of harboring terrorists, but also building weapons of mass destruction. While later evidence failed to support the reasons for invading Iraq, the overall cause remains the same. The United States felt that American national security was at stake, and a war against terrorists in the Middle East was preferable to additional carnage on U.S. soil.

September 11, 2001 attack on the World Trade Center
Courtesy of the Library of Congress Prints and Photographs Division
LC-DIG-ppmsca-02137

Since containing the spread of communism during the Cold War was also related to protecting American national security, the Vietnam War tends to fall into this same category. However, when asked about this war, most students are torn. It is easy with the advantage of hindsight to say the war in Vietnam was a costly mistake, and a slight majority of students usually take this position. However, forty years after the fall of Saigon, there are still a large percentage of students who support the American decision to go into Vietnam. Some claim the biggest problem was not the reasons for going to war, but how we chose to fight. Ever since the Korean War had provoked the communist Chinese to send in 300,000 troops that turned what could have been a quick victory into a bloody quagmire, Americans were hesitant to take any steps in Vietnam that might incite a similar response. Therefore, American ground forces never entered North Vietnam. More bombs were dropped on the communists in North Vietnam than in all of World War Two combined, and North Vietnamese harbors were mined; but U.S. troops never invaded the North. Instead, they waged a defensive war against a deeply rooted enemy in the South, and when American casualties began to mount up over the years, support at home for the war began to diminish.

Another point made by students in reference to the Vietnam War is the bigger picture that extends from the end of the Second World War to the fall of the Berlin Wall. Seen as one major battle of the larger Cold War, a number of students have pointed out that while we may have lost the *"battle"* in Vietnam, we eventually went on to win the Cold War. Their point is that support for communism in Vietnam, not to mention other spots like Cuba and Eastern Europe, proved to be so costly to the Soviet Union that there was little left in the Soviet economy for basic consumer goods. Therefore, pressure for change within Russian society gradually built up to the point that when Mikhail Gorbachev came to power in the mid 1980s and began to open the door a little for limited reform, the people came crashing through with demands that led to free elections, the breakup of the Soviet Union and the end of the Cold War. With these arguments in mind, the supporters of the U.S. decision to send combat forces into Vietnam after the alleged attack in the Gulf of Tonkin usually build a compelling set of arguments around the principle of national security.

Option four on the spectrum is relatively simple at first glance and seems to speak for itself. While the United States avoided any alliances during the 150 years of isolationism that preceded the attack on Pearl Harbor, we have entered quite a few alliances ever since. Today, America is allied with nations around the world, including places as far away as Japan, New Zealand and Australia. The Organization of American States is our primary alliance in the Western Hemisphere and NATO, the North Atlantic Treaty Organization, which includes Canada and most of the nations of Western and Southern Europe, was our most powerful military alliance during the scary days of the Cold War. The most compelling fact in regard to our allies is that as of 2015, the U.S. maintains a military presence in more than 150 countries around the world, with over 156,000 of its active-duty personnel serving outside the United States and its territories.

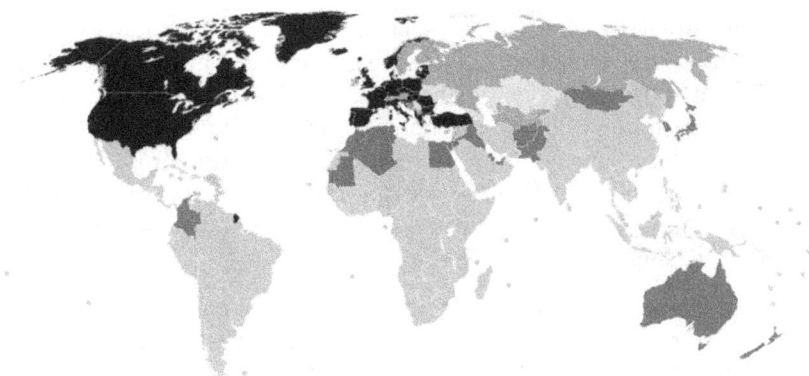

Map of NATO partnerships (countries in dark blue are NATO members)
Courtesy of NATO Cooperations Partners(CC BY-SA-3.0)
https://en.wikipedia.org/wiki/NATO#/media/File:NATO_partnerships.svg

It is usually at this point that students point out flaws in the spectrum. Rather than being able to select one point on the continuum that adequately describes their answer to the essential question about when to go to war, they point out that there may be multiple spots, and these may not be on just one side. For example, a student who maintains that we should only go to war for self-defense may say that this should extend to protecting an ally, but not necessarily fighting to guard national security by containing the spread of communism around the world. Most students agree that if the United States chooses to enter an alliance for mutual self-protection, we should honor that commitment when called to do so. However, what can further complicate the issue is how do we determine who is a legitimate ally? Did we fight in Vietnam to support our ally in the South, or was it more about protecting American national security interests on the other side of the planet?

What tend to be less complicated are the final two options on the spectrum. Option five means that we will fight to protect our trade and economic interests. Since this does not directly involve human life, most students see a clear distinction between options one through four and the other two spots on the continuum. What is more, option five tends to be the most contentious among the students from one year to the next. When students learn that the leading cause behind Congress' decision to declare war on Great Britain in 1812 was attacks by the British navy on American shipping, many say that this was a legitimate reason for going to war. This is further strengthened when they learn that some of these attacks included instances where American sailors were wrongfully accused of desertion from the British navy and were then *"impressed"* into becoming English seamen against their will. Other students then usually bring up that while this may have been a major blow to American nationalism or pride, few lives were actually lost. The United States lost over 2,200 lives in the War of 1812. Was this a price worth paying to insure freedom of the seas for American merchant ships?

The same arguments usually emerge in any discussion about the First World War. As previously stated, the Great War that began in 1914 had complex background causes, and many students say that none of these come close to justifying the loss of 17,000,000 lives. Certainly the assassination of one man does not provide a valid reason for such a horrific war. But in American History classes, students quickly learn that since the United States was pursuing its policy of isolationism and was not committed to any alliances at the time, we chose to maintain strict neutrality. In fact, President Wilson won reelection in 1916 at least partially on the platform that *"he kept us out of the war."*

However, once again, freedom of the seas became a central issue. When a German submarine sank the British passenger liner, *Lusitania*, in 1915, 128 Americans lost their lives. American demands for justice and/or vengeance were only forestalled when the Germans pledged to avoid similar acts in the future. However, the German military and economic situation became increasingly desperate by the spring of 1917. In addition, since the Russians had begun a revolution that would lead them to becoming the world's first communist nation, a treaty would soon be signed that would enable the Germans to shift all of their armies fighting on the Eastern Front to an all out assault on the West. While German troops poured into the trenches of the Western Front in France, there was no way to deal with the British Isles except by taking the gamble to resume u-boat attacks against any vessel entering or leaving a British port. This meant the resumption of submarine torpedo attacks on American shipping. There were other causes too; including the interception of the Zimmerman Telegram suggesting that Mexico could win back land lost in 1848 by joining the German side if and when the U.S. entered the war. German submarine attacks were the leading reason why President Wilson was able to convince Congress to declare war on Germany in April of 1917.

So once again, the question can be raised, does the interference with trade rights justify a war? The American economy might have been dealt a multi-billion dollar blow by avoiding trade with the British and the French, and certainly, it would have been an insult to our pride at a time when nationalism was at an all-time high around the planet. On the other hand, 116,000 Americans lost their lives in the 18 months that the United States was engaged in the First World War. When lives have to be balanced with money, one might expect that most students would choose to avoid any war fought over trade or economic interests. However, that is not the case. This became glaringly obvious during the 1990-1991 school year.

Saddam Hussein and the nation of Iraq had just invaded the neighboring country of Kuwait and were threatening to possibly take over other oil-rich nations encircling the Persian Gulf. President George Herbert Walker Bush worked with the United Nations and pursued a number of diplomatic options before sending in the military, but many Americans at the time did not buy the argument that this war was being fought to liberate an ally. If left unchecked, the Iraqis might threaten much of the world's oil supply, which could then wreck havoc on the American economy, and that of most of our western allies. On the *"going to war"* spectrum, Operation Desert Storm should clearly be matched with option number five: protecting economic interests. However, at the time, most of my students were caught up in the patriotic fervor sweeping the nation, and only a handful were opposed to this war. The fact that the war proved to be a quick and easy victory and at least a short-term success only helped to validate the decision to fight in the Persian Gulf War. Some students indicated that the war even gave a genuine boost to American morale following our loss in Vietnam. What I took from this recent period of history is that there were still plenty of Americans who were happy to go to war to protect trade and economic interests.

M-1A1 Abrams tank during maneuvers in Operation Desert Storm
Courtesy of the US government, Defense Imagery (PD-US Gov)
https://commons.wikimedia.org/wiki/File:Tank_in_Desert_Storm.JPEG

The spot on the spectrum that typically receives the least support from most students is option number six: expansion. How can Americans fight, kill and even die for the purpose of taking land that does not belong to us? A quick survey of American History, however, shows that most of the land that now makes up our nation was acquired directly or indirectly by aggressive wars of expansion. The Revolutionary War, for example, did not just turn 13 English colonies into 13 independent states. The Treaty of Paris ending the war in 1783 provided the new nation with all of the land extending to the Mississippi River. It would take several more wars in the ensuing years against a number of indigenous tribes, including the Creek, the Sauk and the Seminoles, before the land was cleared for American settlement. The Mexican-American War brought in all of the acreage between Texas and the Pacific Ocean, and once again, wars with indigenous tribes were waged to secure the Mexican Cession as well as the remainder of the American West. While the Spanish-American War was ostensibly fought to liberate Cuba, the end result was the American flag flying over the Philippines, Puerto Rico and Guam. When discussing these examples, the majority of my students have always expressed a high degree of moral indignation. When students are asked whether any of this land that helped build our nation should be returned to its original owners, most of them just smile and shake their heads no.

At the present, one of the greatest threats to peace and security in the Middle East, and even around the world, is the Islamic State of Iraq and

Syria, commonly known as ISIS. This group of Islamic extremists has currently built a quasi-state on huge tracts of land extending into Iraq and Syria, particularly since both nations have been plagued by bloody civil wars in recent years. Headlines and videos appear on a regular basis showing the most recent beheadings and acts of terrorism committed by this organization allegedly in the name of Allah. The result is even greater instability in an unstable part of the world, the creation of hundreds of thousands of homeless refugees and another significant threat in the ongoing war against terrorism. Most Americans would agree that something should be done to stop ISIS - but what? Under President Obama, U.S. military efforts have been limited to air strikes combined with financial and military aid to the Syrian, Iraqi and Kurdish forces engaged in combat with ISIS. Should we do more? For the first time, a CBS News poll taken in February of 2015 indicated that a majority of Americans, 57%, were in favor of the U.S. sending ground troops into Iraq and Syria to fight ISIS.

In order to make the decision about going to war in a tough situation like this, a useful determinant has been provided by Richard N. Haass, president of the Council on Foreign Relations and author of *War of Necessity, War of Choice: A Memoir of Two Iraq Wars*. As the title of his book suggests, there are two types of war. The first is the war that is *"justifiable,"* which Haass defines as "a *war of necessity, ... one in which the most vital interests of a country are threatened and where there are no promising alternatives to using force."* These include wars of self-defense, such as World War Two. The other type of war is a war of *"choice,"* which according to Haass, can also be justifiable. By definition, wars of choice *"tend to involve less than vital interests and the existence of alternative policies."* He states that Vietnam was clearly a war of choice, as was the second Iraq war begun in 2003. What is to be determined in the future is what type of war is presented by the threat of ISIS. As their acts of terrorism amass and as other diplomatic options are exhausted, the United States may have to accept that a line has been crossed and that American troops in Syria, Iraq or Libya may have to become part of a *"justifiable war."*

For now, both liberals and conservatives have come up with arguments for why ISIS requires America to engage in a justifiable war. Some liberals would like to help those threatened by such an *"evil"* force, and some conservatives would like to strengthen American national security interests in such a volatile part of the world. However, this is not just a foreign policy decision. Sending in American ground troops means going to war. It means financial costs, the loss of life and some serious moral implications. It is easy to check off *"yes"* on a survey question asking if the United States should put American soldiers on the ground to fight against a morally repugnant force like ISIS. However, as an educator, I wonder how many of those counted as part of the 57% have been asked to examine the broader question of when, if ever, our nation should go to war. Of all the essential questions discussed in my classes over the years, this is the one that usually hits a nerve on a personal level. After all, if the United States were to go to war in the future against ISIS or any other potential enemy, the students sitting in my classes would be the ones most likely asked to do the fighting. Considering these kids will be the ones asked to make the *"ultimate sacrifice"* for their nation, I am constantly reminded how important it is that everyone possess a thorough understanding of the question of when, if ever, the United States should go to war.

Suggested Reading:

Appy, Christian G. *American Reckoning: The Vietnam War and Our National Identity.* New York: Penguin Press, 2015.

Dutton, Sarah, Jennifer De Pinto, Anthony Salvanto, and Fred Backus. "Do Americans want to send ground troops to fight ISIS?" *CBS News.* February 19, 2015. http://www.cbsnews.com/news/do-americans-want-to-send-ground-troops-to-fight-isis/.

Gandhi, Mahatma. *The Essential Gandhi: An Anthology of His Writings on His Life, Work, and Ideas,* Edited by Louis Fischer. New York: Vintage, 1983.

Haass, Richard. *War of Necessity, War of Choice: A Memoir of Two Iraq Wars.* New York: Simon and Schuster, 2009.

Karnow, Stanley. *Vietnam: A History.* New York: Viking, 1983.

Porter, Gareth. *Perils of Dominance: Imbalance of Power and the Road to War in Vietnam.* Berkeley: University of California Press, 2006.

Rohn, Alan. "How Much Did the Vietnam War Cost?" *Vietnam War.* January 22, 2014. http://www.thevietnamwar.info/how-much-vietnam-war-cost/.

Thoreau, Henry David. *Civil Disobedience, Solitude and Life Without Principle.* Amherst: Prometheus Books, 1998.

Tuchman, Barbara W. *The Guns of August.* New York: Presido Press, 1962.

Chapter 13
Taking off the gloves

Unidentified bodies near burning house in My Lai, Vietnam   March 16, 1968
Courtesy of Ronald Haeberle (PD-US Gov)
https://commons.wikimedia.org/wiki/File:MyLai_Haeberle_P33_BodiesNearBurningHouse.jpg

What limits, if any, should be followed in times of war?

The place is small hamlet in South Vietnam called My Lai and the date is March 16, 1968. It is not quite 7:30 in the morning, and the village is just waking up to the usual sounds of birds and insects. Breakfast is being prepared while the residents of the village are gearing up for another ordinary day. The only unique feature of My Lai is the apparent lack of young men. Most of the people visible to the naked eye are women, children and elders.

The quiet sounds of nature are suddenly disturbed by the distant noise of rotor blades. American helicopters can be seen on the horizon and soon, the village is in an immediate state of hysterical pandemonium. The choppers land in a clearing just beyond the huts and American soldiers dressed in their khaki fatigues leap out ready to fire their M16s. They see an old man across the clearing carrying a cane. Mistaking him for the enemy and believing his cane to be a weapon, they fire, instantly ending his life. They then proceed to enter the village.

Accounts of what happened next are still in dispute, but this much is clear. By the end of four hours, My Lai has been burned to the ground, the rice has been destroyed and the livestock slaughtered. A number of women have been raped and up to 500 of the Vietnamese people who lived in or around the village are dead. Pictures taken that day, and later sold to Life Magazine, show piles of corpses where women and children as young as two years of age have been assembled and executed. One young woman, after being sexually assaulted, has had her body ripped open by a knife or a bayonet from her vagina up to her neck.

Among the Americans, there is just one casualty: a soldier accidentally shot himself in the foot. Otherwise, there is no clear evidence that the Americans ever encountered any hostile opposition. By nightfall, the U.S. soldiers have returned to base, and the body count for the day is recorded as another American victory. It would take over a year for the story of what had happened that day in My Lai to leak out, and when it did, it eventually led to one of the most controversial trials in recent American history. The defendant was a lieutenant by the name of William Calley. For much of my teaching career, I have ended the school year by having the U.S. History classes conduct a mock trial of the events that occurred that day at My Lai.

Most of the students initially believe the case strongly favors the prosecution. After all, there are plenty of survivors who can serve as eye witnesses, there are the pictures taken by staff photographer Ronald Haeberle and there is plenty of circumstantial evidence leaving little doubt that Calley and his men did not kill anyone that day in the "*heat of battle.*" Further investigation, however, provides a case for the defense.

First of all, Calley is not a *"criminal"* in the usual sense of the term. He had no criminal record back in the states, and unlike many other Americans who fought in Vietnam, he did not wait to get drafted, he enlisted. Second, military intelligence had indicated that My Lai was part of a Viet Cong "*hot zone,*" and that any of its residents should be considered hostile. After all, the Viet Cong (the V.C.) were known to use guerilla tactics, including land mines, booby traps and ambushes. They did not wear uniforms and frequently included women, children and older people. Calley had only been in Vietnam a few months but his unit had already suffered casualties at their hands. To Calley and the men under his command, the residents of My Lai may appear to be harmless civilians, but in actuality, they were either V.C. or were at least V.C. sympathizers. This would help to explain the lack of young men in the village that day. In Calley's view, the men, all members of the Viet Cong, had fled into the jungle upon hearing the sound of the choppers that morning leaving behind *"civilians"* they thought would be safe.

A third part of Lieutenant Calley's defense was that he was just following orders. He claimed he received these orders from his superior, Captain Ernest Medina just the day before telling him to *"leave no one left alive in My Lai."* However, the orders were not in writing, and there is some dispute over their wording. In addition, while the Uniform Code of Military Justice states that a soldier can be convicted for the crime of failing to obey an order, the Code explicitly states that this is only for the failure *"to obey any **lawful** general order or regulation."* Obeying orders did not work as a defense by the Nazis in the Nuremberg Trials after World War Two and it would be problematic in the court marshal trial of William Calley.

That leaves just one other defense used every year by the students, and for the purposes of this essential question regarding the rules of warfare, it is arguably the most relevant. Killing unarmed civilians may be cold-blooded murder under normal circumstances, but in times of war, a case can be made that the rules are different; in fact, there may not be any rules at all. The defense usually points out that the Viet Cong did not play by the rules, that they frequently tortured and/or killed any civilians thought to be sympathetic to the South Vietnamese government or to the Americans. If one side follows the rules of warfare while the other does not, those following the rules put themselves at an enormous disadvantage. They argue that in the second half of the 20th Century, combatants do what they have to in order to achieve victory. In modern warfare, there are no rules.

Richard N. Haass, mentioned in the previous chapter as the president of the Council on Foreign Relations, states that the subject of war involves two critical issues: the decision to go to war (jus ad bellum) and the decision on how to fight one (jus in bello). In addition, this latter question focuses on three criteria: proportionality (how much force should be used), targeting (avoiding non-combatants), and means (avoiding certain classes of weapons). While the trial of Lieutenant William Calley primarily involves the second standard, the other two are relevant. Haass provides a useful tool to apply to this case as well as any other conflict when addressing the essential question regarding the limits that should be followed.

In his real trial, Calley was convicted and received a life sentence. However, it should be noted that after serving just three years under house arrest, Richard Nixon released him with a presidential pardon. Nixon was concerned that since no one else was ever convicted of a crime for the events that occurred in My Lai, Calley had unfairly been made a scapegoat. For the students, however, the My Lai mock trial is still relevant today, particularly in light of the recent conflicts in Afghanistan and Iraq. The mock trial experience has proven to be a terrific jumping off point into a closer examination of the larger essential question.

A practical consideration with this essential question is how can rules governing warfare be properly enforced. If one side violates the acceptable rules, there are only two ways to bring justice. One is for the victor to bring the loser to trial. While the Allies in the Second World War brought numerous Germans and Japanese to trial upon the war's end, there was not a single American, Englishman or Soviet soldier ever tried by an international court. The other is for a nation to enforce the rules upon its own combatants. This is why prosecuting teams in mock trials conducted by students have two options available to them when it comes time to press charges. At the international level, there are the Nuremberg Principles, which provides definitions for *"War Crimes"*, *"Crimes Against Peace"* and *"Crimes Against Humanity."* For the United States, which purports to follow rules during times of war, there is The Uniform Code of Military Justice. Murder, for example, is defined by this code as *"unlawfully killing a human being without justification or excuse."* While this sounds simple, one could drive a Mack truck through the loophole *"without justification or excuse."*

Probably because of the enforcement problems, rules governing warfare are relatively recent. The Enlightenment of the 17th and 18th Centuries attempted to apply reason to almost everything, including warfare. This soon evolved into an age where soldiers fought like *"gentlemen."* They proudly wore brightly colored uniforms and marched out in the open under brightly colored flags and banners. Music in the forms of drums, fifes and bagpipes added to the pageantry. Military conscription did not yet exist, so forcing someone to fight against his will was not an issue. Weapons were primarily limited to sabers, muskets and cannons; torture was seldom used and the rights of prisoners were generally respected. Victory was secured when the losing general turned over his sword to his opponent. Even though the number of casualties grew exponentially during the Napoleonic

Wars as well as the American Civil War, this was primarily due the use of the draft, more sophisticated weaponry and the primitive medical procedures still in use. After all, most historians generally recognize the end of the Civil War by the gentlemanly act of Robert E. Lee gallantly turning over his sword to Ulysses Grant at Appomattox Court House in April of 1865.

If there is one axiom about war that has been consistently true, however, it is that if one side develops a new weapon that will help to achieve victory, no matter how deadly, it will always be used. The Industrial Revolution that was roaring across nations like Great Britain, the United States, France, Germany, Italy and Japan by the late 19th Century brought a host of these new weapons. Some, like the hand-cranked Gatling machine gun and the submarine, had already been put to limited use, but they would hit their apex in the First World War. Much of the world frowned upon the submarine and its malevolent torpedoes as a cowardly way to conduct naval warfare, but when faced with the enormous British navy and its huge battleships, the Germans did not hesitate to use them. The Wright Brothers had just achieved their first successful flight at Kitty Hawk 11 years before the start of the war, but by war's end, each side had hundreds of airplanes engaged in aerial combat and dropping bombs on enemy trenches. Both sides even made use of poisonous gas, and while this might appear to be a form of chemical warfare by today's standards, the only real reason why this practice did not continue into the next world war was the fear that changes in wind patterns might turn the deadly chlorine into friendly fire. By far, the deadliest weapon that dominated the battlefields of World War One was the machine gun, a direct byproduct of the Industrial Revolution. If new inventions and technology meant a faster and more efficient way to produce goods, the machine gun applied this same principle to the killing of people. The use of each of these new weapons stirred up dissent from the purveyors of the rules to govern warfare, but they soon became accepted by all sides.

Vickers machine gun crew, July 1916
Courtesy of John Warwick Brooke and the collections of the Imperial War Museums
(PD-UKGov)
https://commons.wikimedia.org/wiki/File:Vickers_machine_gun_crew_with_gas_masks.jpg

After witnessing the horrors of trench warfare in the First World War, the nations recoiled a bit and began to write treaties that would place stricter rules on how war was to be conducted. Limits were placed on the use of airplanes, particularly over civilian targets, and navies were regulated in the number of battleships that could be built. The Versailles Treaty ending the war prohibited the Germans from constructing submarines, and at one point, a ridiculous treaty was even signed intended to outlaw the use of war altogether. While these treaties and conventions were well intentioned, the dawn of an even deadlier world war by the late 1930s immediately demonstrated their impracticality. Estimates of the number of people killed in the Second World War run over 60 million people, which was about 3% if the 1940 world population.

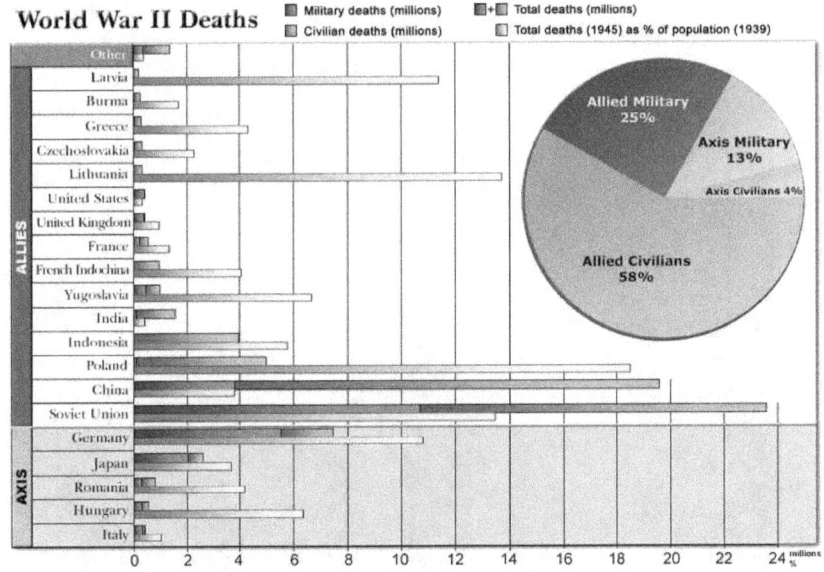

World War II casualties by country
Courtesy of Dennis Nilsson (PD-self)
https://commons.wikimedia.org/wiki/File:WorldWarII-DeathsByCountry-Bar-chart.png

The first to test the boundaries of these new agreements were the Italians and Germans in their support of Francisco Franco during the Spanish Civil War. This brutal conflict, waged between 1936 and 1939, pitted the Republicans, supported by the Soviet Union and other liberal factions, against the Fascists, propped up by Benito Mussolini and Adolph Hitler. In a number of respects, the Spanish Civil War was a sneak preview for the horrific global conflict that would start just a few years later. Ernest Hemingway popularized the Spanish Civil War in his novel, *From Whom the Bell Tolls*, which portrayed the guerilla tactics employed by the Republicans. On the flip side, Pablo Picasso used his art to make a strong anti-war statement against the indiscriminate air bombing of the Spanish village of Guernica, a civilian target. Despite the modern abstract style, the painting undoubtedly depicts the horror of the populace as bombs rain down from above and took the lives of hundreds of noncombatants. The civil war in Spain clearly demonstrated the naïveté of those who had recently negotiated the international treaties attempting to set limits on modern warfare. Franco ended up winning the Spanish Civil War and then ironically kept his country neutral during World War Two. The actual fighting in Spain, however, provided a glimpse of things to come.

Bombing of Guernica 1937
Courtesy of the German Federal Archives (CC BY-SA-3.0-DE)
https://commons.wikimedia.org/wiki/File:Bundesarchiv_Bild_183-H25224,_Guernica,_Ruinen.jpg

It is difficult to pinpoint exactly when the Second World War began. Was it as early as 1931 when Japanese forces invaded and captured Manchuria from the Chinese? Or was it 1937 when China itself became the target of Japanese aggression? How about 1935 when Mussolini's Italy assaulted Ethiopia? Or possibly it was in March of 1939 when Nazi forces occupied the remainder of Czechoslovakia not already claimed as a result of the British and French attempt to appease Hitler in Munich the previous year. Most historians maintain the war became a legitimate world war on September 1, 1939 when the Nazis invaded Poland, leading to a formal declaration of war by France and Great Britain. Regardless of the official start, there is no denying that the rules of warfare were quickly thrown out the window as the Axis nations unleashed blitzkrieg upon their neighboring targets.

Japan's occupation of Chinese coastal cities included the horrifying Rape of Nanking, a six week period when Japanese troops committed acts of mass rape and looting as well as the massacre of at least 200,000 Chinese civilians. To the shock of the world, the German invasion of Poland, which included rapid troop movements, Panzer tank divisions, and the use of dive-bombers, was completed in less than six weeks. The following spring, Hitler's blitzkrieg ignored the neutral rights of Belgium, the Netherlands, Luxembourg, Denmark and Norway as he sought to gain naval ports for his submarines and a backdoor into France. By June, the Fuhrer was dancing a jig in the shadow of the Eiffel Tower in celebration of his capture of Paris, something the Germans had failed to accomplish during the entire First World War. The British Expeditionary Force miraculously escaped a complete defeat by the Nazi onslaught at Dunkirk. Given that the United Kingdom was an island nation protected by a powerful navy, Hitler was forced to unleash another type of unprecedented warfare.

In the early days of the Battle of Britain, Hitler's air force, the Luftwaffe, mostly targeted military and industrial sites. However, as the British Royal Air Force began to put up a valiant defense, Nazi airplanes turned the Blitz into an attack on civilian homes, mostly under the cover of darkness. Every night, the air raid sirens would scream while thousands of civilians scurried into the subway tunnels and other underground bunkers where they would spend the night wondering what would be left of their homes in the morning. Children were sent north for their protection, but the remainder of the population suffered through a form of warfare unlike anything the world had ever seen. It is estimated that during the Blitz, 32,000 civilians were killed and 87,000 were seriously injured. Two million houses, 60 per cent of London, were destroyed. The human suffering endured in the Battle of Britain was still fresh in the minds of English pilots when they dropped their firebombs on German cities just a few years later.

Birmingham, England Blitz 1940
Courtesy of Ministry of Information Photo Division Photographer (PD-UKGov)
https://commons.wikimedia.org/wiki/File:Birmingham_Blitz_D_4126.jpg

The gloves had come off and this was just the start. In the summer of 1941, Nazi divisions attacked the Soviet Union without any warning. The three and half million troops employed made up the largest invasion force the world had ever seen. Crack units of the SS followed in the wake of the regular German army, effectively removing 20,000 Russian villages off the map. Since Hitler's concept of lebensraum meant the superior German master race needed more *"living space,"* the inferior Slavic people were in the way and had to be removed. Millions were used for slave labor and the rest were mass murdered. In many cases, the residents of a village were rounded up in the town square and then machine gunned. In others, Soviet civilians were gassed in the same chambers used for the Jews in the concentration camps. It is estimated that somewhere between 20 and 22 million Russians died in World War Two and the vast majority were civilians. This was over 10 per cent of the population.

Behind the lines, Hitler and the Nazis wrestled with another problem. What was the fastest and most efficient way to eliminate the millions of Jews, Gypsies, homosexuals and other undesirables that Hitler wanted removed in order to purify the master race? Bullets and exhaust fumes from trucks had all been used, but this had proven to be too slow and too costly. The Wannsee Conference was held in 1941 to take up this issue, and after several days of elaborate planning by Nazi officials dressed in full uniform, dining on the finest foods and wines, what resulted was the *"Final Solution."* Six enormous death camps were to be constructed, all located in Poland. Chelmno, Belzec, Treblinka, Sobibor, Auschwitz-Birkenau, and Majdanek were all constructed to take the lives of up to another 12 millions people. Trains bearing cattle cars would bring the undesirables from all over Nazi-occupied Europe to these six camps where showers sprayed poisonous Zyklon B gas in place of water. After about 30 minutes, slave labor carted off the bodies to be cremated in massive ovens, which in many cases, ran 24 hours a day, seven days a week. This was the Nazi Holocaust, and to this day, nothing before or since has surpassed the criminality of this form of limitless warfare.

Gatehouse at Auschwitz 1945
Courtesy of the German Federal Archives
Bundesarchiv, B 285 Bild-04413 / Stanislaw Mucha / CC-BY-SA 3.0
https://commons.wikimedia.org/wiki/File:Bundesarchiv_Bild_175-
04413,_KZ_Auschwitz,_Einfahrt.jpg

Unrestrained acts of warfare were not limited just to the Axis powers. As the British and Americans turned the tide of battle against the Germans by 1943, bombs began to fall on German cities. As previously stated, British consciences were not too troubled since German bombs had continued to fall on their cities. The Americans, however, were a different story. Maintaining their neutrality up until the Japanese attack on Pearl Harbor near the end of 1941, the United States had constantly admonished the warring powers to respect the rights and lives of civilian noncombatants. While British bombers dropped their payload on German cities under the cover of night, the Americans suffered much higher casualties by clinging to the idea that daytime raids would allow more accuracy in the effort to hit military and industrial targets, thereby avoiding the loss of civilian life. This heavy loss of the American flyers, however, could only last so long. In four raids between February 13 and February 15, 722 heavy bombers of the British Royal Air Force and 527 American bombers dropped more than 3,900 tons of high-explosive bombs and incendiary devices on the German city of Dresden. The bombing and the resulting firestorm destroyed over 1,600 acres of the city center and killed approximately 25,000 civilians. For every nation, including the United States, the rules of warfare had quickly disappeared.

39th Bombardment Group dropping high-explosive bombs over Japan
Courtesy of the United States Army Air Force (PD-USGov-Military-Air Force)
https://commons.wikimedia.org/wiki/File:39th_Bombardment_Group_B-29_Superfortress.jpg

As the war came to its conclusion, the Japanese would suffer a far worse fate. Many Americans believed this was payback for the surprise attack on Pearl Harbor, which at the time, was a clear violation of the acceptable rules of warfare. It has also been suggested that American racism toward the Japanese played a role. After all, Japanese Americans were forced into internment camps during the war, something not experienced by German or Italian Americans. In his July 25, 1945 diary entry, as President Truman was writing about the atomic bomb, he referred to the *"Japs"* as *"savages, ruthless, merciless and fanatic."* After Hiroshima and Nagasaki had been leveled a few weeks later, Truman wrote in a letter that, *"When you have to deal with a beast you have to treat him as a beast."*

Regardless of the motives, the fire bombing of Japanese cities took up to a million civilian lives. In a single night, March 9, 1945, U.S. warplanes dropped 2,000 tons of incendiary bombs on Tokyo, a city built largely out of flammable wood and paper. Over the next 48 hours, almost 16 square miles in and around the Japanese capital were destroyed, and between 80,000 and 130,000 Japanese civilians were incinerated in the worst single firestorm in recorded history.

Despite the fact that the Japanese army, navy and air force were all but destroyed by the early summer of 1945, Japan still refused to surrender. In fact, the Japanese continued to fight on with a fanatical fury that even included the use of suicidal kamikaze airplanes that flew into the decks of American warships. It was under these circumstances that President Harry Truman, who had just taken over in April after Franklin Roosevelt had suffered a fatal stroke, was confronted with a decision that has been the subject of a raging debate ever since.

The idea to build an atomic bomb stemmed from revolutionary developments that had been fomenting in the world of physics since before the turn of the century. However, it should be noted that much of the motivation behind Albert Einstein's letter to President Franklin Roosevelt suggesting a massive undertaking to build a nuclear weapon originated from the fear that the United States could not allow Hitler and the Nazis to build a bomb first. In other words, America should construct a nightmarish weapon that clearly violated the acceptable international rules of warfare before the other side could beat us to the punch. This is why Leo Szilard and some of the other scientists who participated in the Manhattan Project signed a petition asking President Truman not to use the atomic bomb against Japan after the German threat to build a nuclear device had been removed with the surrender of the Nazis in May of 1945.

From all accounts, President Truman never gave the petition or the idea of not using the atomic bomb much consideration. By the time he received word that the bomb had been successfully tested in the New Mexico desert that July, he was more than ready to use it in order to bring a speedy end to the war in the Pacific. After all, his military experts had already predicted that an invasion of Japan would cost the United States and its allies between half million and a million casualties. Two billion dollars had been spent on the Manhattan Project, and there was no way Harry Truman could ever look any wife or mother in the eye and explain why her husband or son had died in an invasion of the Japanese islands while the president sat on a two billion dollar investment that could already have ended the war. In addition, Joseph Stalin was about to honor his promise to declare war on Japan, and after seeing how communism was spreading to the nations newly "*liberated*" by the Red Army in Eastern Europe, President Truman wanted to minimize that same opportunity in Asia. Other options, like a demonstration of the bomb on a deserted island or a negotiated settlement were never considered.

Panoramic view of Hiroshima after the bomb
Courtesy of the Library of Congress, Prints and Photographs Division
LC-USZ62-134192

As a result, on August 6, 1945, the world entered the Nuclear Age. At approximately 12:15 local time, an atomic bomb detonated several hundred feet above ground zero in the Japanese city of Hiroshima. Most of the victims were civilians and the lucky ones simply vaporized. Those further away faced horrible deaths that resulted from the blast, from burns or from radiation poisoning. The Japanese were too dazed by what had hit them to communicate anything that resembled a willingness to surrender, so three days later, a second atomic bomb leveled the city of Nagasaki. Within the first two to four months of the bombings, the acute effects of the atomic blasts killed 90,000 to 146,000 people in Hiroshima and 39,000 to 80,000 in Nagasaki; roughly half the deaths in each city occurred on the first day. The people of a third Japanese city, Kokura, understand the arbitrary nature of this new kind of warfare probably better than most others. The American bomber, the *Enola Gay*, that dropped the bomb on Hiroshima, had Kokura as a secondary target, but since there was no cloud cover over Hiroshima on August 6, Kokura was spared. Three days later, when Kokura had become the primary target, cloud cover blanketed the city, so the American B-29, the *Bockscar*, turned towards the city of Nagasaki. Kokura was spared for the second time in three days. The question of life or death for thousands of civilians came down to the weather.

Needless to say, the debate over President Truman's decision raises the essential question over the limits to fighting a war just as effectively as the killings by Lieutenant Calley in My Lai. While classes in the past have placed Truman on trial for charges such as "*War Crimes*" and "*Crimes Against Humanity*", Truman's rising popularity over the past several years makes this decision a tough case to prosecute. Therefore, a simple debate over the decision has proven to be been more effective. A good resource to use for this activity is a website called *The Authentic History Center* put out by Michael Barnes, a high school American history teacher from West Michigan. The site is based on primary sources from American popular culture and includes a series of pages on the decision to drop the atomic bomb. Here, students can find well-developed positions on both sides of the issue. Arguments against Truman's decision include "*the bomb was for defense only,*" "*the bomb was illegal,*" "*there were alternatives to the use of the bomb,*" "*the bomb was used more to scare Russia than to defeat Japan*" and "*the bomb was inhumane.*" In defense of President Truman, the site argues "*the bomb saved lives,*" "*the decision was made by a committee of shared responsibility,*" "*the Japanese were given fair warning,*" "*the atomic bomb was in retaliation for Japanese barbarism*" and "*Truman inherited the war policy of bombing cities.*"

Since 1945, the small number of atomic weapons has grown into a mammoth arsenal of thousands of hydrogen super bombs. Most can be delivered within minutes by intercontinental ballistic missiles. In theory, one nuclear submarine in the American or Russian navy can annihilate over 200 cities. Whether life as we know it could survive a full-scale nuclear war is open to some debate since the death and destruction that would occur is purely theoretical. Hiroshima and Nagasaki are the only two population centers ever targeted by nuclear weapons, and the two bombs that fell on those cities are puny in comparison to today's super bombs. So why is it that these weapons of mass destruction have not been used over the past 70 years? Is it because to do so would clearly violate the acceptable rules of warfare? There have been a number of treaties governing the use of nuclear weapons. After the Cuban Missile Crisis almost pushed the world beyond the brink of nuclear Armageddon in 1962, treaties were signed to ban above ground testing of atomic weapons as well as to prevent the proliferation of these weapons to countries that did not already possess the technology to build them. Further treaties were signed in the 1970s and 1980s to significantly reduce the stockpile of nuclear weapons. However, at the risk of stating the obvious, the primary reason why nuclear bombs have not fallen is because to start a nuclear war would be suicidal. A first strike by the United States on the Soviet Union or vice versa would lead to a deadly counterstrike. This primal fear was depicted in a number of Cold War films like *Fail Safe*, *Dr. Strangelove*, *War Games* and *The Day After*, all of which I have used in some form or other in my classroom. The same factor has also prevented a more limited nuclear war in other parts of the world, such as between India and Pakistan. The reality is that nuclear war in the world today has been prevented mostly by fear, not out of respect for the rules governing warfare.

While the only nuclear explosions over populated cities occurred in the remaining days of World War Two, there have been a host of wars fought since then with conventional weapons. Therefore, the essential question about what limits, if any, should be followed in times of war has not lost its relevance. When presented to my classes, the first step has been to pose a simple question with just two possible answers: rules or no rules? There are always some students who argue that attempting to implement or follow rules during times of war is futile. According to them, people die in war, so what is the point in attempting to follow rules? Does it really matter whether the casualties were wearing uniforms or what type of weapon ended their lives? Besides, rules in war can never be effectively enforced, and if one side attempts to follow them, it will only put its soldiers at a major disadvantage.

The majority of students in most classes support the position that we should still follow rules during times of war, so the next question is what rules? Many argue that weapons of mass destruction like nuclear missiles and biological and chemical armaments should be prohibited. Too many innocent bystanders and noncombatants will be killed or hurt, and there will be irreversible damage done to the environment. Carried further into a slippery slope argument, the use of these weapons could also take us down the path towards the end of all human life, so there is usually little disagreement over the need to respect this rule.

The next rule usually leads to some lively discussion. What about respecting the rights of a neutral country? At first glance, the Japanese attack on Pearl Harbor clearly violated this rule. Therefore, Pearl Harbor is frequently cited as an argument to support President Truman's decision to bomb Hiroshima. When the shoe is placed on the other foot, however, some of these students struggle with the question of neutrality. Take the case of Cambodia. In 1969, Cambodia was a small neutral nation that happened to share a border with Vietnam. After learning the Viet Cong had bases in Cambodia that were being used to launch attacks on U.S. forces in South Vietnam, President Nixon ordered the secret bombings of those sites. He later sent in ground forces into what had publicly been proclaimed to be a neutral country. When news leaked about Cambodia, there were protests on college campuses across the nation; at one, Kent State University in Ohio, National Guard bullets killed four students.

For years, I have also had classes conduct mock trials based on President Nixon's actions in Cambodia. There are a number of issues that emerge from these trials, including an examination of achieving short-term goals versus accepting the long- term effects of our actions. However, the main issue of this trial has always centered on the question of neutrality. In the end, it comes down to how neutrality should be defined. A simple definition is *"the state of not supporting or helping either side in a conflict."* Was Cambodia helping the communists by tolerating Viet Cong bases in their nation? On the other hand, could the attempt to drive out the V.C. be considered a step towards helping the South Vietnamese or the Americans? More often than not, when one nation violates the neutral rights of another, there will always be claims that the neutral country was not really neutral.

Nixon announcing attack on Cambodia April 30, 1970
Courtesy of Jack E. Kightlinger, National Archives and Records Administration (PD-USGov)
https://commons.wikimedia.org/wiki/File:NixononCambodia.jpg

As might be expected, the most important rule that gets batted around during these discussions involves civilians. There are a large number of students who consistently argue that warring nations should avoid the loss of life for women, children, senior citizens and other noncombatants. These are the people who are not fighting on the front lines, they are not attempting to hurt or kill anyone, and they probably had no say in starting the war. Cities should not be bombed, blockades should not be enforced that might starve the masses, and nothing should be done to endanger a nation's water supply or sanitation facilities. The problem with this position again involves a definition. How should one define a "*civilian*?" Modern warfare usually requires the effort of every person. Propaganda is generally issued to mobilize complete support for a nation's war effort, including asking each individual to provide money, work in armaments factories and endure a host of shortages resulting from the shift of economic resources towards the effort to win the war. Therefore, an attack on the enemy's civilian population will reduce its capacity to wage a long-term war. Where exactly should the line be drawn between civilians and actual combatants?

There is one final rule that engenders much debate in the classroom sessions taking up the question over the limits on waging war. What about prisoners? In most wars, there have been rules governing the treatment of prisoners of war. They should be properly fed, clothed and housed, and they should receive appropriate medical attention. Most important, and at times most controversial, they must not be tortured. Back in 1865, Henry Wirz, the commander of the Confederate prisoner-of-war prison, Andersonville, was executed for the treatment of northern prisoners. The same punishment was dispensed to German and Japanese prisoner-of-war camp commanders after the Second World War. Students frequently point out that we have a moral obligation to observe this rule, even if American prisoners are being abused. After all, we are supposed to be "*the good guys,*" we do not want to sink to the level of our enemies. However, even if one accepts this line of thought, there is a complicating factor.

What if the torture of a captured prisoner will lead to information that will prevent the loss of American life? According to the Cybercast News Service (CNS), the CIA recently learned facts as a result of water boarding that prevented a deadly attack on Los Angeles. While CNS is clearly a conservative news source, the sheer possibility that this story could be true lends itself to a deeper understanding of this issue. CNS maintains the CIA used "*enhance techniques*" of interrogation on al Qaeda leader Khalid Sheik Mohammed that caused him to reveal information that allowed the U.S. government to thwart a planned attack on the city of Los Angeles. The alleged attack, called the "*Second Wave*", planned to use East Asian operatives to crash a hijacked airliner into a building in Los Angeles.

This story may or may not be true, but for the sake of argument, lets assume it is. The effectiveness of torture as a means to gain useful information is in itself an issue, but once again, for the sake of argument, lets assume the information was revealed only through the use of the water boarding and that it saved American lives. If preventing the loss of life can be used to justify torture in this one case, does that legitimize its use in similar cases in the future?

Within every essential question, which by definition does not have a single answer that will garner universal agreement, there are a host of other related questions. Some of these are pleasurable to discuss; others raise blistering arguments that can potentially end friendships. Nevertheless, in a truly democratic society, they must be fully addressed so that citizens will have a deeper understanding of the past and will be better prepared to handle the future. War has always been a major theme throughout history, and despite the nuclear deterrent that has so far prevented the start of World War III, it does not look like wars will be disappearing any time in the near future. Albert Einstein once said, "*I know not with what weapons World*

War III will be fought but World War IV will be fought with sticks and stones." Therefore, it is absolutely essential that every citizen in our democratic society must be able to formulate answers to the questions regarding the limits we should follow whenever our nation goes to war.

Suggested Reading:

Barnes, Michael. "The Decision to Use the Atomic Bomb." *Authentic History Center.* December 2, 2014. http://www.authentichistory.com.

Bilton, Michael, and Kevin Sim. *Four Hours in My Lai.* New York: Penguin Books, 1992.

Grayling, A.C. *Among the Dead Cities: Is the Targeting of Civilians in War Ever Justified?* London: Bloomsbury Publishing, 2006.

Hemingway, Ernest. *For Whom the Bell Tolls.* New York: Scribner, 1995.

Lucas, Fred. "Some Senators Wary of Waterboarding, Even to Save Lives." *Cybercast News Service.* July 7, 2008. http://www.cnsnews.com/news/article/some-senators-wary-waterboarding-even-save-lives.

Persico, Joseph E. *Nuremberg: Infamy on Trial.* New York: Penguin Books, 1995.

Chapter 14
The flow of humanity

Moment of Mourning
Courtesy of Defend International (CC BY-2.0)
https://www.flickr.com/photos/29325846@N07/20957140678

What is the best way to control human migration?

The place is a Mediterranean beach near Bodrum in the southwestern part of Turkey and the date is September 2, 2015. The body of a three-year-old boy lies face down in the sand, waves gently lapping around his head. The boy's name was later identified as Alan Kurdi, and he originated from Kobane, Syria; a city that was often at the center of clashes between Western forces and ISIS, the Islamic State. The fighting in this part of the world was a direct byproduct of a civil war that had raged in Syria for the last four years. Alan and his family were caught in the middle, and like hundreds of thousands of other refugees, the Kurdi family simply wanted to escape. A picture of Alan's body had been taken and flashed by the news media around the world. Because of the innocence and youth portrayed in this disturbing visual image, the picture struck a primeval nerve. More than anything, it pushed the question of human migration to the front page of newspapers around the world. As much as people living in the affluent comfort of Western nations, including my students, prefer not to think about the motives behind recent migration patterns, the picture forced many in the West to hold some uncomfortable conversations.

According to news reports, Alan Kurdi was in one of two boats, carrying a total of 23 people that set off separately from Turkey's Bodrum peninsula headed to the Greek island of Kos, where they could have attempted to enter the European Union. The reports indicated that the family's ultimate destination was Canada. Instead, according to officials, the boat capsized, and Alan's body washed up a few miles to the northeast in Turkey, not far from a beach resort. The dead included five children, including Alan's 5-year-old brother, and one woman. Seven others were rescued and two reached the shore in life jackets. The boy's father, Abdullah, survived.

Aegean Sea Map
Courtesy of Atilim Gunes Baydin (CC-BY-SA-3.0-migrated)
https://commons.wikimedia.org/wiki/File:AegeanSea_map_modified.png

In June, Alan's family tried to get permission to emigrate to Canada – where Abdullah's sister, Teema, lived in Vancouver, but their refugee application was rejected by Canadian authorities. The family had two strikes against them. First, like thousands of other Syrian Kurdish refugees in Turkey, the United Nations would not register them as refugees. Second, the Turkish government would not grant them exit visas. The family was among the millions killed or on the run from the Islamic State's continuing campaign of destruction in Syria and Iraq. But at least until the next horrific image comes along, Alan became the most powerful symbol of the conflict that has engulfed the region as well as the issues posed by immigrants seeking a better life.

Refugees like Alan made the 800-mile journey from Kobane through Turkey, trying to reach that nation's Aegean coast. Bodrum has been described as *"Turkey's most glamorous seaside getaway."* However, the refugees did not descend upon the area in search of sightseeing or swimming. Kos is another jewel of the Aegean – spectacular beaches, mountain villages, ancient ruins. But at this time, Kos was less known for its beauty than for its ever-evolving refugee crisis. Six hundred migrants arrived each night on the island of about 30,000. Since January of 2015, a staggering 125,000 refugees found their way to Kos and other Greek islands. Alan's family likely wanted to be part of the 600 people coming to Kos daily to fight for food and registration. As bleak as this sounds, it was clearly better than what they had left behind. At its closest point, Kos is about 2.5 miles across the Aegean from Turkey. Alan's journey across this treacherous stretch of water probably included a rubber dinghy or a similar small boat. Smugglers who typically charged more than $800 per person to cross under the cover of night operated many of these vessels.

What was the end result? A 3-year-old ended up dead on a beach in Turkey. News headlines every day were filled with stories like Alan's, but it took a picture to actually gain the public's attention. As refugees from the Islamic State and other turbulent parts of the world besieged European trains, crowded the French port of Calais, and died on the shores of Libya or in trucks in Austria, it is clear that Alan was just one of countless many.

It has always been somewhat difficult to make the American public care about the plight of people in distant lands, and it has equally been a challenge for educators to create empathy with their students for immigrants and refugees. Only a few students will raise their hands in discussions focused on the troubles of people seeking a better life. These students often will remind the other students that most of us have ancestors who faced comparable difficulties. Some of the more astute might even suggest that life is a crapshoot where no one comes into this world with the opportunity to choose their parents or the environment where they will be born and raised. Should those of us with the good fortune to come of age in comfortable, middle class homes in places like New York, St. Louis or Seattle be able to slam the door in the faces of those who had the misfortune to come into the world in places like Tegucigalpa, Kolkata or Kobane? The picture of little Alan Kurdi's body brought this question to the surface. But the question of how to best regulate the flow of human migration has been with us for thousands of years. Regardless of the discomfort it may cause, it is a question that must be thoroughly examined in order to better understand the planet we all share.

The issue first emerged in modern times with the advent of the modern nation-state. Part of the process of coming out of the Dark Ages was the invention of the modern country that possessed clearly delineated borders. Cross an invisible line somewhere in the Pyrenees and you were traveling from the nation-state of France into the nation-state of Spain. Over time, the French had come to speak a different language, supported a different government, and in many cases, followed a different religion. The rise of modern nationalism made the differences between the nation-states even more pronounced. Many people were now willing to fight, kill or die while carrying their nation's flag into battle. Holidays, rituals, and customs – they have all come to vary from one nation to another. Canadians do not celebrate their independence on July the 4th. With the invention of new technology that has made international travel a matter of hours rather than months, borders have taken on a new meaning. A direct flight from Abu Dhabi to New York takes just 14 hours. However, in a world that has become just as concerned with the spread of Ebola as it has the fear of international terrorism, borders have taken on a new importance. Most modern nation-states have become almost obsessed with guarding the sanctity of their borders and regulating the flow of migrants.

The United Nations recently released data showing that 232 million people, or 3.2 percent of the world's population, currently live outside of their countries of birth. The motives behind this demographic phenomenon are complex, but for the sake of simplicity, they can be divided between the *"push"* and the *"pull."* The first involves reasons why people want to leave their country of birth. At one time, Alan's family was probably content in Syria. However, a civil war that began over the effort to oust Bashar al-Assad, the nation's long-standing dictator, evolved into a brutal conflict where ISIS emerged to exploit the situation to its own gain. The result has been death, destruction, fear and instability. Depending on the time and the place, other push factors have included lack of employment or entrepreneurial opportunities, political and/or religious persecution, shortages of farmland, famine, drought and overpopulation.

The pull factors entail the reasons why people want to enter a particular country. Alan's family was hoping to reach Canada. After all, besides the physical and psychological advantages that come from linking up with family, Canada offered job opportunities, a considerably higher standard of living and a relatively peaceful lifestyle. Similar pull factors exist today in nations like Australia, the United States, and many other countries located in Western Europe and parts of South America. Some of the more common pull factors include more land, economic opportunities, better government welfare programs, superior schools, political freedom, cultural opportunities and a chance to pursue a new lifestyle.

People have been pushed and pulled to migrate for thousands of years. However, the floodgates to worldwide migration first opened with the journeys of Christopher Columbus. Starting in the late 15th Century, Europeans explored and colonized three continents: North America, South America and Australia, opening up land opportunities for millions of European and Asian migrants. The fact these areas were already populated by millions of indigenous souls mattered very little. From then until the present, free or relatively inexpensive land, the economic resources and opportunities, and the escape valve offered from the problems of the past acted like a magnet to attract a steady stream of immigrants. Even before 1776, the 13 British colonies were already open to settlement for people coming primarily from nations in Northern and Western Europe. Anyone who could arrive on his or her own power was welcome to stay. The door to immigration remained wide open throughout the first century of the United States' history. In fact, with the exception of the indigenous tribes and the former slaves whose ancestors had been dragged out of Africa in shackles, every American was either an immigrant by the late 19th century or the descendent of one.

The explosion of the Industrial Revolution in the United States during the late 1800s along with the consequential tension between labor and management created more hostility between the native born and the recently arrived immigrants, a prejudice aptly named nativism. Those who had hailed earlier from the British Isles or from nations in Northern Europe looked and sounded like *"Americans"* – in fact, like most Americans, they also belonged to Protestant religious denominations. They therefore assimilated much faster and spawned less nativism. The only significant exception to this pattern was the millions of Irish who came to America in the 1840s to escape the massive famine resulting from the potato blight that infected the destitute farms of the Emerald Isle. In addition to their more than apparent poverty, the Irish stirred up the ire of nativists because most were Roman Catholic.

The situation with immigration to America greatly changed around 1880. The push factors in Northern and Western Europe diminished, thereby reducing the number of immigrants who sought to enter the United States through Ellis Island, the nation's busiest inspection station that had opened in 1892. On the flip side, poverty, religious persecution and other push factors drastically grew in nations like Italy, Greece, Hungary, Poland and Russia. This meant the new immigrants coming to America tended to speak languages that were more distinct, and often wrote in alphabets new to most Americans. The Italians and Poles were mostly Catholic; the Greeks were Greek Orthodox and a large number of the Russians were Orthodox Jews trying to flee the horrors of the Pogroms that had been unleashed on their communities. In other words, the new immigrants stood out more than the old and tended to need more time assimilating into the great American melting pot. This greatly contributed to the rising nativism of the late 1800s.

The flow of humanity

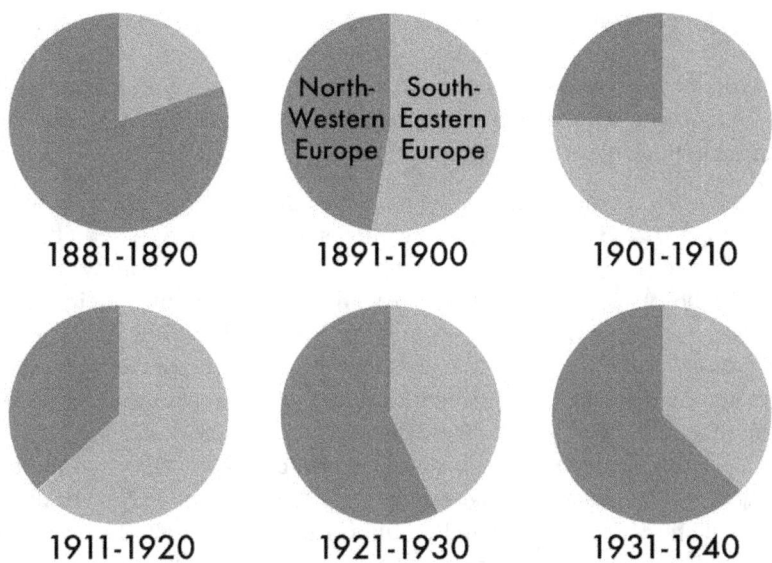

European immigration to the Unites States 1881-1940
Courtesy of Wikimedia Commons (PD-user)
https://commons.wikimedia.org/wiki/File:European_immigration_to_the_United_States_1881-1940.png

Of all the immigrant groups, no nationality stood out more than the Chinese. First arriving during the California Gold Rush of the late 1840s, many of the Chinese soon ventured into opening businesses like restaurants, dry goods stores and laundries catering to the needs of the gold seekers. Thousands also worked for the Central Pacific Railroad, which was blasting its way through the Sierra Nevada Mountains in an effort to link up with the Union Pacific. The result was the Transcontinental Railroad, an amazing engineering feat accomplished in 1869. However, hundreds of the Chinese died in the process. There is no question that the Chinese possessed physical features that set them apart. There is also no question that whether by their own volition or because of American prejudice, they did not assimilate well into U.S. society, often being segregated into "*Chinatowns*" in almost every American city. Finally, there is no doubt the Chinese worked hard and achieved a respectful level of success. Nothing attracted more animosity from native-born Americans than the jealousy and resentment stirred up by economic accomplishment. This all combined to make the Chinese the first victims of U.S. immigration restrictions. The Chinese Exclusion Act was signed into law on May 6, 1882. Although the Chinese composed only .002 percent of the nation's population, Congress passed the act to placate worker demands and assuage prevalent concerns about maintaining white "*racial purity.*" The legislation proved very effective, and the Chinese population in the United States sharply declined.

This was just the start. Despite the welcoming sentiments expressed in the Emma Lazarus poem on the recently erected Statue of Liberty that invited in the "*huddled masses yearning to breath free,*" nativism was on the rise. By the 1920s, restrictions were placed on all immigrants, but in a manner less transparently prejudiced than the Chinese Exclusion Act. The Immigration Restriction Act of 1921 limited the annual number of immigrants who could be admitted from all nations to 3% of the total number of people from that country who were already living in the United States in 1890. The Immigration Act of 1924 further reduced the cap to 2%. The members of Congress that passed this legislation knew exactly what they were doing. Without specifying the targeted group as they had in 1882, the laws were clearly aimed at the new immigrants coming in from Eastern and Southern Europe. Since their total numbers in the United States were comparatively small prior to 1890, the two or three percent quota would also be considerably smaller than the demand. Meanwhile, nations like the United Kingdom, France, Germany, Denmark and Sweden could send many more immigrants since their total numbers before 1890 were much higher, but by the 1920s, they could not even fill their quotas. So much for welcoming "*the wretched refuse of your teeming shore.*"

Immigration to the United States continued to decline in the 1930s due to the Great Depression. In fact, this is the only decade in American history when more people left the United States than came in as immigrants. Immigration restrictions also played a key role with the outset of the Second World War in the late 1930s. Many Jewish refugees from Nazi Germany were turned away when quotas had been filled, and the result is that more people died in the gas chambers. In 1939, the MS *St. Louis* was a German ocean liner carrying 908 Jewish refugees from Germany. After they were denied entry into Cuba, Canada and the United States, they were finally accepted by various European nations. However, when the Nazis later engulfed some of these nations in Europe during World War Two, it is estimated that a quarter of the ship's passengers died in concentration camps.

By the end of the war in 1945, the United States was forced to confront the issue of political and religious refugees. This was furthered by the onset of the Cold War. If refugees from communist nations like the Soviet Union,

China, North Korea, Cuba, Vietnam or any of the nations of Eastern Europe sought political asylum in the United States, it was almost always granted. After all, it was an embarrassing form of propaganda directed at the Eastern Block nations when their citizens preferred the freedom and capitalistic opportunities available in the West. Today, there are nearly one million Cuban exiles living in the United States, the vast majority in South Florida. Between 1989 and 2006, approximately 325,000 Soviet Jews settled in the United States. During World War Two, less than 30,000 Jews had been allowed to immigrate per year. Six million died in the Holocaust, a fate arguably much worse than the anti-Semitism faced by Soviet Jews. Was the wider door for Jewish Soviet refugees the result of America learning from its past, or was it mostly a byproduct of the Cold War?

By the 1960s, the unfairness inherent in the Quota System became increasingly apparent. President Lyndon B. Johnson's Great Society "*declared war on poverty*" by creating new programs like Medicare, Medicaid, Project Head Start and Food Stamps, but it also contained legislation aimed at reforming the nation's immigration laws. The result was the Immigration and Nationality Act of 1965 that abolished the national origins quota system from the 1920s and replaced it with a preference system that focused on immigrants' skills and family relationships with citizens or U.S. residents. Numerical restrictions on visas were set at 170,000 per year, with additional limits on individual nations. The biased quotas were gone, but what replaced them involved so many loopholes and exceptions that law schools were soon teaching entire courses on immigration law. Further reform came during the Reagan years of the 1980s.

So what are the basics of America's current immigration policies? U.S. immigration law is enormously complex, and there is much confusion as to how it works. In simple terms, there are just two questions that have become contentious political issues. First, who should be permitted to legally immigrate into the United States in any given year? Second, what should be done with the estimated 11.3 million immigrants who did not enter the United States legally? Anyone who has followed the subject of immigration reform, particularly as it was debated in the 2016 presidential election, knows that these two questions have received a significant amount of media attention.

Current law provides a worldwide limit of 675,000 permanent immigrants per year, with certain exceptions made for close family members. Congress and the President determine a separate number for refugee admissions. Overall, the policy governing refugees is based on four principles:

the reunification of families, admitting immigrants with skills considered valuable to the U.S. economy, protecting refugees and promoting diversity. There are specific limits set in each of these four areas. Potential migrants in foreign nations seeking admission into the United States can apply in the closest American embassy. In high demand nations like Mexico or the Philippines, they may find their names sitting on waiting lists for years or even decades.

Because of these limits, many migrants have entered the United States illegally. Some came as temporary visitors but failed to leave after their visa deadline expired. Others snuck over the border in a variety of creative ways. As of 2014, it was estimated that there were 11.3 million unauthorized immigrants in the U.S., making up about 3.5% of the nation's population. Mexicans make up about half of all unauthorized immigrants, 52%, though their numbers have recently been declining. Six states alone account for 60% of unauthorized immigrants – California, Texas, Florida, New York, New Jersey and Illinois. Unauthorized immigrants make up about 5.1% of the U.S. labor force. There have been many solutions offered to solve this problem ranging from the granting of general amnesty to massive government efforts focused on rounding up and deporting 11.3 million people. Knowing that many of these illegal immigrants have children born on U.S. soil only further exacerbates the issue.

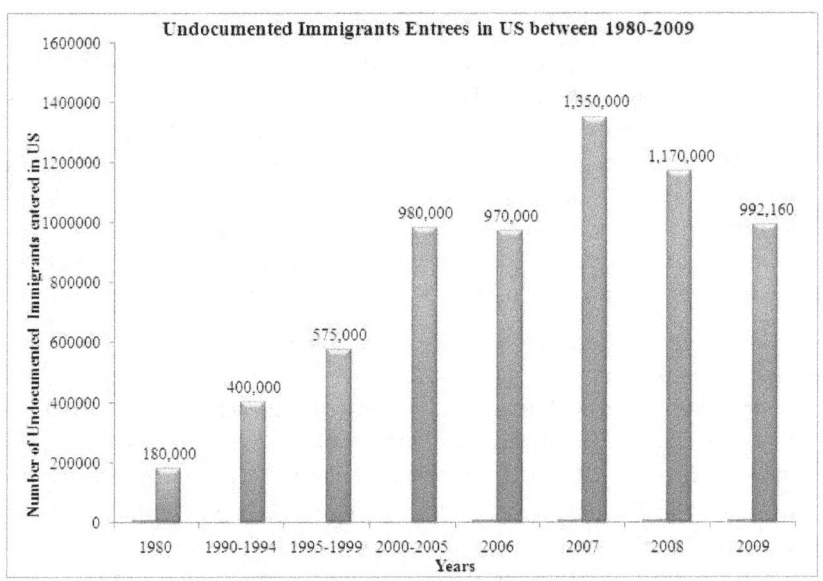

Undocumented Immigrant Entrees in U.S. between 1980-2009
Courtesy of Gshikula1 (CC BY-SA-3.0)
https://commons.wikimedia.org/wiki/File:Undocumented_Immigrants_Entrees_in_US_between_1980-2009.JPG

Another complicating factor involves enforcement along the border. Rather than debating the merits of allowing more or fewer immigrants into the nation, politicians love to talk about the porous quality of the nation's perimeter, particularly between the United States and Mexico. Should there be more enforcement officials? More money allocated? What about a higher fence or a huge wall? These questions are purely pragmatic; they ignore the larger moral issue that emerges anytime one nation chooses to fence itself off from a neighbor. There is also an equity issue. Some of the politicians running for President in 2016 focused on the problems with the border dividing the United States from Mexico. When is the last time a politician talked about building a bigger fence along the border between America and Canada?

Then there is the question of refugees. As stated earlier, someone applying to enter the United States, or for that matter, many other countries, has a much better chance of admittance if he or she can be granted status as a refugee. But who should grant this status, the receiving nation? What about the United Nations? And how should a refugee be defined? One definition of a refugee is *"a person who has been forced to leave his or her country in order to escape war, persecution, or natural disaster."* However, each term in this simple definition is subject to debate. *"Forced?"* What if conditions are such that a person or family simply chooses to leave? Is this forced? *"Escape?"* Does the escape always have to be permanent? What if conditions in the home country improve? Or better yet, what if international relief can bring about this improvement? Should refugees be repatriated when this occurs? What about *"war"*, *"persecution"* or *"natural disaster?"* Just how bad do conditions have to be to justify the establishment of refugee status?

So what is the best way to address the flow of human migration in the classroom? Like many political issues, this one might best be approached as a debatable issue, with two major arguments on each side: one practical and one moral. The practical arguments involve the advantages and disadvantages of one nation opening its door wider to the admission of more immigrants. For example, in classroom debates over the years, students have consistently pointed out that immigrants are more willing to take the lower-paying jobs that natives tend to scorn. In an affluent society like our own, where the ever-expanding middle class sends its kids to college in order to take white-collar jobs, someone still has to work as custodians, sanitation workers, fast food staff and migrant farm laborers. In addition, immigrants aid the economy in the long term because as they assimilate and move up the socio-economic pyramid, they contribute more in the way of taxes and provide an expanding market for domestically produced goods.

These same students have pointed out that immigrants contribute their intellectual prowess and their creative energy in the production of new inventions and cultural achievements. They are quick to identify Albert Einstein, Alexander Graham Bell and Levi Straus as immigrants to the United States. However, to further reinforce this point, students can be asked what these people all share in common: Madeline Albright, John Muir, Irving Berlin, Joseph Pulitzer, Ang Lee, Felix Frankfurter, Cary Grant, Henry Kissinger, Isaac Asimov, Joni Mitchell, Bob Hope, Charlize Theron, Frank Capra, Max Factor, Eddie Van Halen, Edward G. Robinson, I. M. Pei, Arnold Schwarzenegger and Neil Young. Yes, they are all immigrants to the United States and each has made important contributions to the betterment of their new society. Going one step further, ask students if they are grateful for these inventions: Microsoft Word, Siri, ATM Machines, Greek Yogurt, Google, Rechargeable Batteries, eBay, Hotdogs, Loudspeakers, Processed Cheese, Basketball, Video Gaming Systems, Yahoo, Bicycles, Blenders, HDTV, PET Scanners, Hairdryers, Portable Flash Drives, Remote Controls, LASIK Eye Surgery, Automatic Car Transmissions and You Tube. Once again, immigrants who came to the United States were responsible for all of these inventions. A more open door to immigration tends to attract the more ambitious, the risk-takers, and the people with surplus energy. The end result can be an explosion of new innovation.

On the flip side, other students have produced practical arguments in favor of tighter limits on immigration. They start by pointing out that as of 2014, the U.S. population was 319 million, and while the population growth of most other Western nations has leveled off or even declined, that of the United States is still growing. According to the Pew Research Center, the nation's population will rise to 438 million people by 2050, and fully 82% of the growth will be due to immigrants and their descendents. While the United States will still be blessed by an enormous bounty of open land and space, immigrants typically settle in urban areas in order to find employment. New York City was projected to have a population of 8,550,971 by 2020. The city hit that level prior to 2015. Anyone familiar with property values in New York or who has ridden a subway during rush hour can only shudder when thinking about more immigrants pouring into the Big Apple.

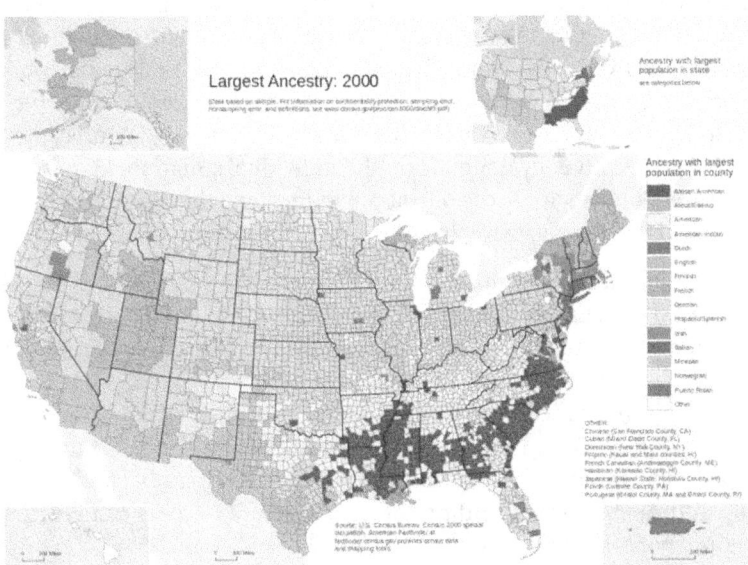

2000 Census Data: Top U.S. ancestries by country
Courtesy of the U.S. Census Bureau (PD-USGov-DOC-Census)
https://commons.wikimedia.org/wiki/File:Census-2000-Data-Top-US-Ancestries-by-County.svg

In addition, students point out economic and national security arguments, some of which date back to the nativists of the mid 19th Century. *"Immigrants will take jobs away from native born residents." "Immigrants will add to the nation's labor supply, thereby lowering wages." "Immigrants will be a drain on the nation's social services and will be a burden to taxpayers." "It was immigrants who hijacked the planes that flew into the World Trade Center on 9/11 and who will continue to pose a threat to national security."* There are numerous studies both in favor and against these assertions, but the perception among a significant part of the population is that they are true, and they always have been. This same set of arguments can be made in any nation, but the irony is that as previously stated, the United States was largely built and populated by immigrants.

The moral arguments on both sides of the issue are reflected by the analogy of a lifeboat. If a passenger liner has just gone down and there are survivors in the water who are seeking rescue on a nearby lifeboat, those with the good fortune to be on the boat are confronted by a tough moral dilemma. There are always some students who argue that no one can morally sit back and watch others drown, particularly if a few more can be squeezed onboard. Those who are more concerned with insuring their own survival point out that taking on more passengers could tip the lifeboat and endanger the lives of everyone. Besides, whatever food or water is onboard will have to be shared with the additional passengers, thereby reducing the long-term chances of survival for those who are still dry. Of course, the application of this analogy depends on the individual situation. Like so many other essential questions, the one about controlling the flow of human migration can best be answered by applying it to a specific example.

In the late summer of 2015, tens of thousands of refugees and migrants began arriving in Europe from the Middle East, Africa and South Asia. Little Alan Kurdi was just one small child riding this colossal wave of immigrants. The response of the European nations varied. Some of their responses raised comparisons with the darkest days of World War Two. Hungary enclosed asylum seekers in razor wire, Czech officials numbered their arms with indelible ink, and Slovakia issued anti-Muslim decrees. However, Germany and Austria, transcending their past, offered access at railway stations and borders across Europe.

The moral imperative of the immediate crisis seems clear. Each European nation is a lifeboat. The amount of room available is subject to debate, but how can those onboard watch as immigrants like Alan Kurdi literally drown? A long-term solution is harder to see. The U.N. Convention on Asylum was created in 1951 as Europe struggled to aid millions who had fled Nazism and communism during World War Two. But those arriving on the continent in the summer of 2015 are part of a postwar record, with almost 60 million people fleeing long-running conflicts around the world, pushing the system to the limits. More than 4 million Syrians alone have fled the civil war that followed President Bashar Assad's crushing of the 2011 Arab Spring that had taken place there. Nearly half have sought shelter in Turkey. Lebanon took in 1.1 million, equal to almost a quarter of its own population, while the burdened governments in Jordan, Iraq and Egypt also took in their share.

Despite shocking images of refugees suffering to reach Europe, such as the widely shared photograph of Alan Kurdi's body lying on the Turkish beach, Syria's immediate neighbors are still dealing with the bulk of the crisis. Each of their lifeboats is precariously full, while there is clearly still more room available in most of the European lifeboats. Despite the arguments made earlier, the United States is large enough and wealthy enough to potentially take in millions of immigrants. As of September of 2015, the U.S. had taken in only about 1,500 Syrian refugees.

Syrian refugee at Reyhanli refugee camp, March 31, 2012
Courtesy of Freedom House (CC BY-2.0)
https://www.flickr.com/photos/syriafreedom/6899058036/

Throughout history, war, oppression, poverty, and other forms of human misery have plagued many parts of the world. These in turn, have driven people to move elsewhere in pursuit of dreams for a better life. The United States has consistently ranked high as a magnet to attract these migrants, and in general, the situation in the present is not all that different from what it was a century earlier. According to Otis L. Graham, author of *Unguarded Gates: A History of America's Immigration Crisis* and a professor emeritus at University of California-Santa Barbara, public attitudes between 1915 and the present are similar in a number of respects. Just like today, there was widespread concern among American workers and people who sympathized with American workers. The volume of immigration in 1915 was unprecedented and had been running high, just at it is in the present. According to Graham, the concern about labor markets and the impact on the American worker was strong – and it is still strong. There was considerable concern about community standards and crowding in the streets in 1915. There was concern about crime.

That said, Graham has noted two differences between 1915 and the present. Today, there is much concern about population growth, which according to Graham, is an offshoot of the 1960s environmental movement combined with the more than 323 million people now living in America. In 1915, the population of the United States was barely over 100 million. There were a handful of intellectuals who worried about the numbers and the pressure on the environment, but the country was much more thinly settled back then. The second difference, according to Graham, is that the civil rights movement of the 1950s and 1960s has profoundly impacted our tolerance for public discrimination. The immigration reform talk today is almost entirely devoid of the racist language that 100 years ago, was taken for granted. Despite some of the recent rhetoric heard in the 2016 presidential debates, what was commonly said in 1915 was far more shocking.

Graham has written that Americans have always had mixed minds regarding immigrants. One week, George Washington or Thomas Jefferson might be found welcoming immigrants, and the next week, they were complaining that there were too many. It has been a strong theme throughout American life to be ambivalent about immigration because people have always perceived both the benefits and the costs. Just like there were a growing number of immigrants seeking entry into the United States in 1915 from Italy, Poland or Russia, today the pressure is simply originating from different places, such as Mexico, India and even Syria. The locations and circumstances may have changed, but the essential question remains the same.

Should America be willing to take in more passengers into its lifeboat? And what do we do about those that "*snuck*" onboard? Just like with all other essential questions, there is no simple solution to this quandary. But for millions of people around the globe, this essential question is in dire need of an answer. For our collective moral conscience, the answer better be one with which we can all live.

Suggested Reading:

Graham, Otis L. *Unguarded Gates: A History of America's Immigration Crisis*. Lanham: Rowman and Littlefield Publishers, 2003.

Krogstad, Jens Manuel, and Jeffrey S. Passel. "5 Facts About Illegal Immigration in the U.S." *Pew Research Center*. November 19, 2015. http://www.pewresearch.org/fact-tank/2015/11/19/5-facts-about-illegal-immigration.

Lee, Erika. *At America's Gates: Chinese Immigration During the Exclusion Era, 1882-1943*. Chapel Hill: University of North Carolina Press, 2003.

Osborne, Linda Barrett. *This Land is Our Land: A History of American Immigration*. New York: Abrams Books for Young Readers, 2016.

Passel, Jeffrey S., and D'Vera Cohn. "U.S. Population Projections: 2005-2050." *Pew Research Center*. February 11, 2008. http://www.pewhispanic.org/2008/02/11/us-population-projections-2005-2050/.

Schrag, Peter. *Not Fit for Our Society: Immigration and Nativism in America*. Berkeley: University of California Press, 2010.

"232 Million International Migrants Living Abroad Worldwide-New UN Global Migration Statistics Reveal." *United Nations*. September 11, 2013. http://www.un.org/en/ga/68/meetings/migration/pdf/UN press release_International Migration Figures.pdf.

Chapter 15
All men are created equal

Protest in Ferguson, Missouri August 17, 2014
Courtesy of loavesofbread (CC BY-SA- 4.0)
https://commons.wikimedia.org/wiki/File:Ferguson_Day_6,_Picture_44.png

What is the best way to achieve equality?

The place is Ferguson, Missouri in the northern suburbs of St. Louis and the date is Saturday, August 9, 2014. The temperature is in the mid 70's, a little cool for this time of year. Shortly before noon, Michael Brown, and his friend, Dorian Johnson, left the Ferguson Market. A camera had just recorded him stealing a box of Swisher cigars. Standing six feet, four inches tall and weighing nearly three hundred pounds, Brown had no problem pushing away the store clerk. Despite his size, Michael Brown was still a teenager. He had just graduated from an alternative education program at Normandy High School in St. Louis County eight days earlier.

At 11:47 a.m., Darren Wilson, a 28 year-old white officer with the Ferguson Police Department, responded to a call of a baby with breathing problems and was motoring just east of Canfield Drive. Like Michael Brown, Wilson was six feet, four inches tall, but was considerably lighter at just 210 pounds. Four minutes earlier, a police dispatcher reported a *"stealing in progress"* at the Ferguson Market and described the suspect as a black male wearing a white T-shirt, khaki shorts, yellow socks and a red St. Louis Cardinals hat. The dispatcher indicated the suspect was accompanied by another male and was running toward a QuikTrip convenience store. The suspect was reported as having stolen a box of cigars. At 12:00 noon, Wilson reported that he was back in service and radioed two other units if they needed assistance in searching for the suspects. Driving alone in his squad car, he made his way up Canfield Drive. Reports of what happened next differ widely among sources and witnesses, but Ferguson, Missouri, and for that matter, the entire nation, would never be quite the same.

Seeing two young men that met the dispatcher's description, Wilson drove up to Brown and Johnson in the middle of Canfield Drive and ordered them to move off the street and onto the sidewalk. Wilson continued driving past the two men, but then backed up and stopped close to them. A struggle took place between Michael Brown and Officer Wilson after Brown allegedly reached through the window of the police SUV, a Chevrolet Tahoe. Wilson's gun was fired twice during the struggle while it was inside the vehicle, with one bullet hitting Brown's right hand. Brown and Johnson fled and Johnson hid behind a car. Wilson got out of his vehicle and pursued Brown. Brown stopped and faced Wilson and then moved toward him. Wilson then fired at Brown several times in total, with at least six shots striking him in the front. In the entire altercation, Wilson fired a total of twelve bullets; the last was probably the fatal shot. Michael Brown was unarmed and moving toward Wilson when the shots were fired. Witness reports differed as to what Brown was doing with his hands when he was shot. Less than 90 seconds passed from the time Officer Wilson encountered Brown to the time of Brown's death.

A combination of peaceful protests and civil disorder broke out the day following Brown's shooting and lasted for several days. This was in part due to the belief among many that Brown was surrendering, as well as longstanding racial tensions between the majority-black population and the majority-white city government and police. As details of the shooting emerged from investigators, police grappled with establishing curfews and maintaining order while members of the Ferguson community demonstrated in the vicinity of the original shooting. On August 10, a day of memorials began peacefully, but some crowd members became unruly after an evening candlelight vigil. Local police stations assembled approximately 150 officers in riot gear. Some people began looting businesses, vandalizing vehicles and confronting police officers that sought to block off access to several areas of the city. In the following days, the situation intensified. On one side, peaceful protests were accompanied by acts of violence that led to the burning and destruction of property. The other side included local police, state troopers and units of the Missouri National Guard using tear gas and military-grade weapons. Believing accounts that Brown had his hands up in surrender when he was shot, protesters chanted, *"Hands up, don't shoot."* Protests, both peaceful and violent, along with vandalism and looting, continued for more than a week.

A grand jury was called and given extensive evidence from Robert McCulloch, the St. Louis County Prosecutor. The prosecution took months to present their evidence in secret, a highly unusual process. It was not until November 24 that McCulloch announced that the grand jury had decided not to indict Darren Wilson. According to the grand jury, Wilson had shot Michael Brown in self-defense. The announcement set off another round of protests and riots that lasted for several days. Once again, burning and looting accompanied peaceful demonstrations. The events in Ferguson that stretched from early August to the last weeks of November received considerable attention throughout the United States and elsewhere, attracting protesters from outside of the region and generating a vigorous debate about the relationship between law enforcement and African Americans. There were other shootings involving white policemen and black victims before and after the killing of Michael Brown. They stretched from Florida to Cleveland and from New York City to Baltimore. However, most would credit Ferguson, Missouri as the birthplace of the current Black Lives Matter Movement.

It has been argued that this contemporary movement has lacked leadership and focus, that its goals remain somewhat nebulous. In the March 14, 2016 issue of the *New Yorker*, Jelani Cobb wrote that the Black Lives Matter Movement *"eschews hierarchy and centralized leadership, and its members have not infrequently been at odds with older civil-rights leaders and with the Obama Administration – as well as with one another."* She states that it has been described as *"not your grandfather's civil-rights movement,"* to distinguish its tactics and its philosophy from those of 1960s-style activism. Is the movement directed at giving African Americans a greater political voice in cities like Ferguson or is it more about economic disparities?

What about aiding the minorities who are victimized by unfair fines and prison sentences handed down by the criminal justice system? Or is the Black Lives Matter Movement aimed at broader issues? There is still an enormous gap separating the races in this country, and it is not just economic. Blacks and whites inhabit different worlds, and most whites cannot begin to fathom the prejudice that many blacks still encounter on a sometimes-daily basis. Frustration and anger have been building for decades if not for centuries, and the Black Lives Matter Movement might simply be viewed as the latest manifestation of a malady that has infected American society since the early 17th century.

When I first mentioned the events unfolding in Ferguson to my students in an all-white classroom in suburban St. Louis, one of the boys immediately blurted out, *"Who's Ferguson?"* The others laughed at his naïve ignorance, since Ferguson had been dominating the headlines for several days, but the reality was much more serious. Just fifteen miles from where violent protests had taken place the night before, there were bright students who had never heard of Ferguson. As far as most of my white, middle class students were concerned Ferguson might just as well have been a million miles away. They knew there were poor neighborhoods in and around St. Louis, but they made no connection between economic gaps and race. After all, the modern Civil Rights Movement led by Martin Luther King had ended discrimination long before they were born, or at least that is what most believed. Why was there a need for this new Black Lives Matter Movement?

Seeing this as a teachable moment, I immediately launched what seemed to be an unrelated activity. Asking for two volunteers, I suggested we hold a class pushups competition. Before the two students commenced doing their pushups, I encouraged speculation about who would win so the class would feel more of an emotional investment in the competition's outcome. Then, just before yelling, *"go!"* I pulled out a knapsack filled with books weighing about 35 pounds and said that one of the contestants would have to wear the backpack. There were immediate protests, but when I told them I never promised a fair contest, they eventually agreed to go along. After about 30 seconds, with the book bag student lagging far behind, I told the rivals to stop and then turned to the class and asked if this was a fair contest. They simultaneously screamed *"no!"* I then asked the most important question of the activity: *"How do we make this a fair competition now that it has already begun?"*

Their initial answer was to have the student wearing the knapsack loaded down with books immediately take it off. *"Okay, that's better, but is it now a fair contest? After all, the student who was wearing the bag is far behind in the number of pushups he has completed. How can we make it fair now?"* After a few suggestions like making the other student wear the bag for a while or giving the student who is behind some extra time to catch up, they finally acknowledged that since the contest had already begun, there was no way to make it perfectly fair. The student wearing the book bag was already more tired than his competition, so no matter what we do to rectify the situation now, the end result will still be tarnished.

I then asked the class if they saw a connection between our activity and the competition that has characterized our society for the last 400 years. Our capitalist economy has always been based on the principle that individuals should have the freedom to compete fairly for their share of the economic pie. However, from the day the first slaves were sold in Jamestown, Virginia in 1619, African Americans have been burdened by wearing the heavy book bag. A combination of slavery, Jim Crow segregation and endemic discrimination has allowed whites to gain a significant lead. Although the modern Civil Rights Movement might be comparable to allowing the one student to pull off the heavy knapsack, the competition is still not fair.

At this point, I provide the following numbers taken from a Pew Research Center study made in 2013:

	Black	White
Median Household Income	$39,760	$67,175
Poverty Rate	28%	10%
Mean Family Net Worth	$6,446	$91,203
College Graduation Rate	21%	34%
Home Ownership	44%	73%
Male Prisoners per 100,000	4,347	678
Marriage Rates (18 or Older)	31%	55%
Life Expectancy	75.1	78.9

After spending time explaining and discussing these numbers, the clincher question is asked. Has the Civil Rights Movement of the 1960s created a fair contest, or is there still a need for a new movement? Before that question can be addressed, a larger essential question must be raised – what is the best way to achieve equality?

First, terms need to be understood. In this case, *"equality"* is not referring to economic equality. The best way to distribute wealth was discussed in an earlier chapter; in this context, equality refers more to equal opportunity. Second, a distinction should be made between the historic drive to establish individual rights for everyone versus the assurance of equal opportunity for groups that have traditionally faced different forms of discrimination.

The movement to protect individual rights such as free speech, privacy or the separation of church and state dates back to England's Glorious Revolution of the late 17th Century. This focus on individual rights for all citizens has continued to gather momentum ever since. These rights make up the dominant theme in the American Declaration of Independence, the U.S. Constitution and the French Declaration of the Rights of Man and Citizen. They have sustained liberal revolutions around the world and have taken on almost a sacred quality for millions of people.

In 1920, the American Civil Liberties Union, the A.C.L.U., was founded with the primary intent of going to court in defense of these civil liberties. To A.C.L.U. lawyers, it is far better to veer on the side of giving people too much liberty than it is to allow the government to chip away at our constitutional rights. This has even led to a few cases where the A.C.L.U. has come into opposition with other liberal organizations created to protect the civil rights of certain minority groups. For example, when A.C.L.U. attorneys took the village of Skokie, a community on the northern outskirts of Chicago with a large Jewish population, to court in 1977, they were put into the position of defending the First Amendment rights of the American Nazi Party. Skokie had passed an ordinance prohibiting the Nazi uniform and swastika from appearing within city limits. The A.C.L.U. saw this as a violation of our individual rights. If this ordinance were allowed to stand, it would take the nation down a *"slippery slope"* making it easier to deny any unpopular group the right to free expression. Some of the A.C.L.U. lawyers were even Jewish! However, to them, their real client was the First Amendment, not an extreme group of fanatics dressed up like storm troopers. Ironically, after winning their case in the U.S. Supreme Court, the Nazis decided not to march in Skokie. They had proven their point, as well as gaining two years of free publicity. The more important point here, however, is that a distinction must be made between the ongoing drive to guarantee individual civil rights and the Civil Rights Movement.

Many people view the modern Civil Rights Movement as a series of events that dominated headlines between the mid 1950s and the late 1960s.

The reality is far more complex. Over the past two hundred years, there have been a variety of collective efforts to improve the lives of people of color. In the first half of the 19th Century, abolitionists, both white and black, advocated through their sermons and writings an end to slavery. Some still harbored racist ideas and believed that with the end of slavery, the best solution would be to send former slaves back to Africa. Most of my students are surprised to learn this is the background story of the African nation of Liberia, a country whose name even reflects the recently earned freedom of the former American slaves that were to add to its population. Monrovia, its capital city, takes its name from President James Monroe. Even though there were approximately 200,000 free blacks living in the United States on the eve of the Civil War, most had no interest in migrating to Liberia. They were born in America and had no desire to leave.

There were others opposed to slavery, but they were pragmatic enough to realize there was little chance of abolishing an economic institution so deeply entrenched in the South. These people became free soil advocates because the compromise solution they sought was the prohibition of slavery spreading to the free soil of new territories in the West. By the 1850s, these individuals organized themselves into a new political party, one that is still very much with us today: the Republicans. When one of these Republicans, Abraham Lincoln, ran for president in 1860 and managed to win, even though it was with barely 40% of the popular votes, it triggered the secession of South Carolina and five other states, taking the nation on the path to civil war. Even after the war had begun, it is worth noting that President Lincoln still did not think of himself as an abolitionist. Lincoln's goal as the cannon balls were fired at Fort Sumter in April of 1861 was to preserve the union, not the eradication of slavery. The Abolitionist Movement had become loud and inflammatory over the years, but it was always just a small percentage of the population. However, it still helped to provide a foundation for other movements in the future.

The next effort to establish greater equality between the races occurred during the Reconstruction years following the Civil War. After President Lincoln's assassination in April of 1865, leadership passed to a group of Radical Republicans in Congress. As a result of their efforts, the requirements imposed on southern states to be readmitted into the union were far more punitive. As for the four million former slaves, new civil rights laws were passed and three new amendments made their way into the Constitution: the 13th formally abolished slavery for all time, the 14th defined American citizenship in such terms that southern states would have to respect the rights of their new *"citizens"* of color, and the 15th provided former slaves, at least the males, with the right to vote. To enforce these measures, the former Confederacy was divided into five military districts and troops were sent to patrol the streets of southern cities and towns. Over the next few years, hundreds of schools were built to educate former slaves, blacks began to vote for the first time and a number of African Americans were even elected to Congress. It proved to be a transitory illusion, but for a short time, it appeared that equality had been achieved.

In the long run, Reconstruction proved to be more a failure than a success. There was talk of providing former slaves with land and the wherewithal to successfully take up farming. However, since this land would have to come from white southerners, and since property had been seen as one of those sacred individual rights since the days of John Locke, the idea of providing former slaves with *"forty acres and a mule"* never materialized. African Americans in the South could celebrate their freedom, their new status as citizens and even their right to vote, but unfortunately, they could not feed ballots to their children. Instead, most former slaves took up share cropping on their old plantations as the only means to survive. From one day to the next, their lives, which revolved around the cotton growing seasons, were not much different than they had been before the Civil War. In addition, while Yankee troops might be on patrol by day, there was not much protection at night from the secret organizations like the Ku Klux Klan that made a concerted effort to terrorize any blacks that dared to assert their equality. Finally, by the 1870s, the nation as a whole had grown weary of Reconstruction. The presidential election of 1876 was one of the closest and most corrupt in history. Who won? Was it Samuel Tilden, the Democrat, or Rutherford B. Hayes, the Republican? A *"corrupt"* bargain was made that gave the election to Hayes in return for the removal of troops from the South. For all intensive purposes, Reconstruction was now dead. White southerners completed the process called Redemption whereby they reclaimed practically all of their political power. Within a few years, Jim Crow segregation in schools, housing patterns and public facilities became the law of the land. Poll taxes and literacy tests were devised to keep African Americans out of the voting booths. In 1896, the *Plessey v. Ferguson* Supreme Court case legitimized this *"separate but equal"* society that in reality, was far from equal.

As the 20th Century unfolded, two threads of African American leadership emerged that would ultimately come to dominate the next 100 years. A former slave, Booker T. Washington, provided the first option. Washington advocated a moderate approach based on education, entrepreneurship and economic advancement. To achieve equality, African Americans would have to prove to themselves as well as everyone else that they were worthy of respect. He established the Tuskegee Institute, a historically black college in Alabama, and in 1895, his Atlanta Compromise called for avoiding confrontation over segregation and the growing number of lynchings.

Booker T. Washington
Courtesy of the Library of Congress
Prints and Photographs Division
LC-DIG-ds-04383

On the other hand, W.E.B. Dubois, the first African American to receive a PhD from Harvard University, pushed for a more militant and confrontational approach. He first rose to national prominence as the leader of the Niagara Movement, a group of African-American activists who wanted equal rights for blacks. Dubois was one of the co-founders of the National Association for the Advancement of Colored People (NAACP) in 1909. He and his supporters opposed the Atlanta Compromise and instead, insisted on full civil rights and increased political representation. Racism was the main target of Dubois' polemics, and he strongly protested against lynchings, Jim Crow laws, and discrimination in education and employment.

W.E.B. Du Bois 1918
Courtesy of Cornelius Marion Battey (PD-old-80-1923)
https://commons.wikimedia.org/wiki/File:WEB_DuBois_1918.jpg

For the first time in history, African Americans were presented with two viable options, each with merit. While they seemed to share similar goals, over time, there would be a significant divergence over whether it would be preferable to achieve equality through racial integration with the larger white majority or by maintaining a distinct black subculture. In addition, there would be big differences over which methods should be employed to achieve these goals.

Despite the efforts of both leaders, the first few decades of the 20th Century saw little progress. Motivated by higher paying jobs in northern cities, six million African Americans fled the cotton fields of the South starting in 1910. This *"Great Migration"* helped to unleash an explosion of cultural achievement collectively known as the Harlem Renaissance. In the nineteen twenties and thirties, African Americans, mostly in cities like New York, Philadelphia, Boston, Detroit, St. Louis and Chicago, were making great strides in such areas as literature, dance, poetry, music and art. However, Jim Crow and the lynchings still continued. In fact, the KKK grew bigger in the 1920s than any other time in the nation's history. Thousands of hooded Klansmen paraded down the streets of Washington, DC, and for a brief period, the Klan took political control over state governments, including those of Indiana and Oregon. The Great Depression in the 1930s only exacerbated a bad situation.

Formation of K.K.K. parade August 8, 1925
Courtesy of the Library of Congress, Prints and Photographs Division LC-DIG-npcc-14036

The three Progressive presidents who occupied the White House between 1901 and 1920, Theodore Roosevelt, William Howard Taft and Woodrow Wilson, did much to help farmers, factory workers and the growing middle class; but for the most part, they ignored the plight of African Americans. In fact, Woodrow Wilson proved to be one of the most racist presidents in history. He once said racial *"segregation is not a humiliation but a benefit..."* The three presidents who followed in the 1920s, Warren G. Harding, Calvin Coolidge and Herbert Hoover, mostly wanted to scale back on the role of the national government; they were not the least bit interested in taking on the task of helping minorities. Franklin Roosevelt, prodded by his wife Eleanor, displayed some empathy toward the plight of blacks, and made it a point to include them in some of his New Deal programs designed to provide employment during the Great Depression. In addition, he later required the integration of defense industries during the Second World War. However, FDR was restricted by the fear that too much progress in the field of civil rights would cost him the political support of white southerners so necessary to achieve reelection. In fact, in his bid for reelection in 1944, Roosevelt dumped Henry Wallace as his vice-president because Wallace was considered too liberal on civil rights issues.

Ironically, the man he chose over Wallace became the first president to display true gumption in the face of white bigotry. Harry Truman was considered a moderate on race issues, but when he became president upon Roosevelt's death in April 1945, he quickly became his own man. Nearing his bid for reelection in 1948, Truman issued an executive order to racially integrate the military. Many predicted race riots similar to those directed at African Americans earlier in the century in cities like East St. Louis, Chicago and Tulsa. However, the soldiers were trained to obey orders, and ordered to share their barracks with men of color, they did so with few problems. This was not the start of a movement; it was the act of a single man. However, it was a seed that would soon grow. Despite the emergence of Strom Thurmond, a segregationist candidate who won white votes in the South, Harry Truman pulled off a political miracle and still managed to get himself reelected.

Six years later, the Supreme Court took up the cause to end racial segregation. Led by Chief Justice Earl Warren, recently appointed by President Dwight D. Eisenhower, the court voted unanimously to overturn the *Plessey* decision handed down 58 years earlier. The *Brown v. Board of Education* decision of 1954 ruled that *"separate but equal"* was *"inherently unequal"* and ordered the racial integration of the nation's public schools to begin with *"all deliberate speed."* As seen by the turmoil in places like Little Rock, Arkansas, where President Eisenhower was forced to send in 1000 troops from the 101st Airborne division in order to enforce the integration of Central High School, this decision proved to be much more difficult to enforce than it was to hand down. In addition, even though it was seen as a major step in the right direction, it too was not the start of a movement.

The *Brown* case resulted from the actions of a few men like Thurgood Marshall and other members of the NAACP who brought the issue of school segregation to the Supreme Court's attention, as well as the nine white men that handed down the *Brown* decision. However, by definition, a movement involves the actions of a large group. The time was becoming increasingly ripe for the start of a movement, but something would have to act as a spark to ignite the explosion. That spark occurred at 6 p.m. on the evening of Thursday, December 1, 1955 in downtown Montgomery, Alabama.

After working all day, Rosa Parks, a 42-year-old seamstress, boarded the Cleveland Avenue bus and took a seat. As the bus began to fill and the driver saw white passengers standing, he asked Parks to give up her seat as was required by law. Legend has it that something inside Rosa Parks detonated and out of anger and frustration, she refused to stand. In reality, Parks was a member of the Montgomery chapter of the NAACP, and she knew they were looking for someone to deliberately violate the law. Regardless, she was promptly arrested, and within days, a bus boycott began that would last for over a year. By late December 1956, the blacks of Montgomery had won the right to sit wherever they wanted on the city busses. More important, a 26-year-old minister named Martin Luther King Jr., who had helped lead the boycott, emerged as a national civil rights figure and a national movement was underway.

From 1956 to the late 1960s, the modern Civil Rights Movement vacillated between the two threads that had been established at the start of the century. Dr. King, following in the footsteps of Booker T. Washington, was certainly more confrontational than his predecessor, but his acts of nonviolent civil disobedience were still more similar to those of Mohandas Gandhi than to a radical revolutionary. In addition, when he stated in his iconic 1963 *"I Have a Dream"* speech that his view of equality meant he looked forward *"to a day when people will not be judged by the color of their skin, but by the content of their character,"* the implication was that integration with whites was the paramount goal.

The sit-ins, marches, demonstrations and protests that made front-page news in the late fifties and early sixties hit their mark. By 1964, Congress passed a major civil rights bill that banned discrimination in education, employment and public facilities. The Civil Rights Act of 1965 along with ratification of the 24th Amendment eliminated the barriers to voting, and a civil rights act passed in 1968 made housing discrimination illegal. Once again, it appeared that meaningful progress had been made.

Beneath the surface, however, African Americans still faced much higher rates of unemployment, poverty and incarceration. Anger and frustration were festering, and the fact that some progress had been made only contributed to the dissatisfaction among those who were still living in crowded housing projects. Even Dr. King understood by the late 1960s that the movement still had a long way to go before it could be declared a success. When he was gunned down on the balcony of his hotel in Memphis, Tennessee on April 4, 1968, he was in town to support a sanitation workers' strike. He understood most of the progress made had been political, not economic.

Long before the assassination of Martin Luther King Jr. and the violent race riots it touched off in 250 American cities, a young African American named Malcolm Little was committing petty crimes in Boston, Massachusetts. When a burglary landed him in prison, it connected him to leaders of the Nation of Islam, a group of African Americans pursuing the second thread of change. Led by Elijah Muhammad, the Nation of Islam was more than an American offshoot of the Muslim faith. Its members were taught to take pride in their African cultural heritage and to confront bigotry and racism squarely in the eye. Malcolm quickly internalized their values and principles, and after he realized that *"Little"* was a surname passed down from the whites that had owned his slave ancestors, he changed his name to a generic X. After his release from prison, Malcolm X soon took on a leadership position within the Nation of Islam and through his speeches and actions, offered himself as the descendent of the more confrontational approach first pioneered by W.E.B. Dubois.

Malcolm once said *"Be peaceful, be courteous, obey the law, respect everyone; but if someone puts his hand on you, send him to the cemetery."* In addition, when offered support from liberal whites, he declined because he was not interested in creating an integrated society where skin color would not matter. Malcolm wanted equality; in fact, he demanded equality. However, he also wanted to maintain a separate identity that would preserve black cultural traditions and pride. With Malcolm X providing the ideology, thousands more would soon provide the actions. The Nation of Islam gunned Malcolm down in 1965, probably out of envy over his rising popularity. By the late 1960s, the Black Panthers had emerged as a major force, advocating an even more militant approach. In the *"Long Hot Summer"* of 1967, race riots exploded in 159 cities across the United States, with the worst taking place in Detroit, Newark and the Watts neighborhood of Los Angeles.

When comparisons between Martin Luther King Jr. and Malcolm X are made in my classroom, as they are in most other American history classes, the responses are generally tied to the race of the students. Most whites favor Dr. King and are quick to point out that his messages about nonviolence and universal brotherhood have earned him a national holiday in celebration of his birthday. As might be expected, most of these students rate the Civil Rights Movement a success and have a hard time understanding the recent events that have unfolded in places like Ferguson, Missouri. To them, the law prohibits discrimination, what else is really needed?

As might be expected, most African American students have a different view. There is no question they have great respect for Dr. King, but they also appreciate the appeal of Malcolm X. Many tell personal stories of confrontations they have had with the police, with suspicious store managers, even with some of their peers in school. They also understand the significant economic disparities that still exist. They agree that the methods of Gandhi may have led to Indian independence from Great Britain, but they also know it took most of the Mahatma's life to achieve this goal. Reflecting on almost 400 years of slavery and Jim Crow segregation, many have little patience for the approaches employed by Booker T. Washington and Martin Luther King Jr. They view the protesters and even the looters in Ferguson as a modern-day expression of W.E.B Dubois and Malcolm X. To them, their approach has proven to be necessary and more effective.

Dr. Martin Luther King and Malcolm X
Courtesy of the Library of Congress
Prints and Photographs Division LC-USZ6-1847

So what is the best way to achieve equality? After reviewing the two threads that stretched from Booker T. Washington and W.E.B. Dubois at the start of the 20th Century up to Martin Luther King Jr. and Malcolm X in the 1960s, one obvious response is to examine and debate the two options offered by the civil rights leaders. Patience versus impatience? Militant confrontation and even violence versus civil disobedience? Negotiation and compromise versus immediate justice? Go to court or hurl Molotov cocktails in the streets? These choices have dogged all minority groups throughout American history that have faced prejudice and discrimination.

For example, Native Americans were torn between leaders that wanted to fight and those who wanted to negotiate the best treaty they could get. Among the Sioux for instance, after attempting years of fierce resistance, Red Cloud traveled all the way to Washington DC in 1870 and met with the Commissioner of Indian Affairs and President Ulysses Grant. The following year, the government established the Red Cloud Agency on the Platte River, downstream from Fort Laramie. Red Cloud had negotiated his best deal and he moved his supporters onto reservation land. From that point on, he made peace with the white majority running the nation. Even when other Sioux leaders like Sitting Bull and Crazy Horse chose to fight, Red Cloud stayed behind. He was nowhere to be seen on that fateful day in 1876 when other Sioux warriors slaughtered George Armstrong Custer and every single one of his men at the Battle of the Little Big Horn. Red Cloud recognized that the Sioux might be able to win a major battle, but they could never defeat the United States as a nation with all of its people, wealth and resources. Divisions within minority cultures of this sort greatly weakened their efforts to achieve equality, but they reflected the strain created by the two threads running throughout American history.

Similarly, women suffragettes were torn between leaders like Carrie Chapman Catt and Alice Paul. Catt had succeeded Susan B. Anthony as the president of the National American Woman Suffrage Association (NAWSA) and played a significant role in bringing about passage of the 19th Amendment. However, under her leadership, Catt tended to follow the *"patience and compromise"* thread. She was content to negotiate for the right to vote on a state-by-state basis, winning New York in 1917, a major achievement since it was the first eastern state to approve women's suffrage. When the United States entered World War One in April 1917, Carrie Chapman Catt made the controversial decision to support the war effort rather than continue to pressure President Wilson for the right to vote. In her effort to win women's suffrage state-by- state, Catt even appealed to the prejudices of the time. In South Dakota, she lamented that while women lacked the right to vote, *"The murderous Sioux is given the right to the franchise which he is ready and anxious to sell to the highest bidder."* In 1894, Catt urged that uneducated immigrants be stripped of their right to vote – the United States should *"cut off the vote of the slums and give it to women."* *"White supremacy will be strengthened, not weakened, by women's suffrage,"* was her argument when trying to win over Mississippi and South Carolina in 1919. Catt supervised dozens of campaigns, mobilized up to one million volunteers and made hundreds of speeches. Yet her approach was appreciably different from the younger generation of women pushing for the same basic goal.

Alice Paul was one those younger women. She was 26 years younger than Carrie Chapman Catt and her approach was more reminiscent of W.E.B. Dubois than Booker T. Washington. Her methods started to create tension between herself and the leaders of NAWSA, who thought she was moving too aggressively in Washington. Paul did not agree with the slower state-by-state approach and wanted to put all of her efforts towards passage of a Constitutional amendment that would immediately require all states to grant women the right to vote. Eventually, disagreements about strategy and tactics led to a break with NAWSA. Paul formed the Congressional Union and later, the National Woman's Party (NWP) in 1916. She went on to organize parades, printed suffragette newspapers and was the first to lead demonstrations in front of the White House. After she and hundreds of other women were arrested for picketing a wartime president, she organized hunger strikes while in jail. The publicity generated by the arrests and hunger strikes proved to be a turning point in the Women's Suffrage Movement. In 1920, ratification of the 19th Amendment finally granted women the right to vote, a goal that had first been laid down 72 years earlier during the Seneca Falls Convention.

Suffragettes June 2, 1920
Courtesy of the Library of Congress
Prints and Photographs Division LC-DIG-npcc-01705

Regardless of the minority group seeking greater equality, there were always palpable differences within each group in terms of goals and especially methods. The divergence between African American leaders like

Booker T. Washington, W.E.B Dubois, Martin Luther King Jr. and Malcolm X can be seen any time a minority group has faced prejudice and discrimination. Since division has only served to weaken the efforts of these movements to achieve success, it behooves these groups to find a consensus on the preeminent answer to the question about how to best achieve equality.

For students, only a careful examination of these leaders and the role they have played in history can lead to a thoughtful response to this vitally important essential question. The chart below provides a focal point for discussions on this matter. Since there are 10 different cells, students can choose the one that best reflects their position regarding both goals and methods.

	GOALS	
METHODS	Equality Through Integration/Assimilation	Equality by Maintaining a Separate Identity
Self-Improvement and Raising Consciousness		
Lawsuits, Election Campaigning and Political Action		
Peaceful Protests and Civil Disobedience		
Acquiring Weapons for Self-Defense		
Planning Acts of Violence and Lawlessness		

Another way to approach the essential question is to examine the need for programs or reparations designed to provide compensation for the past. After all, when an individual is harmed due to the negligence of another, he or she typically seeks justice by filing a civil lawsuit and claiming monetary damages. Our courts are currently choked with cases seeking money for repairs, medical costs, pain and suffering, lost wages, lost abilities and lost lives. In fact, many times, juries award multimillion-dollar decisions purely as a way to punish defendants for their egregious errors. If this sort of compensation can rectify an individual wrong from the past, shouldn't minorities, who have suffered from slavery, segregation and discrimination, be entitled to damages as well?

In 1988, President Ronald Reagan signed the Civil Liberties Act to compensate more than 100,000 people of Japanese descent who were incarcerated in internment camps during the Second World War. This legislation offered a formal apology and paid out $20,000 in compensation to each surviving victim. Because of an executive order issued by Franklin D. Roosevelt in 1942, American citizens of Japanese descent were forced to give up their jobs, homes, businesses and freedom simply out of fear they might aid the enemy after the attack on Pearl Harbor. There is no denying this was a gross injustice and a serious violation of constitutional rights. However, if this wrong, which lasted less than three years, warrants financial compensation, what about money or programs to make up for slavery and Jim Crow segregation, not to mention stolen land and broken treaties?

Referring back to the pushups exercise mentioned earlier, while there might not be a perfect way to make the contest fair, members of the white majority may have to sacrifice some in order to compensate for the sins of the past. The student without the book bag is not the one who required his competition to be weighed down by the books, but he may have to wear the bag for a little while in order to make the competition fair. In the real world, most white students are not responsible for the discrimination of the past, but they may have to accept the fact that a checkmark on the minority status box of a college application may give an African American or a Native American an advantage in gaining admission into a prestigious university. The same goes for the white middle class students who see their tax dollars paying for the bus transportation of blacks into their previously all white schools. To many students, particularly those of color, 400 years of unfair rules and procedures is not rectified just because the heavy book bag is removed.

Affirmative action in some form or other has been around since the 1960s and has become endemic in the world of college admissions, scholarships and financial aid, government contracts to minority businesses and the hiring and promotion policies of many different companies and government agencies. In simple terms, affirmative action, also known as positive discrimination, or by its opponents, as reverse discrimination, is the policy of favoring members of a disadvantaged group who suffer from discrimination. In the past, it has led to quota systems, whereby a certain percentage of jobs or school vacancies had to be reserved for members of a certain group. Because of recent Supreme Court decisions, the latest approach has been to simply give preference in the selection process. The term *"affirmative action"* was first used in the United States in an executive order issued by President John F. Kennedy in March 1961, which included a provision that government contractors *"take **affirmative action** to insure that applicants are employed, and employees are treated during employment, without regard to their race, creed, color, or national origin."* It was intended to promote the opportunities of defined minority groups within a society to give them equal access to that of the majority population. It is often instituted to ensure that certain designated minority groups within a society are able to participate in all provided activities. Almost everyone seems to have a story to tell in regard to these policies, and while they were never intended to be permanent fixtures, at this point in time, they still exist throughout the United States. Even other nations like India have used these forms of preferential treatment to make up for past discrimination against the untouchable castes.

In addition to serving as a form of compensation, many have argued that some type of affirmative action is necessary to insure the diversity needed to reflect the larger community. If a city's population is 67% black, as it is in Ferguson, Missouri, should there not be a significant number of blacks on the city's police force, including in the higher ranks? This might mean minimizing the importance of some exam results, but the tradeoff might help to prevent a combustible racial climate. If a state's population is at least 30% black, as it is in South Carolina, should there not be a significant number of blacks enrolled in the University of South Carolina? After all, their taxes help to subsidize the costs of running the university, and if the 30 percent of the population that is black would like to see more African Americans working as teachers, dentists and attorneys, more will have to admitted into the university.

Opponents, both white and black, have argued that to achieve these goals, standards might have to be lowered, thereby leading to an expansion of incompetence as well as the perception that blacks and other minorities are being patronized. On the flip side, proponents of affirmative action have countered that standards will still be high enough and that fair compensation for the past and increased diversity is a reasonable tradeoff. In addition, affirmative action is generally seen as a temporary remedy that can be reduced or abolished once disparities are minimized.

Affirmative action Supreme Court demonstration February 21, 2013
Courtesy of Joseluis89 (CC BY-SA-3.0)
https://commons.wikimedia.org/wiki/File: Affirmative_Action_supreme_court_demonstration_2003.jpg

Most students initially oppose affirmative action programs, particularly since they understand the impact these policies might have on their access to a college education. However, when the notion of compensation is thoroughly examined in light of the question about the best way to achieve equality, some shift their views. They come to understand that who we are today cannot be divorced from the past. In addition, this understanding cannot be achieved simply by studying a unit on the Civil Rights Movement beginning with Rosa Parks or by attending an assembly during Black History Month.

It took several centuries of bigotry and intolerance to create the inequities that are still around us today. Clay Risen, an op-ed editor for the *New York Times* and author of *A Nation on Fire: America in the Wake of the King Assassination*, contends that we must get rid of the historical view that sees the classical civil rights struggle during the 1950s and 1960s as the definitive struggle. It must be replaced by *"one that looks much further back, and with a much broader lens."* While Martin Luther King, Jr. and the Civil Rights Act of 1964 provided access to public accommodations and voting booths, the larger struggle has been for *"equal access to all the things that white America takes for granted: safe neighborhoods, decent education, and a fair justice system, to name a few."* According to Risen, significant progress has been made, but *"dismal facts abound: Real income among blacks in Washington has not changed in thirty years, more black men are in prison than in college, and blacks have suffered significantly more by any metric during the Great Recession."* As he states, *"there are no easy solutions to these problems."*

The same can be said for resolving the previously mentioned pushups dilemma. However, just because the initial competition was unfair does not mean we cannot search for ways to make it fairer in the present or the future. The first step begins with developing a deeper understanding of the past, one that stretches all the way back to the sale of the first African slaves in Jamestown 400 years ago. The second involves the development of greater empathy towards those that have historically been the victims of history's injustices and inequities. Finally, there must be a greater commitment towards collaboration in the effort to insure equal opportunity for everyone, regardless of the baggage inherited from the past. As my students recently came to realize, even their lives in the sleepy suburbs of St. Louis can be thrown into turmoil after one police shooting. If we are to better understand the nation in which we live, and if we are to continue to search for ways to make it better, it is incumbent upon every citizen to become educated on the best way to find greater equality in our society.

Suggested Reading:

"Chapter 3: Demographics and Economic Data, By Race." *Pew Research Center*. August 22, 2013. http://www.pewsocialtrends.org/2013/08/22/chapter-3-demographic-economic- data-by-race/.

Cobb, Jelani. "The Matter of Black Lives." *New Yorker*. March 3, 2016. http://www.newyorker.com/magazine/2016/03/14/where-is-black-lives-matter-headed.

Curry, George, ed. *The Affirmative Action Debate*. New York: Perseus Books, 1996.

Du Bois, W.E.B. *The Souls of Black Folk*. New York: Dover Publications, 1994.

Morris, Aldon D. *The Origins of the Civil Rights Movement: Black Communities Organizing for Change*. New York: The Free Press, 1984.

Risen, Clay. *A Nation on Fire: America in the Wake of the King Assassination*. Hoboken: John Wiley and Sons, Inc., 2009.

Taylor, Keeanga-Yamahtta. *From #BlackLivesMatter to Black Liberation*. Chicago: Haymarket Books, 2016.

Washington, Booker T. *Up From Slavery*. New York: Dover Publications, 1995.

X, Malcolm, and Alex Haley. *The Autobiography of Malcolm X*. New York: Penguin Books, 2001.

Zahniser, J.D., and Amelia R. Fry. *Alice Paul: Claiming Power*. New York: Oxford University Press, 2014.

Chapter 16
In the eye of the beholder

Robert Mapplethorpe
Courtesy of Flicker (CC BY 2.0)
https://www.flickr.com/photos/centralasian/5894011279/

What is the best way to evaluate artistic expression?

The place is Cincinnati, Ohio and the date is September 24, 1994. A criminal trial is about to begin. The defendants are the Cincinnati Contemporary Arts Center and its director, Dennis Barrie. They have been indicted by a Hamilton County grand jury of two misdemeanors each: pandering and using minors in pornography. For Mr. Barrie, the charges carry a maximum penalty of a year in jail and fines of up to $2,000; for the art center, the maximum fine is $10,000. The trial was in front of an eight-person jury, four men and four women, and would last for about a week and a half. The nation was about to begin its first criminal trial ever of an art museum over the content of an exhibition.

In the spring of 1990, the Contemporary Arts Center (CAC) in Cincinnati, Ohio, held an exhibit of photographs by the late artist, Robert Mapplethorpe. This exhibit, titled *The Perfect Moment*, was controversial in nature from the very outset. There was a great deal of negative public reaction and an attempt to close the exhibit citing the Ohio obscenity statute, which made it illegal for any person to *"promote, display... or exhibit... any obscene material."* Of the 175 pictures in the exhibit, seven were extremely contentious making them the focus of the ensuing trial. Two of the pictures were of naked minors, one male and one female, with a *"lewd exhibition or graphic focus on the genitals."* The other five objectionable pictures were of men posing in unusual sadomasochistic poses.

Mapplethorpe's photographs first achieved notoriety for his celebration and documentation of New York's gay community. His favorite human subjects were himself and his close friend, poet and singer, Patti Smith. His portraits of Smith captured his subject as lonely, independent, sensitive and wild. Andy Warhol, Richard Gere and Grace Jones were also among some of his famous subjects. He expressed his art via pictures of composers, socialites, pornographic film stars and members of the S & M underground. Mapplethorpe's art was explicit in nature, often depicting sexual organs and bondage equipment with his subjects being adorned in leather, spikes and chains.

To many critics and connoisseurs of modern art, Mapplethorpe's photographs expressed a unique vision never before seen. Like statuary dating back to the days of Michelangelo and other Renaissance artists, Mapplethorpe intended the human body in his pictures to be depicted as an object of beauty. In addition, the provocative nature of the images, many of which paid heed to racial diversity and the acceptance of homosexuality, communicated a message of tolerance if not outright acceptance. At the very least, if one of his photographs were hung on a wall, it would be virtually impossible for the image to be ignored. Mapplethorpe's photographs would almost certainly inspire some kind of reaction from the viewer. In the Cincinnati trial, the jury was told by defense witnesses that Mapplethorpe's work was serious, indeed, brilliant art.

That said, it could be safely argued that the photographs inspired a very different reaction from the majority of viewers in the public. The graphically sexual nature of the subject matter tended to provoke a reaction amongst many that ranged from disgust to outright anger. For much of the public, Mapplethorpe's photographs should not be viewed as any form of creative or artistic expression. Many people found no redeeming value in the pictures; instead, the photographs in the exhibit crossed the line into what many might consider to be disturbing, filthy and offensive. Even for those who acknowledged a significant overlap between what is considered to be art and what is considered to be pornography, the exhibit of Mapplethorpe's photographs crossed well over that line and thus led to this criminal trial.

The legal proceedings in Cincinnati raised a timeless question: What is art? To many, the question cannot be answered beyond the vague notion that art is any form of creative expression. The idea is that art, at least good art, is relative and lies in the *"eyes of the beholder."* Since art in its many forms, including paintings, statues, pottery, architecture, poetry, literature, music and dance, has played a vitally important role throughout history, this question has come up repeatedly in my classes.

Over the years, I have found the best way to initiate this conversation in class is by showing students a series of images depicting contemporary abstract art. Painting after painting is projected on the screen, the more abstract, the better. Students are shown examples of the cubist images painted by Piet Mondrian, the Surrealism of Paul Klee and the Abstract Expressionism of Mark Rothko. They see provocative shapes and colorful images, and they are told that many of these paintings sell today for considerable sums of money. In fact, one of Mondrian's paintings sold in 2015 for over 15 million dollars. Towards the end of the slideshow, I slip in the following illustration:

Courtesy of Jack Regenbogen (CC0)

At the end of the presentation, I ask students to select their favorite painting. Several immediately choose the above image, saying they can at least recognize a familiar shape. It is always a fun experience to then reveal that this painting is entitled *Wild Thing*, and that it was created by my son, Jack, when he was still in preschool. His mom and I still have it framed and hanging on our wall even though Jack is now a practicing attorney. However, I doubt we would get much if we put it up for sale at auction. The fact that Jack's masterpiece is usually selected as the class favorite only reveals the dire need for students to examine the essential question, what is the best way to evaluate artistic expression in the context of their history class?

One reason why students struggle with this question is because few have had the opportunity to be exposed to a wide range of art. They tend to respect and value diversity and so are slow to criticize, but when confronted by abstract images seen in paintings by artists such as Wassily Kandinsky, Jackson Pollack or Pablo Picasso, they tend to respond negatively-*"This is art?" "A child could have painted this." "People pay a lot of money for this? I could have created this painting."* Not possessing the credentials to provide much of a rebuttal, I typically respond by saying that you did not create this painting, it emerged as a unique vision from the artist. Whether you initially like the piece or not, it represents a unique creation that emerged from the mind and imagination of the artist.

In some cases, I might treat the painting as a type of Rorschach test and ask the students for the first thought that jumped into their minds after seeing the image. Since most have a ready answer, the students then have to admit the painting did provoke a response. In other cases, I ask if the color of the walls in their bedroom has any impact on their mood swings. Many acknowledge that white walls will provoke a different psychological response than black, red or blue. I then ask if they hung an abstract painting on their bedroom wall, could it have a similar effect? Again, most respond by agreeing that depending on the abstract image, modern art, even if it looks like it was created by a chimpanzee, might be preferable to just staring at a blank wall. I then hit them with the clincher – If an artistic piece was created sometime in the past, might it reflect something from history? Going one step further, is it even possible that the artistic creation had some kind of impact on the past?

To give credit to where it is due, our high school orchestra teacher, Dan Holt, originally raised these questions in my world history classes many years ago. Dan, who recently passed away, inspired a generation of students to love and value classical music. When he came into my classes in the midst of our thematic unit on artistic expression, he not only played samples of music from different time periods, he also began jaw-dropping discussions by raising the intriguing question, does art simply reflect the time period in which it was created, or did it also help to shape the past? It was from Dan, as well as other teachers who have guest-starred in my classes over the years, that I have come to appreciate the role art can and should play in a history class. These questions about how much art reflects and/or helps to shape history have always brought focus to the study of artistic achievements in my history classes.

As mentioned in an earlier chapter, two opposing forces, religious faith and empirical thinking, have fought for the souls of many different cultures throughout history, and this has been reflected in their artistic achievements. In ancient times, religion clearly ruled. It is difficult to look at the architecture, the statues or even the pottery from ancient Egypt, Mesopotamia, India or China and not see the reverence paid to their gods and religious traditions. The same could be said for more recent artistic creations found in sub-Saharan Africa, Australia, Polynesia and the Americas. From the Egyptian Sphinx to the Angkor Wat Buddhist temple in Cambodia, from

Islamic mosques in Timbuktu to Mayan sacrificial alters on the Yucatan Peninsula, religion has dominated the architecture and artwork of societies for thousands of years. There may have been Prehistoric cave paintings in France or Spain that depicted tribal hunts and other scenes from everyday life, but for the most part, artistic achievement was dominated by religious themes.

That all changed with the Greeks. The pendulum began to swing away from religious faith and more towards logic and reason with the rise of the Greek polis, particularly the one called Athens. The Greeks paid heed to their many gods, and their mythology about those gods lives on today as a defining feature of western artistic achievement. However, in reality, the Greeks almost single-handedly invented the notion of humanism. Pictures on vases and pottery may have been of Athena or Apollo, but they were created to represent the Greek conception of the ideal human form. Make no mistake, virtually all of the Greeks held religious views about the Gods influencing human fate, but their overarching values were grounded in the world of humans.

To the Greeks, beauty was seen in the swiftest human runner, the strongest human wrestler and the most accurate human archer. What mattered most was not whether God had handed down laws or commandments to be obeyed but whether humans might create their own laws to govern a civilized society. In the world of architecture, art and sculpture, as well as the dramas, tragedies and comedies performed on stage, the perfect human form or character was almost always the central theme for the Greeks. Logic and reason was the rule, and human anatomy and geometry can sometimes be seen in their creations. To the Greeks, virtually everything in the natural world could be seen through the eyes of science and mathematics. Take for example the golden ratio.

It is thought the Greeks may have been among the first to discover the ratio. Numerically, it is written as one plus the square root of five divided by 2, or as 1.6180339887... The golden ratio appears in many patterns of nature, including the spiral arrangement of leaves and other plant parts. Many believe the golden rectangle, in which the ratio of the longer side to the shorter side is the golden ratio, is aesthetically pleasing. Euclid, Pythagoras and other Greeks saw the golden ratio all around them. It is found in the façade of the Parthenon and in many Greek statues when one computes a ratio where one numerical quality is the distance from the top of the statue to the figure's navel and the second runs from the navel to the bottom of the statue. In ancient Greece, the navel was considered to be the source of human life. The manner in which the Greeks saw and applied these types of mathematical principles to virtually all areas of life speaks volumes about their intense focus on the use of reason.

Fibonacci spiral in nature (This spiral is intimately connected to the Golden Ratio)
Courtesy of Flicker (CC BY 2.0)
https://www.flickr.com/photos/jitze1942/3114723951/

Combined with Roman cultural achievements that continued to blossom for another thousand years after the spread of Greek culture under Alexander the Great, the emphasis on logic, reason, math and science came to define the essence of classical civilization. Religion by no means disappeared, but the artistic achievements of the Greeks and Romans pushed the pendulum far towards the side commonly referred to as humanism and this was reflected in a wide range of artistic achievement. However, the thousand years that followed the fall of the Roman Empire in Western Europe, commonly called the middle ages, forced the pendulum to swing far in the opposite direction.

During the Middle Ages, knowledge and reason took a backseat to ignorance and superstition. The one unifying constant in people's lives was Christianity. The Church made a concerted effort to maintain Greek and Roman culture by copying and housing the great classical manuscripts, and in many cases, monks in their abbeys and monasteries beautifully decorated them. The architectural center of every feudal town in Western Europe was the Church, and in the larger cities, Gothic style cathedrals were constructed to rise up to the heavens. From the statuary to the richly colored stained-glass windows to the hymns sung by their choirs, almost every feature of medieval artistic achievement was intended to glorify God and appeal to the dominant sense of faith. Rather than attempt to enrich life in the here and now, the middle ages was focused on how to best achieve salvation and eternal life in the next world.

Sometime in the 15th Century, the pendulum began to shift back again and this time, the epicenters of this change were the burgeoning commercial cities of northern Italy. Thanks to the wealth generated by trade with the near and far East, cities like Florence, Genoa and Venice began to patronize the arts. The Renaissance, as this development came to be known, did not suddenly materialize in a single day, and most people had no idea they were living in the midst of a cultural transformation. However, beginning with the poetry of Petrarch, the gradual refocus on humanism continued with the paintings and sculptures of Michelangelo, Titian, Raphael, Botticelli and Leonardo da Vinci. The subject matter often remained religious, but by pioneering and perfecting new techniques like the use of perspective, the figures in the paintings took on life-like forms. Values began to slowly shift back towards the current world rather than the next, and this manifested itself in increased interest in everything Greek or Roman. Literacy rose, particularly with the advent of the printing press, and as the Renaissance began to spread to other parts of Europe, names like Cervantes, Erasmus, Rembrandt and Shakespeare all joined the crowd. The tendency was towards questioning and greater rational thought applied to almost every area of life. In the material world, this helped to jumpstart the Commercial Revolution. Even the Church was not immune as Martin Luther, John Calvin and the English king, Henry VIII, among others, broke away to begin new Christian sects as part of the Protestant Reformation. Once again, these changes were all reflected in the artistic creations of the time.

The Birth of Venus by Botticelli
Courtesy of Wikimedia Commons (PD-Art/PD-old-100)
https://commons.wikimedia.org/wiki/File:Sandro_Botticelli_-_La_nascita_di_Venere_-_Google_Art_Project_-_edited.jpg

The metaphor of art acting as a mirror to reflect key developments in any society is relatively easy to find. Almost any culture, past or present, possesses examples of artistic creation that reflect important values and ideas. Locating instances of where art has played a vital role in shaping a society's values or ideas is a different story. One good place to look, however, is with the dawn of the Romantic Movement along with the simultaneous rise of nationalism roughly two hundred years ago.

The Enlightenment, an intellectual movement characterized by logical thought, science and reason, dominated 18th Century Europe. Borrowing from the classical thinking of the Greeks and Romans, Enlightenment philosophers discussed, debated and wrote about how to best apply reason to almost every area of life. Enlightenment thinkers went far beyond the bounds of physics, astronomy, chemistry and anatomy and looked for ways to apply logical thinking to such areas as politics, government, religion and the arts. This was the age when John Locke developed his Theory of Natural Rights, Sir Isaac Newton created the calculus to help prove gravity, Montesquieu originated the idea that three distinct branches of government should share political power, and Voltaire used reason to attack the notion of organized religion.

Therefore, the period of the Enlightenment is most closely associated with the Classical Period in art, music and architecture. Clarity and rational cognition can be heard in the melodies of Mozart, seen in the paintings of Jacques-Louis David and reflected in the Greek columns dominating so many homes and public buildings of this era. Intellectual leaders in the 1700s looked back to the Greeks and Romans for guidance and inspiration. While most believed in God, some came to see his role in creating the universe as being synonymous to the skills employed by a clockmaker in assembling a piece of machinery that would still operate long after it has left the clockmaker's workshop. This style of thinking was clearly reflected in most of the artistic creations of the time.

At the risk of over-simplification, along came Ludwig van Beethoven. Composing mostly in the Classical period, something dramatic happened towards the end of his career. Maybe it stemmed from his anger over losing the ability to hear, but anyone who has ever listened to the *Ode to Joy* in Beethoven's Ninth Symphony can hear the change. The year was 1824, and Europe was still reeling from the French Revolution and the carnage of the Napoleonic Wars. Despite the attempt by the Congress of Vienna in 1815 to turn the clock back to the days of absolute monarchy and a privileged nobility, the forces of liberalism and nationalism had been unleashed, and there was no way to ignore them. Millions clamored for greater freedom, equality and nationalistic pride.

Ludwig Van Beethoven
Courtesy of the Library of Congress
Prints and Photographs Division LC-USZ62-13745

However, this time, logical debate would not be enough. To join the revolutions coming in the 19th and 20th centuries, reason would frequently have to take a backseat to emotion. Just as the French could march off to battle in the early days of the 19th century inspired by La Marseillaise, the Russians were equally aroused at the end of the same century by the blazing cannons in Peter Tchaikovsky's *1812 Overture*. The common denominator in between was the rise of nationalism, and this time, the music did not simply reflect this development, it helped to generate feelings of national pride within the listener.

The Romantic Period in music, art and literature was characterized by intense feelings as well as a healthy respect for nature. In the 19th century, the pendulum was swinging away from logic and reason and towards passions and emotions. The arts certainly reflected this movement, but it can also be argued they helped shape peoples' thinking. Did the operas composed by Richard Wagner in the 1800s only reflect the rise of German nationalism or did they also help to inspire the German people to seek the creation of a powerful German nation-state? When Wagner wrote *Die Meistersinger* in 1867, could he have possibly imagined a young Austrian by the name of Adolph Hitler attending over one hundred performances of this very lengthy opera? Hitler fancied himself an artist and at one point, was turned away from the Vienna Art Academy. Despite the frustrations over his inability to paint, how many of Hitler's ideas about a German master race or the need for lebensraum (living space) were fermented in his early days of exposure to Romantic art and music?

Dan Holt had asked whether art simply reflected the time period in which it was created, or did it also help to shape the past? This has proven on so many occasions to be a wonderful tool in determining the best way to evaluate artistic expression. In the course of my teaching career, here is just a sample of the more specific questions that have been inspired by Dan's query:

> *Did Uncle Tom's Cabin only reflect slavery in the South or did it also play a role in launching the Civil War?*
>
> *Did Upton Sinclair's The Jungle only reflect life in Chicago at the dawn of the 20th century or did it play a role in launching the Progressive Movement?*
>
> *Did All Quiet On the Western Front only reflect the soldiers' experience in the First World War or did it help inspire the rise of pacifism in the years that followed?*
>
> *Did The Great Gatsby only reflect life in the Roaring Twenties or did it contribute to the rising alienation experienced by the Lost Generation?*
>
> *Did Steinbeck's The Grapes of Wrath only reflect life during the Great Depression or did it stir up greater empathy and support for FDR's New Deal?*
>
> *Did Louis Armstrong only write and perform toe-tapping songs that reflected his upbringing in New Orleans, or did his jazz music help to fuel the Great Migration of African Americans towards northern cities?*
>
> *Did folk singers like Woody Guthrie, Pete Seeger and Bob Dylan only compose simple ballads that reflected everyday*

life, or did they inspire the respect for the common man that became a focus of 1960s activism?

Did the rise of rap music starting in the 1980s only reflect the experience of many urban blacks, or did it lay a foundation for much of the leadership in today's Black Lives Matter Movement?

As part of the discussion that typically follows any of these questions, I ask students to think of any music, art or literature that has had a profound impact on their ideas or values. To get them started, I tell them about a personal experience of my own. I explain that when I was about 13 years old, my interest in politics and international events was only embryonic at best. Then one day, I heard a song over the radio – *Ohio* by Crosby, Stills, Nash and Young. Intrigued by the angry tone of the guitar playing, I inquired into the meaning of its lyrics. It spoke about soldiers and President Nixon, and it constantly repeated the refrain about four dead in Ohio. Towards the end of the song, it mentions finding someone dead on the ground. I was more than intrigued and it did not take much effort to link these words to the recent student protests over President Nixon's secret bombings in Cambodia and the ensuing killing of four students at Kent State University by the Ohio National Guard. Suddenly, my interest in current events spiked and the political values I still possess to this day began to coalesce. If protest songs like *Ohio* could fire up the curiosity and interest of one adolescent, what impact would they have on the millions of others listening to the radio and buying the LPs? Once again, I ask the students did this song only reflect the events of the time, or did it have an impact on the thinking of millions of baby-boomers just coming of age?

Kent State University Massacre
Courtesy of Flicker (CC BY 2.0)
https://www.flickr.com/photos/nostri-imago/4427918003/

Considering that film has become a contemporary art form that combines the visual with the auditory, it possesses even greater power than any other medium. Therefore, it also enters the conversation generated by Dan's question. Dalton Trumbo's *Johnny Got His Gun* is a good example. As a book published in 1938, the tome about an American soldier recovering from his horrific wounds in the First World War clearly reflected the rise of pacifism in Great Britain and across the Atlantic in the United States. While the lead character, Joe Bonham, lays in bed slowly realizing an artillery shell has taken his arms, legs and face leaving him with a workable mind but no way to communicate with the outside world, the reader is left with a sense of despair and anger over the senselessness of war. Did the book simply reflect the thinking of many at this time, or did it feed a growing pacifist movement that contributed to the United Kingdom and the United States both looking the other way as Hitler prepared for war? Interestingly enough, the film version of the book was released in 1971, a time when student protests across the United States were pressuring the Nixon Administration to find a quick exit out of the war in Vietnam. Once again, the question could be raised, did the film simply reflect the growing antiwar movement or did it contribute to its growing popularity?

Similar questions might be raised about the influence of film on the Civil Rights Movement that dominated much of the second half of the 20th Century. The African American slaves seen in the 1939 film, *Gone With the Wind*, appeared to be happy and content with the watermelon culture of the antebellum South. In 1989, the film *Glory* purposely aimed to correct this debilitating stereotype. Not only did it tell the true story of the Massachusetts 54th regiment, an all-black unit who fought courageously in the Civil War, but it also included a scene that at first, made little sense. Robert Gould Shaw, the leader of the regiment, is out training on his own early one February morning. Even though Shaw was white, as the officers in all-black units were up until the time when President Truman integrated the military in 1948, he came from an abolitionist background and clearly supported the goal of enabling the men under his command to achieve their *"glory."* Riding on a horse, he uses his saber to slice through watermelons mounted in a line of pikes. Watermelons in Massachusetts in February? The event clearly never happened, but the point of the scene is not hard to ascertain. The image resonated in the minds of millions of viewers, and the point was to literally obliterate the *"darkie"* stereotype that dated back to the days before the Civil War and was carried into the 20th Century by films like *The Birth of a Nation* and *Gone With the Wind*. *Glory* simply followed in the wake of earlier films like *A Raisin in the Sun*, *In the Heat of the Night* and *The Autobiography of Miss Jane Pittman*. How much did *Glory* and these other films reflect the changes taking place and how much did they also influence them? Dan posed his question in regard to music, but it might be even more relevant in the medium of film.

One movie proved to be so explosive it led to a Supreme Court case. In 1988, *Mississippi Burning* was released to tell the tragic story of three civil rights workers murdered during the Freedom Summer of 1964. While the film was criticized for playing loosely with the truth and for focusing too much on white FBI agents rather than the victims of the Klan's violence, the film's director, Alan Parker, clearly intended to provoke an angry response from the audience. A combination of violent scenes, tough language and a rhythmic sound score appealed more to the viewers base instincts than to any sense of logic or reason. After seeing the movie in a Wisconsin theater, Todd Mitchell, a young black man, was so enraged he attacked a young white boy. He was subsequently convicted of aggravated battery in the Circuit Court of Kenosha County. However, according to Wisconsin statute, Mitchell's sentence was increased because the court found he had selected his victim based on race. When the Wisconsin Supreme Court ruled Mitchell's First Amendment rights were violated because he was being punished for his thoughts in addition to his actions, the U.S. Supreme Court agreed to hear the case. The unanimous decision in the case of *Wisconsin v. Mitchell* upheld the state hate crime statute. A major verdict affecting the entire nation was the last domino to fall in a line where the first resulted from the emotional power of a film.

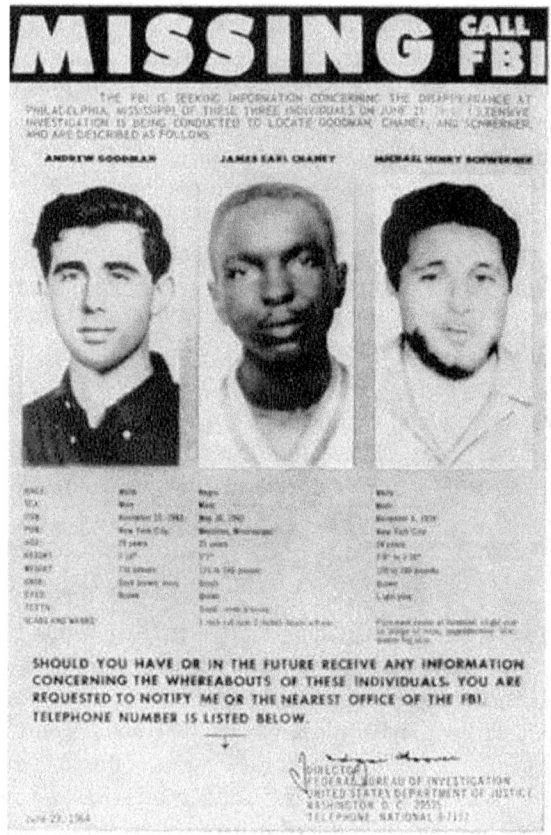

FBI poster of missing Civil Rights workers
Courtesy of the Federal Bureau of Investigation (PD-USGov-FBI)
https://commons.wikimedia.org/wiki/File:FBI_Poster_of_Missing_Civil_Rights_Workers.jpg

In addition to Dan's question, there is one other point that must be considered in any examination of the best way to evaluate artistic expression.

Whether viewing art, listening to music or contemplating the meaning of a poem, how can one determine if a piece of artistic expression has any redeeming value? After all, the Mapplethorpe photographs were not just considered by many to be obscene, they were also judged to lack any kind of artistic merit. This once again conjures up the question of relativity examined in chapter four. Applied here, the cultural relativist would say that all art is *"in the eyes of the beholder"* and that there are no fixed standards by which to judge artistic expression. Others would strongly disagree. The marketplace might be a guide since some paintings command much higher prices than others and some recording artists clearly outsell others. However, the marketplace is incredibly fickle, and what sells today may quickly be forgotten tomorrow. The Mapplethorpe defendants were acquitted, but this was seen mostly as a major affirmation of First Amendment freedom of speech rights. The court case said nothing about the artistic quality of the pictures and it is assumed this decision would be left up to those who now had the freedom to view the photographs.

Peter Hoekstra, a Republican congressman from Michigan and an opponent of the National Endowment of Arts, once said, *"art is whatever people want to perceive it to be, but that doesn't mean the federal government should fund it."* Hoekstra, in addition to other critics of the court ruling, believed the Mapplethorpe decision opened the door to too much tolerance in the evaluation of artistic expression and this would lead society down a slippery slope jeopardizing its values. Dan Holt's question would force many to acknowledge that artistic expression does hold a certain sway over what people think and therefore, how they behave. In that regard, the moral gatekeepers who wanted to shut down the Mapplethorpe exhibit have a valid point. However, while many see homoerotic artistic expression as a threat, consider the opposite end of the spectrum. Visualize the Nazis burning books by Ernest Hemingway, Upton Sinclair, Jack London, Helen Keller, H.G. Wells, Victor Hugo, Joseph Conrad, Fyodor Dostoyevsky and Leo Tolstoy. Given a choice between these two opposing ends of the spectrum, maybe it is better to ere towards too much freedom of artistic expression rather than too little.

On October 12 of 1997, the *New York Times* ran a piece by Amei Wallach that posed the questions, *What is art, what is good art and who gets to decide?* Several experts were asked these questions; here is a sampling of their responses:

Thomas McEvilly, professor of art history at Rice University, said *"It is art if it is called art, written about in an art magazine, exhibited in a museum* or bought by a private collector." In other words, if it is art according to the so-called "*art system*," that makes it art. He also stated that many people, like my students, do not understand art the same way they do not understand molecular biology until they study molecular biology. If people are going to understand art, they must study art.

Robert Rosenblum, another professor of art history at New York University and curator at the Guggenheim Museum, essentially agreed with his peer at Rice University. He stated that "*there has to be consensus about good art among informed people – artists, dealers, curators, collectors.*" According to Rosenblum, the process begins when someone says that something is good, but "*if you put it up a flagpole and nobody salutes it, then there's nothing there.*"

Richard Prince, an artist, had a different view. He said that 10 people in a room talking about art could never agree about whether something is good or bad. According to Prince, "*I think its good when I can put myself in another artist's shoes, and wish I could have done that, or could see myself doing it.*" Good art must create a level of empathy with at least some people within the viewing audience.

Jenny Holzer, another artist, has a similar position. She believes the viewer can rely on the artist's representation; "*he or she has no reason to lie.*" According to Holzer, the art patron "*with a combination of sensitivity and knowledge will perceive that something is art and is good.*" It is probably not surprising that the artists possess more flexible standards for art and are not as concerned about achieving a larger consensus.

Speaking of standards, Philippe De MonteBello, director of the Metropolitan Museum of Art in New York City, believes that the need for accepted criteria by which to evaluate art has diminished in recent times. He believes that the "*change began with Impressionism when you had a division among people who saw the academic painters as the accepted norm and the avant-guardists represented the others.*" According to De MonteBello, there is no consensus about anything today. "*Even the notion of standards are in question.*" However, that does not mean art is less important today than in the past. In fact, he believes it probably matters more. Just look at the millions who go to art museums today. Art is in many more households and is in the awareness of many more people than ever before. "*You could argue that because art is so ubiquitous it is even harder to make judgments.*"

Then there are those who look at the bigger picture. Linda Weintraub, freelance curator and author of *Art on the Edge and Over: Searching for Art's*

Meaning in Contemporary Society 1970's-1990's, states that *"when you think about art, you have to think about life. If art doesn't sensitize us to something in the world, clarify our perceptions, make us aware of the decisions we have made, it's entertainment."* In other words, art, and certainly good art, must have a positive impact on the viewer.

Finally, Morley Safer, co-editor of *60 Minutes*, has a significantly dissimilar view. He had the opportunity to view a Robert Ryman retrospective at the Museum of Modern Art. Ryman is an American artist identified with the movements of monochrome images, minimalism, and conceptual art, and is best known for abstract, white-on-white paintings. After strolling through the show, Safer walked through the museum's permanent collection. *"It was like going from an absolute desert to a perfect spring day."* Regardless of the existence of standards by which to evaluate art or the lack thereof, the bottom line is that everyone will still have his or her own individual opinion.

In the course of examining the question about how to best evaluate artistic expression in the classroom, there has been one other point that consistently achieves a high level of consensus amongst students. What is good art? Most agree good art must meet the test of time. The Beatles were enormously popular in the 1960s and they are still enjoyed by many of the grandchildren of those who swooned at Beatles concerts from more than fifty years ago. Will they still be popular two hundred years from now? Michelangelo, Rembrandt and Van Gogh are still held in awe around the world, but for every artist, musician or architect who is still admired centuries after their deaths, there are probably hundreds that have been lost and forgotten. The more that artistic expression reflects the ideas and events of a particular period in the past, the more likely it will meet the test of time. However, if it can be shown that a particular painting, poem, song or film also helped to shape the ideas or events from the past, it will achieve a level of historical relevance. This should guarantee its immortality.

Suggested Reading:

Barta, Tony. *Screening the Past: Film and the Representation of History.* Westport: Praeger Publishers, 1998.

Gompertz, Will. *What Are You Looking At?: The Surprising, Shocking, and Sometimes Strange Story of 150 Years of Modern Art.* New York: Penguin Group, 2012.

Hartt, Frederick, and David Wilkins. *History of Italian Renaissance Art.* Boston: Pearson, 2010.

Palmer, Alex. "When Art Fought the Law and the Art Won." *Smithsonian.* October 2, 2015. http:www.smithsonianmag.com/history/when-art-fought-law-and-art-won-180956810/.

Strickland, Carol. *The Annotated Mona Lisa: A Crash Course in Art History from Prehistoric to Post-Modern.* Kansas City: AndrewsMcMeel Publishing, 2007.

Wallach, Amei. "Art; Is It Art? Is It Good? And Who Says So?" *New York Times.* October 12, 1997. http://www.nytimes.com/1997/10/12/arts/art-is-it-art-is-it-good-and-who-says-so.html?pagewanted=all.

Weintraub, Linda. *Art on the Edge and Over: Searching for Art's Meaning in Contemporary Society, 1970's-1990's.* New York: Art Insights, 1996.

Chapter 17
The struggle for power

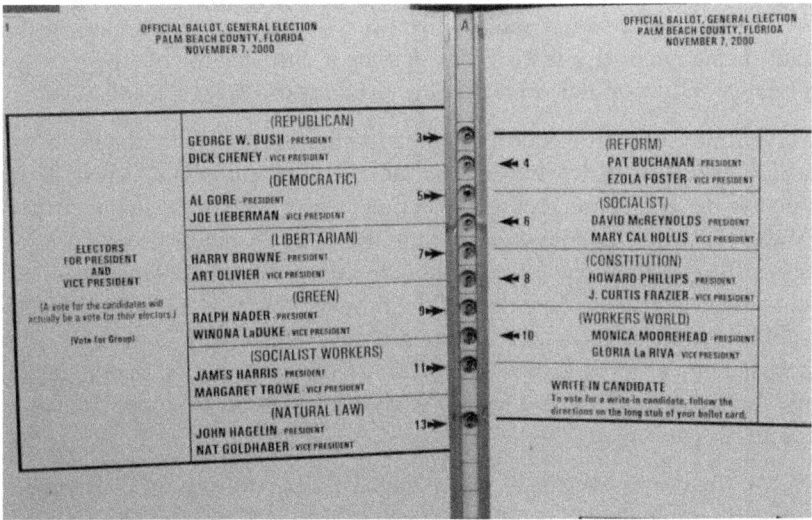

Palm Beach County, Florida official ballot for the 2000 United States Presidential election
https://commons.wikimedia.org/wiki/File:Butterfly_large.jpg (PD-ineligible)

Why are there competitive factions in a democratic society?

The place is the U.S. Supreme Court building in Washington, D.C. and the date is December 12, 2000. In one of the most controversial and contentious decisions handed down in recent history, the Supreme Court has just announced a narrow five to four decision stating there will not need to be any further recount of the votes in Florida from the presidential election held the month before. For practically six weeks, the nation has been torn apart between Democrats and Republicans over the outcome of this election.

George W. Bush, the past governor of Texas and the Republican nominee, has claimed the victory based on winning a majority of electors in the Electoral College. Al Gore, the vice-president for the last eight years and the Democratic nominee, also claimed a victory saying that after a recount of the votes cast in Florida, he will have the majority of the electors. It all came down to Florida. Lost in the haze of controversy is the fact that Gore won a clear victory in the popular vote. Despite his winning margin of over half a million votes, the Constitution requires only a majority of the 537 electors to determine the victor; the popular vote is irrelevant. This marked the fourth election in U.S. history in which the eventual winner failed to win a plurality of the popular vote (after the elections of 1824, 1876 and 1888).

Complicating the election was the presence of another candidate on the ballot, consumer advocate Ralph Nader, representing the Green Party. Sensing dissatisfaction among the populace with both of the major parties, Nader ran with the goal of increasing the nation's political conversation about the environment and other liberal causes. Although Ralph Nader did not win a single state, his share of the popular vote was 2.7%. Since he arguably won these votes more from Gore than Bush, many Democrats, who accused him of spoiling the election for Al Gore, have vilified Nader. In fact, my teenaged daughter set up her first email account to include "blamenader" as part of her address.

On the evening of the election, held Tuesday, November 7, the major networks originally projected that Gore had won in Florida. Later that evening, they reversed themselves, giving Bush the 25 Florida electors, and with them, the overall victory. Al Gore, who had privately conceded the election, retracted his concession as the results in Florida continued to narrow in the early morning hours to a margin of just 2000 votes. The results in Florida were so close they triggered a mandatory recount. Over the next several days, issues were raised about voting abnormalities in several counties including the disqualification of minority voters, questionable vote-counting procedures, even the shape and layout of the ballot. Gore's cause was also hindered by decisions made by Florida Secretary of State, Katherine Harris, a Republican. The recount stretched from days into weeks, and litigation was filed in the Florida state courts as well as the Federal Courts. Al Gore finally conceded after the Supreme Court ruled there was no need to continue the recount in Florida. Later studies have reached conflicting opinions on who would have won the recount had it been allowed to continue. In the end, George W. Bush *"officially"* defeated Al Gore in Florida by 537 votes out a total of more than six million. In the state of Florida, Ralph Nader had received just over 97,000 votes.

Bush v. Gore finally put the issue surrounding the now infamous election of 2000 to rest. George W. Bush was reelected in 2004, this time with a majority of the popular vote as well as electors. His presidency was responsible for beginning and waging the war on terrorism after the 9/11 attacks in 2001 that ultimately brought thousands of American troops to fight in Afghanistan and Iraq. He also had to wrestle with other problems, including a major hurricane that practically destroyed New Orleans and a significant economic downturn beginning in 2007. It is anyone's guess as to how different the nation might have looked by 2008 had Al Gore won the election in 2000. Many Americans took pride in our constitutional system that provided for a peaceful transition in power despite the high level of emotion and controversy. However, the election of 2000 only exacerbated the partisan gap that has existed in the United States from the beginning of our nation. One result of this breach is a staggering dysfunctionality in our government at the present.

After 240 years as an independent nation, how have we reached this point? In the halls of Congress, differences between Democrats and Republicans have made it almost impossible to provide a government that effectively meets the needs of the people. The nation is currently begging for immigration reform that has not been forthcoming. Republicans keep talking about repealing President Obama's Affordable Care Act even though the necessity for some kind of national health care program was first suggested back in the days of the Truman Administration. And at the present, our government lumbers on with a national debt approaching 20 trillion dollars. The growing gap between liberal Democrats and conservative Republicans has reached the point where it is not only difficult to communicate with each other, but in many areas, it is difficult to live with each other. The state of Colorado could potentially vote Democratic or Republican in a national presidential election, but anyone familiar with the state knows there is world of difference between life in liberal Boulder and everyday existence in conservative Colorado Springs.

We collectively take pride to live in our democratic nation, but we have increasingly divided ourselves between liberals and conservatives. Why are there competitive factions in a democratic society? The knee jerk answer might be that humans are different from each other, and it is only natural for them to divide based on these differences. Yet our founding fathers did not believe this to be true and discouraged the division of the populace into competing factions. The words *"political party"* are not found anywhere in the Constitution. After the Constitution was completed in the summer of 1787, it was decided that at least nine states would have to vote to ratify the document in order for it to become the foundation of our government. To encourage support for ratification, Federalists like John Jay, Alexander Hamilton and James Madison published a series of articles collectively known as *The Federalist Papers*. In Federalist No. 9, James Madison, who is considered to be the "*Father of the Constitution*" and went on to become our fourth president, addressed the destructive role of a faction in breaking apart the republic. He continued the discussion in Federalist No. 10 where he discussed the question of how to guard against factions, which he defined as "*a number of citizens, whether amounting to a minority or majority of the whole, who are united and actuated by some common impulse of passion, or of interest, adverse to the rights of other citizens or to the permanent and aggregate interests of the community*". The question Madison then attempts to answer is how to eliminate the negative effects of faction.

James Madison
Courtesy of the Library of Congress
Prints and Photographs Division LC-DIG-ppmsca-19166

Observers of today's balloting procedures might point out the significant role played by the major political parties in conducting elections. After all, according to the Constitution, any natural born citizen who has been in the United States for at least the last 14 years is eligible to run for president. Without parties, there might be thousands of names on the ballot. How could the voter possibly make an informed and intelligent decision? If James Madison were here today to answer that question, he might say the Electoral College was created to take on the nominating process, which today is done by the political parties. Once the electors had narrowed the list of thousands of candidates to the top three, assuming that none had a majority, the House of Representatives would then select the winner. If Madison knew about the massive role today played by political parties/factions in choosing a president, he would probably role over in his grave.

To James Madison and many of our other founding fathers, factions or parties would be more concerned with gaining or keeping power than with effectively providing for the needs of the people. They would do more harm than good, and should be avoided at all costs. When this point comes up in class, many of my students nod their heads in agreement. Yet, the admonition against forming parties or factions was almost immediately disregarded. As previously stated, those in favor of ratifying the Constitution in order to create a stronger central government, including James Madison, immediately began to organize the Federalist Party. They soon labeled their opposition as the Anti-Federalists. From that time to the present, with only a brief interruption during the "*Era of Good Feelings*" in the 1820s, America has been divided between two major political parties.

In addition, the competition between the early political parties in presidential elections was sometimes surprisingly fierce, and would put today's mud-slinging campaigns to shame in comparison. The election in 1800 involved our second president, John Adams, running for reelection as the Federalist candidate. Meanwhile, the Anti-Federalists had morphed into the Democratic-Republicans, and they chose George Washington's former Secretary-of-State, Thomas Jefferson, as their candidate. Adams and Jefferson were two men who had once been close friends but had now become bitter political rivals. The campaign between the two reached a level of personal animosity seldom equaled in American politics.

The Federalists attacked the fifty-seven-year-old Jefferson as a godless radical who would unleash the forces of bloody terror upon the land. With Jefferson as President, so warned one newspaper, "*Murder, robbery, rape, adultery, and incest will be openly taught and practiced, the air will be rent* with the cries of the distressed, the soil will be soaked with blood, and the nation black with crimes." Others attacked Jefferson's deist beliefs as the views of an infidel who "*writes aghast the truths of God's words; who makes not even a profession of Christianity; who is without Sabbaths; without the sanctuary, and without so much as a decent external respect for the faith and worship of Christians.*"

On the other side, Adams was ridiculed from two directions: by the supporters of Alexander Hamilton within his own party and by the Jeffersonian-Republicans from the outside. For example, a private letter in which Hamilton depicted Adams as having "*great and intrinsic defects in his character*" was obtained by Aaron Burr and leaked to the national press. It fueled the Republican attack on Adams as a hypocritical fool and tyrant. His opponents also spread the story that Adams had planned to create an American dynasty by the marriage of one of his sons to a daughter of King George III. According to this unsubstantiated story, only the intervention of George Washington, dressed in his Revolutionary military uniform, and the threat by Washington to use his sword against his former vice president stopped Adam's scheme. Ironically, even though Jefferson won the election and went on to serve for two terms, he and Adams later reconciled and returned to their former friendship. In fact, they were still exchanging affable letters between Massachusetts and Virginia when they both died on the same day, July 4th, 1826, 50 years to the day that the document they both had played such a large role in shaping was signed.

In subsequent elections, matters only went from bad to worse. In 1828, John Quincy Adams, the son of our second president, was running for reelection against the same man he had controversially defeated in 1824: Andrew Jackson. The campaign grew so ugly that not only were personal attacks lobbed against each of the candidates, some were even directed at Jackson's wife over the issue of whether she was divorced from her first husband before marrying again. Jackson was accused of adultery and vilified for running off with another man's wife, and Rachel was accused of bigamy. Once again, despite the vicious nature of the campaign, Jackson went on to victory and to serving two terms.

Up until the mid 19th Century, the contentious nature of partisan politics was nasty but mostly personal. There were some divisive issues, like internal improvements and the tariff, but the focal point of most elections was more on the man than on the issues. This began to change by mid century with the rise of slavery as the primary issue of the day. Only a small percentage of the population ever considered themselves to be abolitionists, but after the United States acquired the southwest region in the Mexican-American War, the spread of slavery became a growing, hotly contested issue. By the 1850s, the Democrats, the party created in the days of Andrew Jackson to succeed Jefferson's Democratic Republicans, were weakened by their division into northern and southern factions. In the North, Democrats like Stephen Douglas advocated the principle of popular sovereignty, which meant that slavery should be allowed to spread only if the people in the new territory voted in its favor. Most Democrats in the South naturally supported the spread of slavery without any restriction.

Meanwhile, the Whigs, a party formed to replace the Federalists after they had collapsed around 1815, were so weakened by the spread of the slavery issue that for all intensive purposes, they all but disappeared. In their place came the Republicans, a new party formed largely on the free soil position that slavery should be kept out of all new territories and states. The election of the Republican, Abraham Lincoln, in 1860, was the first time an issue supplanted personal attacks in a presidential election. In this case, the partisan politics of the day went on to start a Civil War that cost up to 750,000 American lives.

In the years that followed the Civil War, political apathy pushed issue-driven politics off of center stage. The years between 1865 and 1900 were filled by the rise of Big Business, industrialization, rapid urbanization, westward expansion and the arrival of millions of immigrants. While there was a plethora of problems and issues, most were either overlooked or were handled on a state or local level. In the national spotlight, laissez faire policies that dominated our free enterprise system in the late 19th Century kept the federal government's role to a minimum. People did not expect the President or Congress to do very much, and they basically got what they expected. Whenever I ask students to name any presidents between Abraham Lincoln in 1865 and Theodore Roosevelt in 1901, I generally get blank stares. For the most part, they were collectively forgettable and what is more, it did not really matter if they were Democrats or Republicans. Since neither party paid much heed to the problems of farmers, factory workers and other ordinary people, by the 1890s, millions of voters turned to the Populist Party, the most significant third party in American history.

Populists were elected into state legislatures and several governors' mansions, particularly in the Midwest. In addition, about 45 Populists served in Congress. However, after William Jennings Bryan, the Populist candidate for president, lost the election to the Republican, William McKinley, in 1896, the Populists soon disappeared. This was partially due to the fact that the core of their membership was lower class workers and farmers, not the growing middle classes. It can also be explained by a phenomenon that has occurred repeatedly throughout American History; whenever a third party arises to meet the specific needs of a particular group of people, one or both of the other two major parties will begin to address those same needs. When the growing middle class took up the banner of the Populists a decade later in the form of Progressivism, modern American politics would never be the same. The only question that remained is which party, the Democrats or the Republicans, would permanently assume the challenge of pushing the government to help farmers, factory workers and any other group in need of help or protection.

The struggle for power

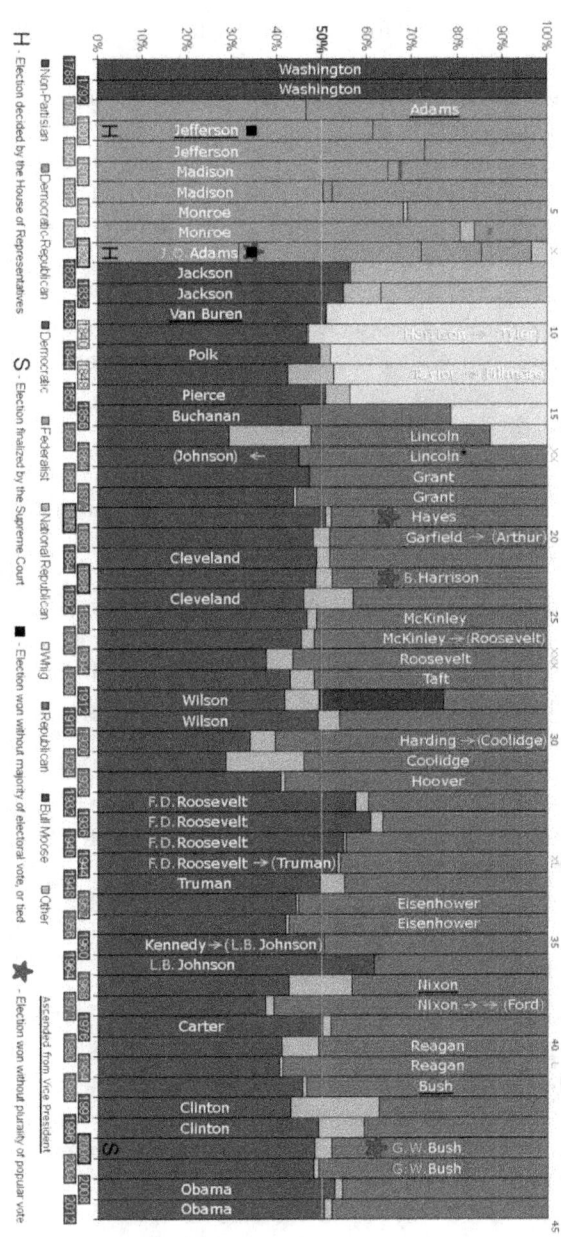

Political Parties in the United States
https://en.wikipedia.org/wiki/Political_parties_in_the_United_States#/media/File:PartyVotes-Presidents.png (CC0 1.0)

The Progressives stood for many things, but the common denominator was an expanding role for government on the local, state and federal level. Progressives wanted to break up the growing monopolies and trusts, protect factory workers in the workplace, provide a "*Square Deal*" to labor unions, protect consumers from unsafe products, conserve natural resources, regulate banks and expand more political power to the people. The consummate Progressive leader took the form of our youngest president, Theodore Roosevelt. He became president almost by accident. As governor of New York, his hyperactive energy drove so many of the Empire State's politicians mad they were delighted when he was chosen as the vice-presidential running mate in William McKinley's drive for a second term in 1900. When Roosevelt became president upon McKinley's assassination a few months into his second term, politics in the 20th Century drastically changed from what it had been in the 19th Century.

It should be noted that Theodore Roosevelt called himself a Republican. So did William Howard Taft, the man TR chose as his successor when he decided not to run for reelection in 1908. Both men were considered Progressive leaders, and both brought about Progressive achievements in the form of "*Square Deal*" programs designed to protect workers and consumers. In addition, unlike modern-day Republicans, both sought the expansion of government to aggressively break up monopolistic trusts. However, when Taft assumed office, Roosevelt, needing an outlet for his unlimited supply of energy, went off on a lengthy safari to Africa. Upon hearing reports about Taft's lethargy, Roosevelt soon bought into the perception that Taft was not the Progressive reformer that he had wanted to take his place. In reality, Taft broke up twice as many trusts in his one term than Roosevelt did in almost two, but this was a case where perception trumped reality. When Roosevelt returned to the states, he soon began to plot his campaign to unseat Taft in 1912.

The presidential election of 1912 proved to be one of the most interesting and important elections in U.S. history. The candidates were William Howard Taft, the incumbent who ended up winning the Republican nomination; Theodore Roosevelt, who after losing the Republican nomination, decided to run as a third party candidate; Woodrow Wilson, the Democrat; and Eugene Debs, the representative of America's small but growing Socialist Party. This was the only presidential election in American history to pit a former president, a current president and a future president against each other. In addition, Progressivism had become so popular and endemic that leaders within both major parties had designs on adopting its core values. Who would carry the Progressive banner into the 20th Century and beyond?

With only a few exceptions, candidates in previous elections had refrained from overt campaigning. Roosevelt changed this by giving speeches around the country. He traveled some 10,000 miles and visited 34 states, where he spoke out in favor of such Progressive causes as a minimum wage, conservation, women's suffrage, safer workplaces, and the eight-hour workday. At one point, he was shot before a speech in Milwaukee, yet still managed to speak for 90 minutes with a bullet lodged in his chest. In addition, he called Taft a *"fathead"* with *"the brains of a guinea pig,"* and Taft responded in kind, saying Roosevelt's followers were *"radicals"* and *"neurotics."* According to Alan Lessoff, a history professor at Illinois State University who specializes in the Progressive Era, *"Roosevelt felt it was hard to sit on the sidelines when this guy was messing up." "And Taft was no slouch, so he resented it terribly."*

Political cartoon from 1912 Presidential election
Courtesy of Charles Lewis Bartholomew (PD-US)
https://commons.wikimedia.org/wiki/File:IF_Teddy_Roosevelt_Woodrow_Wilston_WH_Taft_1912_political-cartoon.jpg

As November approached, Taft essentially gave up as a candidate. He complained in a letter "*there are so many people in the country who don't like me.*" To make the situation even worse, Vice President James S. Sherman died in office that October, temporarily leaving Taft without a running mate. Meanwhile, Woodrow Wilson ran a vigorous campaign based largely on such progressive ideas as completely smashing monopolies and significantly reducing the tariff so as to improve the standard of living of most Americans. According to Lewis L. Gould, author of *Four Hats in the Ring: The 1912 Election and the Birth of Modern American Politics*, Wilson "*was a fresh face, an articulate guy, mildly progressive, southern roots, northern background.*"

In the end, Taft became the only incumbent president to come in third in his own bid for reelection. The good news for him was that he became the only former president to serve on the Supreme Court, a position that was probably more suitable for his reflective nature than the White House. Despite his vigorous campaign, Roosevelt could not overcome the weakness created by the division within his former party and came in a distant second. Wilson was the winner. Even though he had only 42 per cent of the popular vote, he ended up with over 80 per cent of the Electoral College.

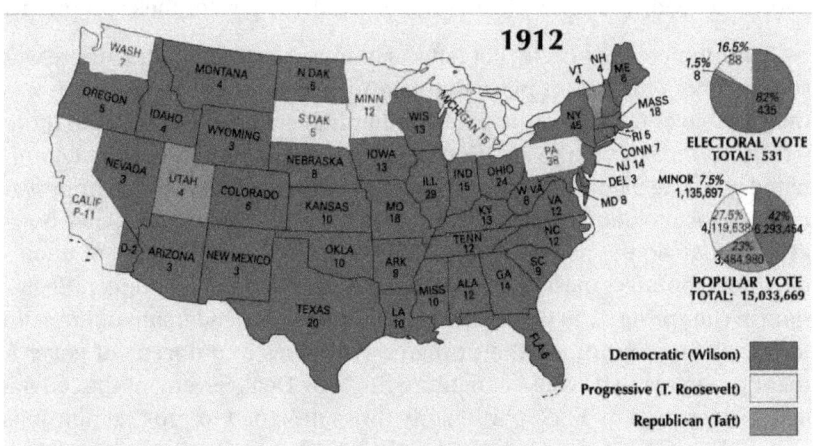

1912 Electoral Map
Courtesy of the National Atlas of the United States (PD-USGov-Atlas)
https://commons.wikimedia.org/wiki/File:1912_Electoral_Map.png

According to Lewis L. Gould, the 1912 election presented "*the most distinguished field that has ever run for president in modern times.*" He added that the consequences of the election were profound. The Republican Party, for instance, would never be the same. And according to Alan Lessoff, "*ever since the 1912 campaign, the conservatives in the Republican Party have had the upper hand.*"

Taft had been nominated by the conservative faction of the Republican Party, the side that placed a higher premium on freedom for businesses rather than increased governmental restrictions. Ever since the 1912 presidential election, the Republicans have been more in favor of economic freedom for businesses, lower taxes, and less government intervention in the economy. Meanwhile, the Democrats ended up adopting Progressivism so thoroughly that progressive values are still the leading characteristic of the Democrats right up to the present. In terms of domestic reforms, Wilson helped to create the Federal Reserve System to better control the nation's banks, a considerably lower tariff to make goods more affordable for the masses, passage of more anti-trust legislation and the formation of the Federal Trade Commission to further regulate businesses. In addition, during his tenure, amendments were added to the Constitution creating the federal income tax, allowing for the direct election of senators and granting women the right to vote. Ever since, the Democrats have been the party in favor of an expanded role for the federal government, programs to help people in need, and higher taxes on the wealthy to pay for these programs.

To complete the puzzle that reflects modern partisan politics, there was still one more important piece that had to be put into place, and that was the variable of race. It would take another half century to achieve that objective. At the start of the 20th Century, both major parties were still dominated by white bigots or at least by leaders who did not make the improvement of race relations a priority. The Great Depression in the 1930s, however, witnessed the rise of massive human suffering in the form of unemployment, homelessness, lost savings and even widespread hunger. Beginning in the spring of 1933, the Democrats under the leadership of Franklin Roosevelt soon morphed their progressive values into dozens of government programs that would constitute the New Deal. Several of the federal agencies created by FDR, particularly those designed to provide new jobs or to aid sharecropping farmers, quietly included the participation of African Americans. This was done in a limited manner, however, so as not to cost the Democrats the votes of white southerners in the next election. The start of the Second World War also witnessed the gradual evolution of race and politics as blacks were integrated with whites in colossal defense industries.

The first Democrat to openly defy the white segregationists who had been part of the Democratic coalition since before the Civil War was Harry Truman. At the risk of costing him his bid for reelection in 1948, Truman issued an executive order to fully integrate all branches of the military. This move contributed to the glacial drift of the Democrats, at least in the North, towards adopting the agenda of the modern Civil Rights Movement. Although poll taxes and literacy tests still prevented a significant number of African Americans from voting in the South, 68% of the Nonwhites that did cast a ballot in 1960 gave their support to the Democratic candidate, John F. Kennedy. Four years later, that number rose to 94% in favor of the Democrat, Lyndon B. Johnson. This was a complete reversal from the previous century when African Americans who had voted during the days of Reconstruction almost universally cast their ballots for the Republicans, the party that had liberated them from slavery.

Kennedy, who narrowly won the presidency, was at first concerned about appeasing white southerners so as to retain their support in his bid for reelection. However, by the second half of his term, he had decided to support passage of an important Civil Rights Act in Congress. Just five days after his assassination on November 22, 1963, Johnson, who had been his vice-president, stated *"no memorial oration or eulogy could more eloquently honor President Kennedy's memory than the earliest possible passage of the Civil Rights bill for which he fought so long."* The following July, the most important piece of civil rights legislation ever passed went into effect and the partnership between blacks and the Democratic Party was sealed.

As might be expected, many white southerners were not happy with the direction taken by the party they had traditionally supported for over a century. In 1968, five southern states again turned away from the Democrats and gave their support to a third party candidate, George Wallace, the white segregationist governor of Alabama. This defection contributed to the election that year of Richard Nixon, the Republican.

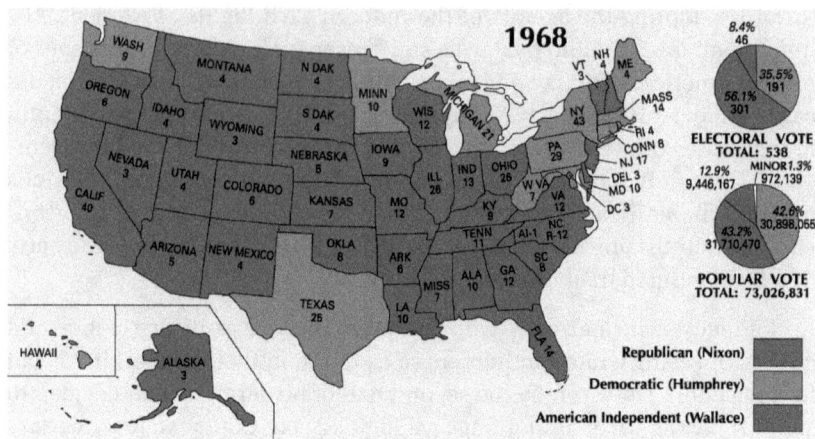

1968 United States Presidential election map
Courtesy of the National Atlas of the United States (PD-USGov-Atlas)
https://commons.wikimedia.org/wiki/File:ElectoralCollege1968.png

Seeing the opportunity opening up in the South, Nixon employed his *"Southern Strategy"* during his first term where he systematically made veiled racist appeals to white voters. He was reelected in 1972 in a landslide election that included victories in 49 out of 50 states. By 1980, the shift was complete. In that year, every southern state except for Georgia, the home state of the Democratic candidate, Jimmy Carter, went for the Republican candidate, Ronald Reagan. Meanwhile, 86% of the nonwhite vote went to Carter. From that point up to the present, it is safe to say that the Democrats have become the party who represent the interests of all people seeking government protection, assistance or relief; including most African Americans and other minorities.

President Ronald Reagan
Courtesy of the Library of Congress
Prints and Photographs Division LC-DIG-highsm-15747

Reagan's election was also noteworthy for another reason. The "*Reagan Revolution*" was more like a counterrevolution, but it also contributed to the current state of modern partisan politics. Reagan, whose two terms dominated the 1980s, managed to create a new coalition by effectively combining two groups. One consisted of those who possessed conservative economic values and favored smaller government, deregulation of major industries and dramatic tax cuts. The other included the New Right: social conservatives and Fundamentalist Christians who opposed secular humanism and were concerned with such issues as church and state, patriotism, pornography and abortion. Reagan's charm, sense of humor and charisma welded this coalition together so tightly that to this day, the Republican Party still looks up to him as its defining iconic figure. It is difficult at the present to find a Republican candidate making a speech without mentioning Reagan's name.

At the present, what are the essential differences that divide most liberal Democrats from the more conservative Republicans? This would seemingly be one of the most important questions that every educated American citizen should be able to intelligently answer, but that is often not the case. In fact, when I raise this question with my students, even high school seniors, I generally receive blank stares. To hook their interest, I usually tell them the story of my wife, who moved to New Orleans with me shortly after our wedding. When we registered to vote, the closed primary system employed by Louisiana at the time required each citizen to put down Democrat, Republican or Independent on the registration form so there could be no cross over voting in party primary elections. Walking home afterwards, I asked my wife what she chose, and she said Republican. Since she was currently taking classes to become a special education teacher, I was a bit surprised. After all, it had always been my understanding that the foundation of both parties generally consisted of a certain set of values, and the values of many teachers, especially those who want to work with special needs students, were primarily linked to those of the Democratic Party. I immediately asked her why she chose Republican, and even though this conversation took place more than 35 years ago, I have never forgotten her answer: *"I didn't know what else to put, that's how my parents always voted."* To be fair, my wife was only 19 at the time, and as she said back then, none of her history teachers had ever discussed this subject. They may have done a stellar job teaching about the past, but no connection was ever made to the political present. There is no doubt that my wife is not alone. As a result of this omission in the social studies curriculum of many schools across the nation, millions of people like my wife struggle to apply whatever understanding of history they possess to making intelligent political decisions today.

Of course, part of the problem lies in the reality that trying to delineate the fundamental differences between a liberal Democrat and a conservative Republican is far from an exact science. It brings to mind the quote from the Supreme Court Justice, Potter Stewart, who could not define pornography, but *"knew it when he saw it."* Every time I get into a political discussion with my brother-in-law in Ohio, it soon becomes clear to most observers who is the liberal Democrat and who is the conservative Republican. However, trying to explain WHY we differ on so many political issues is much harder to teach or understand. In fact, there were years when I would purposely combine my classes with those of another teacher who I knew to be on the opposite end of the political spectrum just so our students could hear the contrast in our political values. We also wanted them to see how two adults could disagree on politics and still remain friends; something that recently seems lost on many members of Congress.

I have always believed it is better to openly and honestly approach this subject, as messy as it might seem, rather than shy away from it due to concerns about political exactness. With that said, here goes. By definition, liberals value change while conservatives prefer to maintain the status quo. This point, however, probably applies more to lifestyle choices than it does political values. One person might prefer a change of scenery more than another, but this does not mean he or she will vote for the Democrat in the next election. Another person may dress more conservatively, but this has little to do with his or her political preferences.

A better metaphor may be the *"head versus the heart."* Conservative Republicans often take pride in the fact they approach society's problems with logic and reason, in other words, with their heads. Liberal Democrats, on the other hand, work more from the emotion and compassion that comes from the heart. When conservatives see a homeless person begging for money on the street, they may tend to rationalize that the vagrant should apply for any of the many jobs openings they see posted all around them. Logically, giving money will only discourage the beggar from getting on his own two feet and seeking lasting employment. When liberals see the same scene, they assume the homeless person has fallen on hard times, something that could happen to any of us. Thinking more from the heart, their empathetic compassion compels them to give what they can. This scenario naturally translates to many political issues, particularly those where the question involves the role of government in helping those with a wide array of problems and needs.

That brings up another distinction between liberals and conservatives: the role of government. Two to three hundred years ago, conservatives and liberals held positions almost opposite to that of today. In Colonial times, conservatives valued a stronger government that would step in to protect the interests of those with land or property. Liberals cut from the mold of Enlightenment thinkers like John Locke, Voltaire and Thomas Jefferson preferred a weaker government that only existed to protect the rights and liberties of the people. The view that we should get by with as little government as possible has evolved over the centuries into the Libertarianism of today. Libertarians overlap with modern-day Republicans in that both prefer less government in the economy. Businesses should be as free as possible from government rules, regulations and taxes to pursue true liberty in the marketplace. On the other hand, Libertarians tend to agree with modern-day Democrats on many social issues. Both tend to favor less government so that individuals are free to express themselves, smoke marijuana or seek an abortion.

While true Libertarians have formed a small but active political party of their own, there are issues where they will agree or disagree with both Democrats and Republicans. In today's political arena, however, the differences between the two major parties over the role of government are relatively clear. Modern-day Republicans have evolved from their ancestors that wanted to nominate William Howard Taft as their candidate in the 1912 presidential election. They wanted fewer progressive reforms, less government interference in the economic arena and little to no income taxes. They essentially supported laissez faire policies that favored business in all of its forms, shapes and sizes. As Calvin Coolidge, the conservative, Republican president from the 1920s liked to say, "*the chief business of the American people is business.*" Sixty years later, Reagan's supply-side economic theory was based pretty much on the same principle. Not much has changed today.

On the other hand, modern-day Democrats can best trace their lineage back to the Populists and the Progressives. With further refinement from Franklin Roosevelt's New Deal, Harry Truman's Fair Deal, John F. Kennedy's New Frontier and especially Lyndon B. Johnson's Great Society, the role of government grew in fits and spurts throughout much of the 20th Century. Taxes have increased, particularly on the wealthy; regulations have been enacted to protect workers, consumers and the environment; and there are multitudes of programs designed to help the poor in such areas as food, education, housing and health care. Democrats are more inclined to trust in and support big government the same way Republicans tend to trust in and support big business.

This point was made clear from research cited in 2010 by Thomas Byrne Edsall, the journalist and academic best known for his weekly opinion for *The New York Times* and author of the book, *The Age of Austerity: How Scarcity Will Remake American Politics*. According to Edsall, the Pew Research Center asked voters, "*If you had to choose, would you rather have a smaller government providing fewer services, or a bigger government providing more services?*" White Republican men chose a smaller government by a 92-7 margin and white Republican women made the same choice by an 82-12 margin. Conversely, white Democratic men chose bigger government by a 53-35 margin and white Democratic women by 56-33. This is an ideological gap between Republicans and Democrats of 57 points among white men and 49 points among white women.

Related to the role of government as a wedge separating liberals from conservatives is the dichotomy between two related values: liberty and equality. Conservatives in the past as well as the present value liberty, at least in the economic arena. Should there be a higher minimum wage? The conservative would say no because it will deprive business owners of the liberty to decide what they can afford to pay their employees. Should property taxes be raised to provide better funding for local schools? No says the conservative because it will reduce the homeowners' liberty to decide how they would best like to spend their hard earned money. Should emission standards be raised on automobiles in order to reduce air pollution or global warming? Again, most conservatives would say no because car manufacturers will be denied the liberty to build a product that will best maximize their profits. No matter the question, the conservative Republican in the United States will typically prefer less government and more liberty so that individuals can freely own their property, run their businesses and keep all or at least most of their income rather than paying high taxes to support unnecessary government programs.

Most people are familiar with the first line from President Lincoln's Gettysburg Address, *"Four score and seven years ago our fathers brought forth on this continent, a new nation, conceived in **Liberty**, and dedicated to the proposition that all men are created **equal**."* Today, most liberal Democrats place a greater value on the equality component of this sentence. The liberal looks at the enormous wealth discrepancies that have always existed throughout American history and is disturbed by the inherent unfairness. Liberals understand that wealth is distributed not by hard work or by any other manner in which it is *"earned,"* but through the economic law of supply and demand. One person can spend eight or more years earning a doctoral degree, work long hours as a professor and become a teacher that dramatically improves the lives of his or her students. Another is a terrific basketball player. Assuming the professor averages an income of $100,000 per year, he or she will earn $4 million dollars in a forty-year career. LeBron James earned $65 million dollars in one year. Of course, there is a much larger supply of people who can earn the PhD and become a professor than there are basketball players who can shoot buckets like LeBron James, and the popularity of the NBA has created an enormous demand for players with his particular talents. Therefore, most people who grow up accustomed to the tenets of free enterprise fully understand this enormous discrepancy in the distribution of wealth. However, the liberal fails to see how it can possibly be considered fair. Therefore, liberal Democrats call for higher taxes on the rich and more government programs that will effectively share the wealth. Most do not call themselves communists or even socialists; they just place a higher premium on a society where possessions are more equally distributed. Liberty versus equality? The vast majority of Americans value both, but when push comes to shove, most will pick one as being at least a little more important than the other. At the risk of oversimplification, this may be one of the most important factors that separate the modern liberal from the modern conservative.

In addition, issues such as foreign policy divide liberals from conservatives. Related to the higher value placed on equality over liberty, most liberal Democrats are naturally more generous to foreign nations. The liberal is more inclined to help other nations with economic aid, to spread democratic values and to provide relief after an earthquake, hurricane or drought. On the other hand, the conservative Republican tends to favor American interests over those of other nations. He or she understands that Americans make up fewer than five per cent of the world's population and that there are limits to how much help the United States can or should provide. They do not necessarily want to see our nation recede inside the shell of isolationism that dominated U.S. foreign policy up to the start of World War Two, but they favor more discretion when it comes to deciding when and where America chooses to get involved.

Another foundational issue dividing liberals from conservatives involves the value placed on individual rights as opposed to guarding national security. After the terrorist attack on September 11, 2001, Congress responded by passing the Patriot Act. Liberals, particularly those belonging to groups like the American Civil Liberties Union, fumed over the invasion of privacy that would result from the government examining telephone records, reading private emails and even monitoring books checked out of libraries. Conservatives, on the other hand, saw this as a necessary price to enable the government to protect U.S. national security. Most Americans on both ends of the political spectrum support the individual rights contained in the Constitution during times of stability and peace, but when national security is threatened, cracks appear in the foundation. This first occurred with passage of the Alien and Sedition Acts during the Quasi War with France in 1798. The cracks resurfaced during the Civil War when President Lincoln ignored the right to seek a writ of habeas corpus by locking up people suspected to be Confederate sympathizers. During the First World War, Eugene Debs, the Socialist candidate for president, received a ten-year prison sentence for speaking out against America's involvement in the war. This even received the support of the Supreme Court in the case of *Schenck v. United States*, where the court said statements that presented a "*clear and present danger*" to our national security interests were not protected as a form of free speech. Then, shortly after the Japanese attack on

Pearl Harbor, over one hundred thousand Americans of Japanese ancestry were locked up in internment camps so they could not offer any assistance to the enemy. This wedge has repeatedly cropped up to divide liberals from conservatives whenever American national security has been at risk.

Finally, there is one more wedge, and it can frequently be found lurking beneath the surface of many of the others. This is once again the philosophical issue of free will versus determinism. Conservatives tend to believe more strongly in free will; that is, the view that each of us as individuals possesses the innate ability to make our own decisions and to chart our own futures. Why should the government provide food stamps for the poor if people living below the poverty line can simply choose to find a job and work hard to earn a decent income? Why make prisons more comfortable or provide better rehabilitation programs if a criminal can choose to become a more law-abiding citizen? Some even question the creation or continuation of Social Security. After all, if people would simply choose to put aside a certain amount of their savings to prepare for retirement, the government would not have to provide this safety net. In fact, most conservatives believe that too much government only encourages people to choose the easier or lazier path rather than one based on hard work or determination.

Most liberals, on the other hand, veer toward the deterministic side of the spectrum. Since they believe we are all the product of genetics, the environment in which we are raised, and other factors beyond our control, they argue the government should be there to serve those who fall on misfortune. No one chooses to be poor; poverty results from a cycle where most poor people come from a lower socio-economic background. With over two million Americans locked up in jails and prisons, it makes more sense to focus on rehabilitation than punitive measures so that when released, former convicts will be pointed in the right direction. Alcoholics? Gambling addictions? Drug abuse? Once again, the liberal tends to believe people with these problems need help, that they should not be penalized for making wrong choices. People whose parents could not provide stable homes or tuition for college should not have to endure an unfair burden. This position can be clearly linked to the value placed on equality, and while there is no way to guarantee complete equal opportunity, the government can certainly expand its role to provide a more level playing field.

The Pew research cited earlier from Thomas Byrne Edsall's book also included a question relevant to this point concerning free will versus determinism. Voters were asked to choose between these statements: "*Most people who want to get ahead can make it if they're willing to work hard*" and "*Hard work and determination are no guarantee of success for most people.*" White Republican men and women both picked "*hard work*" by decisive margins of 78-21 and 73-24 respectively. White Democratic men and women, in contrast, were far more equivocal, supporting hard work by modest margins of 52-44 and 53-43.

In order to help students understand these fundamental differences between liberals and conservatives in a more personal way, I usually have them take the survey that follows. It is updated every year to best reflect the most current issues, and while far from perfect, it usually raises students' interest in the subject and gives them at least a vague idea of where they belong on the political spectrum. After writing a number ranging between one and five for each statement, they are then instructed to add up all the numbers. Their total score will range between a low of 15, the most conservative number, to a high of 75, the most liberal. A score of 45 will put them squarely in the middle, but while this might mean they are conservative on some issues and more liberal on others, it could also mean they do not understand the issues. Either way, this survey has proved to be a useful teaching tool over the years.

POLITICAL SPECTRUM SURVEY

For each of the following, write a

5   for strongly agree

4   for agree

3   for neutral or undecided

2   for disagree

1   for strongly disagree

1. The United States should work more to cooperate within the United Nations to resolve international conflicts and issues.
2. The United States should be more willing to use its political, economic and military strength to help other nations in times of need without expecting anything in return.

3. The United States should not use its military forces to interfere in the affairs of other nations solely to protect its economic interests.
4. Civil liberties must be protected even if it might undermine our national security.
5. People who live below the poverty line should be provided with enough welfare assistance to meet basic human requirements for as long as the need exists.
6. The wealthier classes in America should be paying a larger share of the taxes.
7. The United States should open its doors wider to welcome immigrants from around the globe.
8. A woman should be able to seek an abortion to terminate an unwanted pregnancy for any reason.
9. The government should guarantee equal health care coverage for every U.S. citizen.
10. Minority status should be a significant consideration in the hiring or promotion policy of any business or government agency with a history of discrimination.
11. Any form of discrimination based on sexual preference should be against the law.
12. There is still a need for civil rights reforms regarding blacks and other minorities, particularly in regard to police conduct and the actions of the nation's courts.
13. The death penalty is unconstitutional and should no longer be used.
14. There should be more restrictions placed on the purchase, ownership or use of handguns.
15. There should be more federal regulations and stricter enforcement to prevent climate change and to take other measures that will protect the environment.

TOTAL

We currently live with a government that often appears to be seriously debilitated. Services from Washington, D.C. will suddenly be halted because of a government shutdown. The spending deficit is approaching twenty trillion dollars, a number most of us cannot begin to fathom. The approval rating for Congress has been steadily declining to an all time low. Much of the problem stems from our inability to communicate, to compromise, to get along.

Why do we have competitive factions in a democratic society? In some ways, this one is easy to answer. We are all different, we come from different backgrounds and we have a different set of core values. There is even some scientific research that says it is all inside our heads. A growing consensus is emerging among political scientists and psychologists that differences between liberal and conservative ideology may be hardwired into our brains. According to political scientist John Hibbing at the University of Nebraska and some of his colleagues that published in *Behavioral and Brain Sciences*, conservatives possess what is called a strong "*negativity bias,*" or physiological fixation on negative stimuli in their environments. Conservatives have a more threat-oriented and reactionary mindset than liberals. If this is true, then differences between liberals and conservatives may be just as physiological as they are psychological.

It was probably somewhat naïve for James Madison and the other writers of the Constitution to believe we would not divide up into factions. It happened immediately after the Constitutional Convention of 1787 and it has continued right up to the present. Certain elections from the past have played an important role in shaping these partisan differences, including those held in 1800, 1828, 1860, 1912, 1968, and of course, 2000. Conflict, argument and debate are the messy components of democracy. On the other hand, so is compromise. Democracy works best when the competing factions make an effort to understand each other and to get along. Therefore, we need to accept that we are all different and that this is simply part of being human. In addition, it is imperative that we must all be able to effectively relate to competing factions.

Suggested Reading:

Condrad, Jessamyn. *What You Should Know About Politics...But Don't: A Non-Partisan Guide to the Issues That Matter.* New York: Arcade Publishing, 2012.

Edsall, Thomas Byrne. *The Age of Austerity: How Scarcity Will Remake American Politics.* New York: First Anchor Books, 2012.

Gould, Lewis L. *Four Hats in the Ring: The 1912 Election and the Birth of Modern Politics.* Lawrence: University Press of Kansas, 2008.

Green, John C., Daniel J. Coffey, and David B. Cohen, eds. *The State of the Parties: The Changing Role of Contemporary American Parties.* Lanham: Rowman and Littlefield, 2014.

Greenspan, Jesse. "Remembering the 1912 Presidential Election." *History.com.* November 2, 2012. http://www.history.com/news/remembering-the-1912-presidential-election.

Hibbing, John R., Kevin B. Smith, and John R. Alford. "Differences in Negativity Bias Underlie Variations in Political Ideology." *Behavioral and Brain Sciences* 37, no.3 (2014): 297-350. Accessed April 19, 2016. http://www.psych.nyu.edu/vanbavel/lab/documents/Jost.etal.2014.BBS.pdf.

Hofstadter, Richard. *The Idea of a Party System: The Rise of Legitimate Opposition in the United States, 1780-1840.* Berkeley: University of California Press, 1969.

Mayhew, David R. *Parties and Policies: How the American Government Works.* New Haven: Yale University Press, 2008.

McWhirter, Cameron. *Red Summer: The Summer of 1919 and the Awakening of Black America.* New York: Henry Holt and Company, 2011.

"Thomas Jefferson: Campaigns and Elections." *Miller Center of Public Affairs.* Accessed April 19, 2016. http://millercenter.org/president/biography/jefferson-campaigns-and-elections.

Chapter 18
Epilogue

The Mayflower
Courtesy of https://www.flickr.com/photos/britishlibrary/11301814715/

What is the best way to use essential questions?

The place is a ship, the *Mayflower*, located somewhere in the middle of the Atlantic Ocean and the year is 1620. On board is a young man named John Howland, and like the other 101 passengers, he is headed to a new life in a new world. John Howland, who boarded the ship as a servant to John Carver, has had a considerable impact on the history of the United States. He is not as famous as William Bradford or Myles Standish, but his notoriety stems from an event that occurred in just a matter of a few minutes. Hundreds of thousands of Americans are unaware they owe their very existence to John Howland and he almost never made it to the New World.

During a gale, Howland fell overboard in the middle of the Atlantic and barely managed to grab a trailing rope. Sailors using boat hooks hauled him back aboard and he went on to live another day. Later, after arriving to help settle the colony at Plymouth and after sitting down at the famous meal celebrated every year as Thanksgiving, Howland married a fellow *Mayflower* passenger, Elizabeth Tilley. They went on to have 10 children and more than 80 grandchildren. Today, more than 2 million Americans can trace their roots back to John Howland. His descendents include three presidents: Franklin Roosevelt, George H.W. Bush and George W. Bush, as well as former vice presidential candidate Sarah Palin. Others include poets Ralph Waldo Emerson and Henry Wadsworth Longfellow, actors Alec Baldwin, Humphrey Bogart and Christopher Lloyd, Mormon Church founder Joseph Smith and child care guru Dr. Benjamin Spock.

How different would the United States be today if John Howland had not managed to grab that rope? For that matter, how many other important developments in the past were shaped by these minor events that have passed without notice? Like other essential questions, this one cannot be answered in a way that will achieve uniform agreement. It is subject to debate and can serve as a focal point for a good, healthy discussion. There are an infinite number of these questions that can be raised in a history class, and this more than anything else is probably what separates the study of history from that of science or mathematics. Essential questions are designed to provoke reflective thinking and by definition, they do not have a single correct answer. It has always been fun and enormously satisfying to facilitate an open-ended discussion centered on a good essential question. They are the single biggest reason why I chose to teach history 37 years ago.

For most of my career, I have employed Socratic seminars as a means to engage students in higher-level thinking. By leading a discussion over an essential question, the hope has been that students would achieve a deeper understanding of whatever topic was being studied. While there have been many memorable discussions over the years, there was always one nagging dilemma. What was my role? On one hand, I wanted to be able to sit back and observe. Students should be able to take greater control and ownership over their discussions, particularly if they are genuinely engaged in the topic. After all, as future citizens, they will not have a teacher present to facilitate the conversations that should take place in a healthy democracy. They must be able to carry on a discourse, even one loaded with some emotional disagreement, without coming to blows.

On the other hand, whenever I attempted to take this backseat role, student discussions included a wide range of opinions not grounded by specific details and examples. They frequently evolved into bull sessions that lacked few connections with the history being studied in class. As a result, I

Epilogue

often stepped into their Socratic seminars to add some meat to the bones, but the end result was that I typically talked too much, and some of the students began to shut down. This dilemma, more than anything else, became the impetus to write this book.

The Socratic seminars throughout my teaching years have always included some ground rules in terms of discussion decorum, especially at the present since I currently teach seventh and eighth graders. No matter the size of the class or the academic level of the students, a certain amount of training must take place in how to conduct and participate in a vigorous discussion. This guidance has always taken time and practice, but ultimately, student behavior has not been much of a problem. The puzzle has always been how to deepen the understanding of the students prior to the Socratic seminar so they could spend more time delving into their ideas and values and less time learning about support examples and details.

The author leading a seminar in his younger days. (CC0)

Over the several months this book was being written, individual chapters have been copied and distributed to my students prior to a scheduled Socratic seminar. The difference has been like night and day. Recently, the students in my eighth grade class sat in a circle and discussed how much power should be given to the people. I sat outside of the circle and took notes to be used in the closure phase that takes place in the final moments of the discussion. One student was chosen to facilitate this particular session, and he did a wonderful job of encouraging student participation and maintaining focus when the discussion began to wander. Every single student spoke up multiple times and I felt bad about ending the session when the bell was about to ring. The level of energy was incredibly high throughout most of the Socratic seminar and the students were still discussing the topic as they packed their bags and left for their next class. I was witnessing the kind of magic that teachers long to see in their classrooms.

In all my years of teaching, I have seldom observed this level of engagement and it is now beginning to occur on a regular basis. Essential questions have always been the focus of my teaching, but now the students are better prepared to answer them. As expected, each student will formulate his or her own response to the questions and a class consensus will seldom be achieved. However, by using this book, as well as other relevant readings before engaging in a Socratic seminar, my students will achieve a deeper understanding of the past.

Ever since I was a young child, I have loved the subject of history. It is so richly loaded with good stories that fuel the imagination and it possesses colossal value in developing the skills necessary for the success of a vibrant democracy. However, history is not the past, it is the study of the past, and there is a vastly significant difference. The study of the past is open to interpretation, and this requires a certain set of skills necessary to achieve a goal that will never be completely reached: objective truth. Essential questions can help to hone these skills. Considering how dysfunctional our democratic government often appears to be, the advancement of these skills may be our best hope for the future.

The essential questions discussed in this book were chosen based on my own experiences in the classroom. They have served me well over the many years of my career and they are still regularly included in my teaching curriculum. However, there is no established list of essential questions that have been created for universal use in history classes across the nation; there is no need for such a list. The point of this book is not to provide an all-encompassing list of essential questions for all history teachers to use; it is to convince people of their inherent value. Different teachers might create different questions as the need arises. These questions can then go on to be used as the focal point for stimulating conversations, the development of critical thinking skills and the attainment of a deeper understanding of the past.

Acknowledgements

It took 37 years to lay a foundation for the writing of this book. There are many people that have had a profound influence over the course of my teaching career and have helped to shape the experiences reflected in its pages. The first was Russell Costanza, my building principal at F.T. Nicholls High School in New Orleans, who understood that the first rule to follow in grooming future educators is to give them the freedom and support to develop their full potential. Next came Craig Larson, the principal of Parkway South High School. Craig always assumed there is room for improvement no matter how satisfied a community might be with its school, so he constantly attempted to expose his faculty to many reform principles, including those espoused by Theodore Sizer and the Coalition of Essential Schools. There have also been a number of fellow teachers over the years that exerted their own influence over what was occurring in my classroom. These include Edward Mihevc, Michael Howe, Daryl Hemenway, Scott Nilsen, Elizabeth Morrison and my good friend for many years, James Hubbard. Finally, there is Devon Metzger, the man who taught me the lesson that the rationale behind what you teach is even more important than the methods. So much of this book sprang from the discussions held in his graduate classes and in our many conversations.

There are also many people who have contributed to this book as it was being written. For starters, there is Rosario Batana, editor at Vernon Press, who provided the necessary guidance to turn a rough manuscript into a publishable book. Next, there is Trevor Kraus, a former student and now a friend who proofread the entire book and reminded me of the writing maxim that less is usually more. I also received much support from a number of family members, including my sister, Debby Jacobson, my daughter Julie Regenbogen and my son, Jack Regenbogen. I am also most grateful to my brother-in-law, Dean Robbins and my sister-in-law, Ann Shaffer, for their feedback, and especially for their support in encouraging me to submit this book for publication. Rounding out the family involvement is my mother-in-law, Radine Robbins, who also read the book and supplied invaluable feedback and advice. Finally, this book would never have made it into print without the assistance and support of my wife for 37 years, Dana. Most of the visuals and the suggested readings are the result of her tireless efforts, and she had the "pleasure" of reading this book more times than I can count. Most of all, I cherish her words of loving encouragement provided when I was most in need.

Index

1

13th Amendment, 162
15th Amendment, 111
17th Amendment, 109
19th Amendment, 267, 268

2

24th Amendment, 111, 263
26th Amendment, 112

A

abolitionists, 5, 301
Adams, John, 299, 300
Adams, John Quincy, 120, 300
affirmative action, 270, 271
African Americans, 65, 66, 184, 253, 255, 258, 260, 263, 309
American Civil Liberties Union, 256, 316
American Revolution, 158, 177, 200
anti-Semitism, 35, 61, 63
apartheid, 134, 135, 136
Aquinas, Thomas, 17
aristocracies, 101
Articles of Confederation, 108
Asian Americans, 64
Assad, Bashar, 247
atomic bomb, 223, 224, 225

Aztecs, 49, 50

B

Balkan Peninsula, 163
Beard, Charles, 180
Beethoven, Ludwig van, 284
biblical creation, 14, 22
Bill of Rights, 109
Black Lives Matter Movement, 184, 253, 254
blitzkrieg, 218, 219
Boers, 134, 135
Bonaparte, Napoleon, 117, 179
Bonus Army, 76, 95
Brown v. Board of Education, 262
Brown, Archie, 94
Brown, John, 5
Brown, Michael, 251, 252
Bryan, William Jennings, 13, 14, 52, 89, 301
Buddhism, 16, 28, 30, 36
Bush v. Gore, 297
Bush, George H.W., 125, 205
Bush, George W., 200, 296

C

Callatians, 47, 48
Calley, William, 212, 213, 214
Cambodia, 227
Camp David, 149

capitalism, 80, 81, 82, 91, 95
Castro, Fidel, 88
Catt, Carrie Chapman, 267
Cherokee, 51
Chinese Exclusion Act, 239
Christianity, 16, 28, 30, 36, 37, 141, 282
Churchill, Winston, 101, 105
Cincinnati Contemporary Arts Center, 275, 276
Civil Liberties Act, 270
Civil Rights Act, 309
Civil Rights Act of 1965, 263
Civil Rights Movement, 93, 185, 255, 256, 263, 289
Civil War, 2, 3, 9, 58, 161, 162
Classical period, 284
Classical Period, 284
Cold War, 93, 94, 122, 123, 164, 193, 202, 240
Columbus, Christopher, 43, 237
communism, 19, 87, 91, 122, 194
Congress, 101, 106, 109, 191, 203, 240, 241
conservatives, 313, 315, 316, 317, 318, 320
Constitution, 109, 111, 180
Constitutional Convention of 1787, 109
Coolidge, Calvin, 261, 314
Cortez, Hernando, 49, 50
Crusades, 33
Cuban Missile Crisis, 226
cultural relativity, 42, 43, 48, 55

D

Darius, 47, 48
Darrow, Clarence, 13, 14
Dawes Act of 1887, 51
Debs, Eugene, 85, 304, 316

Declaration of Independence, 178
democracy, 100, 102, 104, 112
Democratic Party, 309
Democrats, 95, 310, 314, 316
determinism, 79, 80, 317, 318
dictator, 101
dictatorship, 101
dikasts, 100
Discovery Doctrine, 138, 139
distribution of wealth, 77, 78, 79, 80, 88, 91
draft riots, 58
Dubois, W.E.B., 259

E

Edsall, Thomas Byrne, 314, 317
Einstein, Albert, 88, 223, 229
Eisenhower, Dwight D., 193, 262
Electoral College, 109, 296, 299, 307
Emancipation Proclamation, 162
Enlightenment, 17, 107, 176, 214, 283
Epicurus, 20
Eskimos, 45
essential questions, 8, 10, 324, 326
eugenics, 60, 61
evolution, 13, 14, 15, 22

F

fascism, 156
Federalist Party, 299
Ferdinand, Franz, 195
First Amendment, 23, 32, 33, 110, 291
First Great Awakening, 19

foreign policy, 116, 121, 122, 124, 125, 126, 316
free will, 79, 80, 317
French Revolution, 88, 107, 158, 179, 180, 181

G

Gandhi, Mohandas, 197, 199, 265
genetics, 60, 61, 68
genital mutilation, 41
Gibbon, Edward, 21
golden ratio, 280
Gorbachev, Mikhail, 94, 202
Gore, Albert, 296
Gould, Lewis L., 307
Graham, Otis L., 248
Great Depression, 76, 91, 240, 308
Great Society, 93
Greeks, 20, 21, 47, 48, 280
Gulf of Tonkin, 189, 190, 194

H

Haass, Richard N., 207, 213
Hamilton, Alexander, 105, 298, 300
Harding, Warren G., 261
Harlem Renaissance, 260
Herodotus, 44, 47
Hibbing, John, 320
Hinduism, 16, 28, 30, 35
Hiroshima, 223, 225
Hitler, Adolph, 100, 154, 155, 220
Hobbes, Thomas, 173, 174
Holocaust, 221
Hoover, Herbert, 75, 77, 261
Howland, John, 323, 324
Hundred Years' War, 172

Hussein, Saddam, 125, 200, 205

I

Immigration Act of 1924, 240
Immigration and Nationality Act of 1965, 241
Immigration Restriction Act of 1921, 240
imperialism, 51, 140, 141, 195
Indian Removal Act of 1830, 51
Indians, 51, 143, 144
Industrial Revolution, 181, 215, 237
ISIS, 207, 233, 236
Islam, 16, 28, 30, 37
isolationism, 116, 119, 120
Israel, 146, 149
Israel, Elfie, 65

J

Jackson, Andrew, 51, 110, 300
Jay, John, 298
Jefferson, Thomas, 31, 175, 299
Jim Crow laws, 66, 258, 260
Johnson v. McIntosh, 138
Johnson, Lyndon B., 93, 122, 190, 241, 309
Judaism, 16, 28, 29, 30, 35, 36, 37

K

Kassindja, Fauziya, 41, 42
Keith, Kent M., 45
Keller, Helen, 6
Kennedy, John F., 52, 270, 309
King, Martin Luther, Jr., 185, 263, 264
Kipling, Rudyard, 140
Kissinger, Henry, 126, 128

Ku Klux Klan, 258, 261
Kurdi, Alan, 233, 234, 246

L

League of Nations, 119, 127
Lenin, Vladimir, 90, 183
Lessoff, Alan, 305, 307
liberals, 313, 315, 316, 317, 318, 320
Libertarians, 313
Lincoln, Abraham, 162, 257, 301, 315, 316
Locke, John, 107, 175
Loewen, James, 5, 6, 7
Long, Huey P., 91
Lost Cause, 2
Lusitania, 204

M

Maddox, 189
Madison, James, 105, 298, 299
Magna Carta, 106
Mandela, Nelson, 133, 135, 136
Manifest Destiny, 140
Mapplethorpe, Robert, 276, 291
Marshall Plan, 52
Marshall, John, 51, 139
Marshall, Thurgood, 262
Marx, Karl, 19, 86, 90, 182
Maslow, Abraham, 80
Mayflower, 323, 324
Menton, David, 23
Middle Ages, 21, 62, 282
Middle East, 123, 146, 150, 206
Milgram, Stanley, 155
mock trial, 49, 51
monarchs, 101
monarchy, 101
Monroe Doctrine, 120

Muhammad, Elijah, 264
My Lai, 211, 212

N

NAACP, 259, 262, 263
Nader, Ralph, 296
Nagasaki, 223, 225
National American Woman Suffrage Association, 267
National Security Council, 128, 129
National Woman's Party, 268
nationalism, 156, 157, 158, 159, 160, 162, 163, 164, 195, 285
Native Americans, 51, 143, 266
nativism, 237, 238, 240
NATO, 202
Nazis, 54, 60, 153, 154, 218, 220
Neely, Mark E., Jr., 162
Netanyahu, Benjamin, 123
New Deal, 91, 104, 105, 262, 308
Niagara Movement, 259
Nixon, Nixon, 309
Nixon, Richard, 122, 214, 227, 287
Nuremberg, 60, 214

O

Obama, Barak, 123, 207
oligarchies, 101
Orwell, George, 19, 90, 156
Owen, Robert, 85

P

Palestine, 146, 149
Paley, William, 18
Parks, Rosa, 263
Parliament, 107, 175, 177

Patriot Act, 316
patriotism, 156, 157, 158, 162
Paul, Alice, 267
Pearl Harbor, 115, 120, 223, 227
Peasants' Revolt, 172
Persian Gulf War, 125, 205
Plessey v. Ferguson, 258
Populist Party, 301
Populists, 89
Progressive Movement, 89, 90
Puritans, 31, 138
Putin, Vladimir, 166

Q

Quakers, 31

R

Rachels, James, 43
racism, 67
Rape of Nanking, 219
Reagan, Ronald, 93, 270, 311
Reconstruction, 257, 258
religious persecution, 35
Renaissance, 22, 282
Republican Party, 257
Republicans, 95, 301, 314, 316
Risen, Clay, 272, 273
Romans, 20, 21, 48, 281
Roosevelt, Franklin D., 91, 104, 116, 120, 262, 270, 308
Roosevelt, Theodore, 52, 90, 121, 128, 261, 304
Rothschild, Mayer Amschel, 62
Rwanda, 54, 126

S

Salt Acts, 197
Schenck v. United States, 316
Schweikart, Larry, 4
Scopes, John, 13, 14
Second Great Awakening, 20
secular humanism, 19
Seven Years War, 176
Shirer, William L., 155
Skinner, B.F., 80
slavery, 3, 66, 161, 257, 301
Smith, Adam, 80, 81
socialism, 80, 83, 87, 88, 94, 95
Socialist Party, 304
Socrates, 99, 100
Socratic seminars, 65, 324, 325
South Africa, 134, 135, 136
Soviet Union, 90, 91, 93, 94, 124, 202
Spanish Civil War, 217
Spanish-American War, 121
Stalin, Joseph, 90, 224
Steinbeck, John, 18
stereotype, 59, 60, 61, 64, 67
Strasser, Todd, 155
Supreme Court, 32, 138, 258, 262, 289, 295
Syria, 233

T

Taft, William Howard, 90, 261, 304
Tariff of Abominations, 160
Tchaikovsky, Peter, 285
Thirty Years War, 33
Thoreau, Henry David, 197
Tinker v. Des Moines, 186
Trail of Tears, 51, 145
Trotsky, Leon, 90
Truman, Harry, 223, 224, 225, 262, 308
Turner Thesis, 69, 70
Turner, Frederick Jackson, 69

U

Ukraine, 165, 166
Uniform Code of Military
　Justice, 214
United Nations, 120, 124, 129,
　150, 236
United Nations Convention on
　Asylum, 247
United Nations Security
　Council, 124
Universal Declaration of Human
　Rights, 46
universal moral standards, 42,
　45, 46, 54

V

Versailles Treaty, 119, 124, 155,
　216
Vietnam War, 190, 192, 194, 201
Voltaire, 18, 33

W

Wannsee Conference, 221
War of 1812, 120, 159, 204
Warren, Earl, 262
Washington, Booker T., 258
Washington, George, 116
Whigs, 301
Wiesel, Elie, 126
Wiggins, Grant, 9
Wilson, Woodrow, 7, 90, 119,
　128, 204, 261, 304, 306
World War I, 118, 164, 194, 204,
　215
World War II, 116, 218

X

X, Malcolm, 264

Z

Zinn, Howard, 4, 5

www.ingramcontent.com/pod-product-compliance
Lightning Source LLC
Chambersburg PA
CBHW050332230426
43663CB00010B/1832